ALTERNATIVE HEALING METHODS

for EMOTIONAL *and* SPIRITUAL NEEDS

HOW TO INCORPORATE HERBS, ESSENTIAL OILS, AYURVEDA, AND ALTERNATIVE REMEDIES INTO YOUR LIFE

from the author of *Essential Oils for Healing*

VANNOY GENTLES FITE

Alternative Healing Remedies for Emotional and Spiritual Needs: How to Incorporate Herbs, Essential Oils, Ayurveda and Alternative Remedies into your life

FIRST EDITION
First Edition, 2021

Book design by Uplifting Author Services
Cover design by Murphy Rae
Gentles Enterprises is a registered trademark

Library of Congress Cataloging-in-Publication Data

Names: Vannoy Gentles Fite, author
Title: Alternative Healing Remedies for Emotional and Spiritual Needs / Vannoy Gentles Fite

Description: First edition. Independently published. Kindle Direct Publishing. "This book contains recipes using herbal, essential oil, Ayurvedic and alternative remedies to assist in controlling emotional and spiritual needs" – provided by author
Identifiers: ISBN 9798687619271
Subjects: Naturopathy, Spiritual, Alternative medicine
Classification: paperback, eBook

All mail and inquiries should be sent to the author, Vannoy Gentles Fite. Contact information is as follows: vannoylou@gmail.com

Printed in the United States of America

OTHER BOOKS BY VANNOY GENTLES FITE

Essential Oils for Healing (St. Martin's Press 2016)

Essential Oils for Emotional Wellbeing (Llewellyn 2018)

Llewellyn's Book of Natural Remedies (Llewellyn 2020)

CONTACT INFO:

www.amazon.com/author/vannoyfite

vannoylou@gmail.com

IG: @vannoylou

FB: Vannoy Fite, Author

TikTok: @vannoyfite

ALTERNATIVE HEALING METHODS

for EMOTIONAL *and* SPIRITUAL NEEDS

HOW TO INCORPORATE HERBS, ESSENTIAL OILS, AYURVEDA, AND ALTERNATIVE REMEDIES INTO YOUR LIFE

This book is dedicated to:

Michele Marie Gentles McDaniel and Thomas Michael Gentles. You guys are the reason I am the way I am. Good, bad or in-between. We have been through it all together and we will continue the long fight. I love you both and thank you for always loving me, even when I don't deserve it. A better brother and sister does not exist on this Earth. We cling to each other in love and loss.

Count

How do we react,
When we're upset,
Things don't go our way.
Deep breaths.
Count to ten.
A silent prayer.
Don't erupt.
Close your eyes.
Go to your happy place.

Michele Gentles McDaniel
"Words in Amber"

CONTENTS

MY STORY

I was rapidly on my way to living the rest of my life in a wheelchair. My feet, ankles and back were twisted and in pain. I could hardly walk due to my eczema, arthritis and the crippling effects it had on my body and my mind. Depression, panic attacks and anxiety plagued me. I often felt like I would be better off dead than trying to cope with everything going on with my body and my mind. Bi-polar and other types of mental illness run rampant in my family and I was feeling the emotional wear and tear of struggling to live each day. I was an unbalanced mess.

I was young when I discovered herbs. Growing herbs, cooking with herbs, healing with herbs and including herbs in every part of my life, I believe, saved me. This soon turned into a love of essential oils, home remedies, shamanistic healing, yoga, alternative medicine, alternative therapies and finally, Ayurveda. These modalities changed my life, my health and my mental fortitude. Since learning to heal myself physically, mentally and spiritually, I have longed to share my love of natural healing with everyone I meet.

People request all types of healing methods from me since my first book Essential Oils for Healing was released. My new book, *ALTERNATIVE HEALING METHODS FOR EMOTIONAL AND SPIRITUAL NEEDS: How to Incorporate Herbs, Essential Oils, Ayurveda and Alternative Remedies into your life*, covers those ailments of the mind and soul that people need answers for. Each emotional or spiritual need is listed alphabetically and is followed by an herbal recipe, an essential oil recipe, an Ayurvedic recipe and an alternative remedy from around the world.

It seems that the majority of us now want a more natural approach to handling our mental and emotional issues other than Xanax or another over-prescribed drug. Some of the drugs people are taking are causing them more harm than the issues they were meant to heal. The side effects of a lot of these prescribed medications can be potentially very harmful, or even deadly. People want a more holistic and natural way to solve mental and spiritual needs and *ALTERNATIVE HEALING METHODS FOR EMOTIONAL AND SPIRITUAL NEEDS* has the answers that they are seeking.

I have studied natural healing for over 40 years. I have three previously published books on natural healing methods. I am a certified Ayurvedic Life Coach, a certified Herbalist, a certified Aromatherapist and a certified yoga instructor. I have grown herbs most of my life and have made herbal medicines as far back as I can remember for my family. I have had herbal businesses, essential oils businesses, owned a yoga studio, and studied all forms of natural healing my entire adult life. My dining room table is covered right now with sages, mints and balms drying for tea making. I cook and prepare food that heals, not harms, as I am a big believer that food is the answer to healing out lives, both physically and mentally. Food is the medicine of life.

Looking for alternative healing methods has been a huge barrier for a lot of people. Trying to find various ways to heal a cough, for example, can be a daunting task. First you look through an herbal book for recipes and herbs that can quiet a cough, then look for some home remedies, try to find online information for a chronic cough, peruse an essential oil book and all of the remedies are so scattered and confusing that it's hard to focus on any one healing method. People don't have an easy, straightforward way of discovering how to incorporate oils, herbs, Ayurveda, alternative or natural healing into their daily routines…until now.

ALTERNATIVE HEALING METHODS FOR EMOTIONAL AND SPIRITUAL NEEDS offers so much more than the title suggests. Not only does it incorporate the more well-known alternative healing methods such as herbs, oils and Ayurveda, but it also suggests healing with gemstones and crystals, mantras, colors, bathing rituals, prayer, meditation, yoga, and various healing techniques from around the world. All accessible in one, easy to find, alphabetical guide. It could not be simpler for the average person trying to use new healing methods. *ALTERNATIVE HEALING METHODS FOR EMOTIONAL AND SPIRITUAL NEEDS* is a must have for anyone wanting to learn the various techniques of alternative healing.

I often receive messages from teenagers who want to know how to naturally heal their broken heart, mothers of children wanting to boost their child's self-esteem, and elderly people who want to remind me of how they used everyday ingredients in "the old days" to rid themselves of anxiety, insomnia or to boost their energy. Everyone I talk to on a daily basis has either a question or a remedy that I can use as a new opportunity to learn from. *ALTERNATIVE HEALING METHODS FOR EMOTIONAL AND SPIRITUAL NEEDS* is for every person on Earth. It has come to the attention of myself and others how the pharmaceutical companies use the chemical copies of plants, food, trees and flowers to charge astronomical amounts of money for a drug that is inundated with side effects. People are tired of it and want to heal themselves, mentally and spiritually, as naturally as possible, cheaply, and with good results. So instead of using the chemical copies of plants – why not use the actual plant?

ALTERNATIVE HEALING METHODS FOR EMOTIONAL AND SPIRITUAL NEEDS does not follow any one religion, but spirituality is a very important part of the healing process. Whether it is a walk with nature, saying mala beads, burning incense, praying to a Higher Power, sage smudging, reciting mantras, group gatherings, eating for your dosha type, performing rituals or meditating, spiritual quests come in many forms. Many of the recipes in this book include spiritual guidance suggestions, but they are only suggestions. People can incorporate their own types of worship into these healing modalities. Faith is the cornerstone of good health. But it must be the faith that you have perfect trust in. *ALTERNATIVE HEALING METHODS FOR EMOTIONAL AND SPIRITUAL NEEDS* imparts that truth many times over for the reader. A particular religion is not a prerequisite in adopting any of the remedies in this book. You can include your own religion or spiritual beliefs into any of the recipes as you see fit. But having some form of faith is so important to your health and well-being. Feed your faith and watch your whole life improve. Especially your brain and your soul.

The number one reason most people seek alternative healthcare is for emotional needs. *ALTERNATIVE HEALING METHODS FOR EMOTIONAL AND SPIRITUAL NEEDS* provides you with the information you need to heal and treat yourself in the healthiest ways possible. Every demographic, every economic level, all genders, every race/ethnicity, everyone with emotional and spiritual needs is looking for the answers to healing their own issues themselves, without formal medical intervention or chemical medications. *ALTERNATIVE HEALING METHODS FOR EMOTIONAL AND SPIRITUAL NEEDS* will give you the answers that you are looking for.

Much healing and love to you and yours,
Vannoy Gentles Fite

READ BEFORE YOU PRACTICE

Every herb, essential oil, or really anything you come into contact with anywhere on Earth, has the potential to cause harm. It is up to you as a human being to learn which things can help you and which things can harm you. This is especially true of herbs, essential oils, plants, seeds, trees, flowers, and most of nature. Each living thing contains properties. Learning which properties can help you and which ones can harm you is the responsibility that we each bear in our daily lives. Just because an aspirin can help a headache doesn't mean you should take ten of them at once or take them with certain other medications. The same is true of herbs and essential oils. Learn the warnings, the contraindications, the methods and the repercussions of any natural medication you use, just the same as medications you get from the drug store.

Many herbs and oils can counteract medications you may already be taking. They have the potential to exacerbate any illnesses or diseases you might have been diagnosed with. Contact your physician to ensure that any new treatments you wish to add to your self-healing practices will benefit you and not harm you.

Herbs and essential oils can be fragile things while at the same time holding power that is unsurpassed by chemicals. Keep them in a dry, cool dark place, and always pay attention to directions on how to store your herbs and oils. They can last many months, or even years if stored properly.

Following all the rules and precautions included in this book will ensure you have a healthy and enjoyable time practicing your self-healing. Enjoy!

AYURVEDA

Ayurveda is my first true love. The basis behind this healing is that you must balance your body, mind and spirit before healing can take place. In order to do this, you need to find out what your dosha type is. There are tons of tests you can take online to learn about your dosha, but a quick tip is to understand that the doshas are primarily three different personality types and keeping these doshas in balance will prevent you from getting a disease in the future that is usually associated with your particular dosha. Which one do you most identify with? You are not only one dosha, but a combination of the three. Usually one dosha will be the primary dosha, and it is our job to balance our doshas, reduce the dosha that is out of control, and bring healing to ourselves. However, this dosha balancing is not a one-time fix. Balancing your doshas is a life-long quest that you will find yourself relying on time and time again. Read below to see if you identify with any of these descriptions.

The three types of doshas are pitta, kapha and vata. Kaphas are wise, non-judgmental, couch potatoes, big-boned and enjoy inactivity. They usually have sinus issues, weight issues, diabetes, high blood pressure and heart diseases.

Pittas are charismatic, charming, quick to laugh, but equally quick to temper. Pittas are of average build, hot natured and despise heat. Pittas often suffer from heartburn, indigestion, hypertension, strokes and heart issues.

Vatas are quick talkers, multi-taskers, type A's, and suffer from painful illnesses and mental disorders such as anxiety, bi-polar and arthritis. Vatas tend to think very quickly and aggressively and their rampant, out-of-control thoughts often lead to sleepless nights.

Learning about the doshas can help you to prevent illnesses in your future by eating, exercising and medicating yourself to balance your doshas. Reducing your primary dosha can bring you so much peace and joy, but it is a daily struggle you will face throughout your life in order to be happy and healthy in all the areas of your life.

Ayurvedics believe that all illness begins in the gut. In order to heal many of your illnesses, you should first look at your diet. What you eat can affect everything from your thoughts, moods, energy levels, socialization, spirituality, everything! Learning to eat for your dosha and for your illness is the number one way in which Ayurveda can help you to be healthy.

These is the very first baby steps of Ayurveda. Thousands of years of practice go into this healing modality. It is the oldest known form of medicine in the world. If you enjoy the Ayurvedic recipes in this book, I encourage you to foray into the Ayurveda world and buy other books, watch videos and #Ayurveda to learn more.

ESSENTIAL OILS

These little bottles of magical elixir hold untold amounts of healing potential. Essential oils have been used since the Egyptian dynasties ruled the Earth. Many ancient texts extoll the healing powers of essential oils and we still rely on them for much of our healing today.

Obtaining essential oils in the age of online shopping is so easy and quick. I remember thirty years ago when I wanted a bottle of essential oil, it took a lot of planning and a whole day to go to a major city and find a store that would hold the treasure I was seeking. Today it's simply a matter of getting online, pushing a few buttons, and in a matter of days whatever type of essential oil you desire will be delivered to your door.

Essential oils are, to me, what pharmaceutical companies wish they could make with their chemical compounds. While oils are made from plants, flowers, trees and herbs, pharmaceutical companies study the plants and copy the properties chemically to make their expensive medications. These chemical copies are rife with side-effects and are often too expensive for the average consumer to buy.

Essential oils are the oils derived from plants in a very condensed form. To get one ounce of rose oil takes thousands of pounds of roses, which are distilled to produce the oil from deep within the flower. These oils used to be costlier than gold. Every religion and every culture on Earth has used essential oils for their rituals, traditions and for prayer. Every nation has used essential oils in healing and bringing a multitude of usefulness to their cultures.

Learning what essential oils are used for, what therapeutic properties each oil holds, how to use them, and what healing methods are the best practice to obtain healing is the key to using essential oils. *ALTERNATIVE HEALING METHODS FOR EMOTIONAL AND SPIRITUAL NEEDS* gives you an easy guide to learning about essential oils and how to use them. Ensure that your oils are out of reach of children as you go about learning to make wonderful, healing lotions and potions for yourself and your family.

Any medications or diagnosis can be discussed with your physician to clear you for using essential oils. The warnings section of this book should be looked at before using essential oils of any type.

HERBS

Herbs were on the Earth from day one. Can you imagine that first person that tried a peppermint leaf and noticed that their tummy ache disappeared? Or the person who smelled lavender and fell into a peaceful slumber? Watching animals eat certain herbs was a great way for our ancestors to figure out what plants were good for what ailments. I began growing and using herbs over forty years ago. I am a life-long lover of all things herbal. I use herbs daily in my life in the form of medicine, enjoyment, aromas, cooking, teas, potpourri and every way in which herbs can be used. One of my favorite things to do is to blend herbs into new and exciting combinations for my afternoon and nightly herbal teas.

Herbs are so beautiful and so aromatic, it's sometimes surprising to learn what a profound effect they can have on your emotional and spiritual psyche. These recipes are designed to give you the full benefits of the therapeutic properties contained in each and every herb. You will be able to know in a moment's notice which herbs you should use for which emotional or spiritual desire. Herbs are full of therapeutic properties that are often healing, but some can also be harmful. Learning which herbs are good for you and which herbs are not is a life-long project. We can never, ever know it all. But trying to learn all we can about herbs is half the fun.

Herbs can be used in a multitude of ways, ointments, baths, cleaning products, perfumes, teas, syrups, soaps, detergent, bouquets, culinary, sprays, oils, potpourri, the list of how you can prepare your herbs is too massive for any one book to hold. The healing properties of the most widely used herbs is included in this book, as are the warnings, as a first step for you to learn how to heal safely and responsibly with herbs. Herbs are easy to purchase, to use and to learn to love. You have been using herbs for years in your cooking, now you can learn how to use them to benefit yourself and your family in a multitude of ways.

ALTERNATIVE REMEDIES

These healing techniques, recipes and tips are from every timespan, every culture and every corner of the world. Sometimes the old ways and the simple ways are the best ways. Learning that you can make a soup that truly heals from the inside out is great knowledge to be passed down through the generations. Learning that breathing a certain way can help you to stave off a panic attack, or that you can use certain colors or gemstones to give yourself energy as well as a great night's sleep is a valuable commodity.

ALTERNATIVE HEALING METHODS FOR EMOTIONAL AND SPIRITUAL NEEDS utilizes so many different healing techniques: yoga, diet, nature, colors, prayer, crystals, teas, meditation, massage, mantras, affirmations, oils, flowers, food, tips, rituals, and sometimes just plain common sense. You will be surprised at how some of these recipes bring up memories of your grandmother and what she used to whip up to make you feel better all over.

Our spirits and emotions sometimes get stuck in a certain negative field and need a little outside help to bring us back to balance and grounding. These recipes will give you the edge you need to achieve the emotional and spiritual healing and balancing that you are seeking.

HERBAL THERAPEUTIC PROPERTIES AND WARNINGS

AGRIMONY

Warnings: Agrimony is sometimes phototoxic. It is unsafe to use if you are pregnant or breast-feeding. Check with healthcare provider if having surgery or if you have diabetes before using agrimony.

Therapeutic Properties: Anti-bruising, astringent, tonic, anti-diarrheal, vulnerary, febrifuge, anti-inflammatory, diuretic, antibiotic, and styptic.

ALOE VERA

Warnings: Test for allergies. Not to be used orally if pregnant or breast-feeding. Not to be taken orally by children under the age of 12 years. Should not be taken in large amounts internally.

Therapeutic Properties: Vulnerary, anti-inflammatory, laxative, diuretic, immune boosting, antiviral, antitumor, cicatrisant, cytophylactic, antiseptic, antifungal, antibiotic and antiviral.

ANGELICA

Warnings: Angelica may raise or lower blood sugar, so persons with heart disease, hypoglycemic, upcoming surgeries, diabetes or blood pressure issues should not take angelica. Do not take if pregnant. Trying to abort with this herb has poisoned women.

Therapeutic Properties: Carminative, diuretic, antiviral, tonic, stimulant, pulmonary, diaphoretic, antibacterial, expectorant, febrifuge, anti-nausea, diaphoretic, emenagogue, protectant from evil and antispasmodic.

ANISE

Warnings: Not to be used if you have a nervous disorder, are pregnant or nursing or with children under the age of 6 years.

Therapeutic Properties: Carminative, digestive, anti-hysteric, antiseptic, anti-rheumatic, anti-nausea, antispasmodic, diuretic, aperitif, anti-inflammatory, decongestant, cordial, expectorant, sedative, nervine, and aphrodisiac.

ARNICA

Warnings: Should not be taken by diabetics or heart patients, as this is a blood thinner. Can cause depression, skin irritations and should not be taken with any other medications. Only take internally at the advice of a physician.

Therapeutic Properties: Antibruising, antispasmodic, vulnerary, vasodilator, antiarthritic, hair-restorative, antibacterial, anti-inflammatory, gastro-stimulant, nervine, and immune-stimulant.

ASTRAGULA

Warnings: Consult your physician before taking astragula with any other medications. There is a lack of evidence if harmful if pregnant or nursing. Not to be used on children.

Therapeutic Properties: Antibacterial, anti-inflammatory, vulnerary, immune booster, circulatory stimulant, antioxidant and vulnerary

BASIL

Warnings: Pregnant and nursing women should not use basil. Children under 6 years old or persons with epilepsy should not use basil until more research has been completed. Has shown liver cancer in mice research.

Therapeutic Properties: Anti-inflammatory, analgesic, nervine, antidepressant, antispasmodic, antiinfectious, galactogogue, cephalic, antirheumatic, sudorific, antiseptic, tonic, antibacterial, antitussive, antiviral, digestive, expectorant, sedative, diaphoretic, circulatory stimulant, carminative, relaxant, antifungal, purifying and restorative.

BEE BALM

Warnings: Pregnant or nursing women, and children should not use bee balm. Can be phototoxic, also not to be used by those with thyroid issues. May cause drowsiness.

Therapeutic Properties: Febrifuge, carminative, decongestant, anti-nausea, anticatarrhal, relaxant, sedative, diaphoretic, aperitif, calming,

BILBERRY

Warnings: Not to be taken by those about to have surgery, diabetics (as the lowering of blood sugar along with diabetic medicines could cause sugar to go too low), children, pregnant or nursing women, or those with epilepsy should not use bilberry.

Therapeutic Properties: Ophthalmic, antioxidant, anti-inflammatory, circulatory stimulant, antiarthritic, vasodilator, digestive, cytophylactic, antiulcer, and anticarcinogenic.

BLACK COHOSH

Warnings: Should not be used by pregnant or nursing women or children. Long-term usage could increase chances of cancer, according to one study. No one with a chronic illness should take this herb.

Therapeutic Properties: Antianxiety, anti-inflammatory, nervine, herbal estrogen, antiarthritic, antispasmodic, antirheumatic, emenagogue, digestive, relaxant, antibacterial, analgesic and sedative.

BLACK HOREHOUND

Warnings: Should not be used by those suffering from Parkinson's disease, psychotic disorders, schizophrenia, pregnant or nursing women or children.

Therapeutic Properties: Vermifuge, astringent, anti-nausea, pain relief, antispasmodic, anticatarrhal, sedative, nervine, cholagogue, and stimulant.

BLACK PEPPER

Warnings: Persons with stomach issues such as ulcers, colitis, and diverticulitis should not use black pepper.

Therapeutic Properties: Anti-inflammatory, antispasmodic, antiarthritic, aperient, antirheumatic, carminative, analgesic, diaphoretic, antiseptic, antioxidant, antibacterial, digestive, dental usages, decongestant, expectorant, anticatarrhal, cordial, anticarcinogenic, and neuralgic.

BLUE COHOSH

Warnings: Not to be taken by pregnant or nursing women. Can cause birth defects, nausea, anyone with heart disease, cancer or any reproductive disease.

Therapeutic Properties: Laxative, antispasmodic, anti-hysteric, antiarthritic

BORAGE

Warnings: Do not take while pregnant or nursing. Do not take if you have a liver disorder or are taking blood thinners. Do not take 2 weeks before surgery.

Therapeutic Properties: Antirheumatic, cordial, diuretic, demulcent, emollient, febrifuge, anti-inflammatory, anticatarrhal, antidepressant, antiulcer.

BURDOCK ROOT

Warnings: Should not be used by pregnant and nursing women, children under the age of 2 years, or persons with liver disease.

Therapeutic Properties: Diuretic, laxative, bitter, tonic, vulnerary, antibacterial, emollient, antifungal, and diaphoretic.

BUTTERBUR

Warnings: Do not take if you are pregnant or breastfeeding. Do not take if you have any liver issues or ailments.

Therapeutic Properties: Tonic, diuretic, nervine, febrifuge, vermifuge, stimulant.

CALENDULA

Warnings: Do not take if pregnant or nursing.

Therapeutic Properties: Stimulant, antispasmodic, diaphoretic, emenagogue, antipyretic, aperient, vulnerary, vasodilator, analgesic, vulnerary, anti-inflammatory, expectorant.

CARAWAY

Warnings: None found by this author

Therapeutic Properties: Carminative, aromatic, stimulant, anti-hysteric, antibruising, stomachic, analgesic.

CATNIP

Warnings: Occasional nausea by some people when taken in large quantities.

Therapeutic Properties: Diaphoretic, carminative, tonic, antispasmodic, stimulant, emmenagogue, nervine, sedative, anti-hysteric, antibruising.

CAYENNE

Warnings: Can cause inflammation of the mouth, throat or rectum in some people.

Therapeutic Properties: Carminative, aromatic, stimulant, febrifuge, and rubefacient.

CHAMOMILE

Warnings: Can cause allergies in some people. Should not be used during the first 4 months of pregnancy. Can be a skin irritant. Roman chamomile oil is less irritating than German chamomile oil. May cause drowsiness.

Therapeutic Properties: Analgesic, antiallergenic, antibiotic, antidepressant, antifungal, antiinfectious, anti-inflammatory, antimicrobial, antineuralgic, antiphlogistic, antiseptic, antispasmodic, bactericidal, carminative, cholagogue, cicatrisant, cooling, digestive, emenagogue, febrifuge, hepatic, nervine, sedative, sudorific, stomachic, tonic, vermifuge, and vulnerary.

German chamomile- analgesic, anti-allergenic, antibacterial, anti-inflammatory, antirheumatic, antispasmodic, antibacterial, digestive, fungicidal, nerve sedative.

Roman chamomile- antispasmodic, respiratory distress, analgesic, antiseptic, digestive, nerve sedative.

CHICKWEED

Warnings: Can be toxic in large amounts.

Therapeutic Properties: Anti-inflammatory, demulcent, digestive, emollient, sedative, anticarcinogenic, antitumor, antiseptic.

CHICORY

Warnings: None found by this author

Therapeutic Properties: Aperient, sedative, emollient, decongestant, anti-inflammatory, tonic, laxative, diuretic.

CINNAMON

Warnings: Can cause dermatitis. Should not be used if you are pregnant of suspect you are pregnant. Not to be used on children, in baths or directly on the skin. Cinnamon oil is very strong and can burn the skin. It should be mixed with carrier oil (such as jojoba, sesame, grapeseed or your preference). Do not use during chemotherapy.

Therapeutic Properties: Antibacterial, anticlotting, antifungal, antimicrobial, astringent, carminative, cooling, and stimulating.

CLEAVERS

Warnings: Has been known to cause a skin rash in some people.

Therapeutic Properties: Diuretic, tonic, aperient.

CLOVE

Warnings: Can cause dermatitis. Should not be used on children under two years old. Should not be used if you are pregnant or suspect you are pregnant. Clove oil is very strong and can burn the skin. Do not use on children or in baths. Do not diffuse. Do not take with blood thinners.

Therapeutic Properties: Analgesic, antifungal, anti-inflammatory, antimicrobial, antirheumatic, antiseptic, antiviral, aphrodisiac, nervine, stimulant, and good for stimulating immune system.

COMFREY

Warnings: Has shown to have carcinogenic effects in research with rats. Do not take if pregnant or nursing. Do not take if you have liver disease or cancer. Never take comfrey oil by mouth or internally in any way.

Therapeutic Properties: Anti-inflammatory, antirheumatic, anticarcinogenic, antitussive, and menorrhagia.

CORIANDER

Warnings: Can cause stomach issues. Should not be used if you are pregnant or suspect you are pregnant. Coriander is not safe if you have any kidney issues.

Therapeutic Properties: Analgesic, aphrodisiac, antifungal, anti-inflammatory, antispasmodic, carminative, depurative, deodorant, digestive, fungicide, lipolytic, sedative, stomachic, and vermifuge.

CRAMPBARK

Warnings: Relaxes the uterus. Should not be taken with other medications.

Therapeutic Properties: Antispasmodic, nervine, antiasthmatic, anti-rheumatoid.

DANDELION

Warnings: Can cause upset stomach or skin rash.

Therapeutic Properties: Hepatic, aperient, diuretic, depurative, tonic, antirheumatic, stomachic.

DILL

Warnings: Can cause skin rash.

Therapeutic Properties: Antispasmodic, carminative, digestive, disinfectant, galactogogue, sedative, stomachic, and sudorific.

DONG QUAI

Warnings: Not to be used if you are pregnant or nursing, have a heavy menstrual flow, or are on blood thinners.

Therapeutic Properties: anti-depressant, detoxifies, circulatory, antioxidant and anti-inflammatory.

ECHINACEA

Warnings: Not to be taken if pregnant or nursing. Not to be taken if you have asthma. Do not take with any other medications.

Therapeutic Properties: Antibiotic, antiseptic, tonic, antibacterial, depurative, anti-inflammatory, antifungal, antiviral, febrifuge, and an immune system booster.

ELDERFLOWER

Warnings: Uncooked berries from this plant are poisonous. Contains cyanide.

Therapeutic Properties: Immune strengthener, anti-inflammatory, anti-viral, anti-catarrhal, bronchial, and also believed to promote vivid dreams.

EUCALYPTUS

Warnings: Do not use on children. Never take eucalyptus oil internally. Should be used with caution as some strong odors can trigger an asthma attack. Should not be used on the face, on children, or with any other medications. Not to be used if you suffer from high blood pressure.

Therapeutic Properties: Analgesic, antibacterial, antifungal, anti-inflammatory, antimicrobial, antirheumatic, antiseptic, antispasmodic, antiviral, bactericidal, decongestant, deodorant, diuretic, expectorant, mucolytic, and stimulating. Eucalyptus oil can increase circulation, clear the mind, be uplifting and help reduce negativity.

EVENING PRIMROSE

Warnings: Use caution if pregnant or nursing

Therapeutic Properties: Astringent, antispasmodic, hypertensive, liver regeneration, antiarthritic, anticoagulant.

EYEBRIGHT

Warnings: Has caused increased eye pressure and adverse effects in some persons.

Therapeutic Properties: Astringent, anti-inflammatory.

FENNEL SEED

Warnings: Do not use if you are on birth control, and have occasional clotting, or breast tumors. Stop taking if you experience nausea or vomiting.

Therapeutic Properties: Carminative, aromatic, digestive, antispasmodic, stimulant, diuretic, galactogogue, rubefacient, expectorant, antiemetic, diaphoretic, hepatic, digestive, antiseptic, stomachic and antibruising.

FEVERFEW

Warnings: May cause mouth ulcers. Do not take if you are pregnant, nursing or taking blood thinners.

Therapeutic Properties: Anti-inflammatory, vasodilator, relaxant, digestive.

FLAX SEED

Warnings: This is a laxative. Do not use if nursing.

Therapeutic Properties: Emollient, demulcent, digestive, anticatarrhal, anti-inflammatory, decongestant, laxative.

GINGER

Warnings: Do not use if pregnant or nursing. Should not be taken by persons on blood thinners. May cause stomach distress in heavy doses.

Therapeutic Properties: Stimulant, carminative, carminative, rubefacient, aromatic, aphrodisiac, digestive, anti-nausea.

GARLIC

Warnings: May cause rash in persons allergic to garlic. Not to be used if you are nursing or pregnant. Do not take if you also take blood thinners.

Therapeutic Properties: Antiseptic, antimicrobial, antiseptic, anticarcinogenic, antibacterial, antifungal, diaphoretic, detoxifier, cholagogue, hypotensive, antispasmodic, anticatarrhal, anti-inflammatory, carminative, antiviral, expectorant, rubefacient, stimulant, tonic, vulnerary.

GINKGO BILOBA

Warnings: do not take large amounts over an extended period of time. Do not take if you are on blood thinners or are having an upcoming surgery as it causes bleeding.

Therapeutic Properties: Antiasthmatic, antidepressant, antibiotic, stimulant, circulatory, antioxidant, shock, nervine, congestion, antiinfectious.

GINSENG

Warnings: Do not use if pregnant or nursing. Do not use if you have lupus. No one with a chronic condition should take this without first consulting your physician.

Therapeutic Properties: Vasodilator, stimulant, aphrodisiac, stimulant, tonic.

GOLDENSEAL

Warnings: Uterus stimulant. Do not take if pregnant. Do not use if you have high blood pressure. Do not take internally.

Therapeutic Properties: Tonic, astringent, anticatarrhal, laxative, digestive, cholagogue, emenagogue, expectorant, hepatic, antibiotic, vulnerary, immune stimulant, antibacterial, antiviral, antitumor.

GOTU KOLA

Warnings: Do not use if you have ever had cancer or take antidepressants or sedatives. Careful monitoring for rash. Do not use if pregnant or nursing.

Therapeutic Properties: Antibiotic, promotes circulation, antibiotic, antidepressant, antirheumatic, hypotensive, anti-inflammatory, memory boosting.

GREEN TEA

Warnings: Do not take if you are on blood thinners. Can cause allergic reactions in people.

Therapeutic Properties: Stimulant, astringent, nervine, stimulant, nervine, cephalic.

HAWTHORN

Warnings: Not to be taken if you have seizures or any heart condition. Do not take with any other medications.

Therapeutic Properties: Antispasmodic, sedative, circulation booster, digestive, antidiarrheal, stomachic.

HIBISCUS

Warnings: Unsafe for pregnant women.

Therapeutic Properties: Antiallergenic, anticoagulant, antihaematomic, anti-inflammatory, antimicrobial, antiphlogistic, antiseptic, antitussive, cholagogue, cicatrisant, cytophylactic, diuretic, emollient, expectorant, febrifuge, fungicidal, hepatic, mucolytic, nervine, and splenic.

HOLY BASIL

Warnings: can cause low blood pressure. Should not be taken with blood thinners as basil can increase bleeding.

Therapeutic Properties: Aromatic, disinfectant, protectant.

HONEYSUCKLE

Warnings: The berries are mildly poisonous.

Therapeutic Properties: Antibacterial, antifungal, and enhances intuition.

HOPS

Warnings: Do not take with any other medication or if you suffer from seizures.

Therapeutic Properties: Antiseptic, astringent, analgesic, digestive, nervine, sedative, hypnotic, analgesic, antibacterial, immune stimulant.

HOREHOUND

Warnings: Do not take if you have any type of heart disease.

Therapeutic Properties: Decongestant, expectorant, tonic, antiasthmatic, purgative, vulnerary, antibruising.

HORSETAIL

Warnings: Can cause dermatitis.

Therapeutic Properties: Astringent, diuretic, vulnerary.

JUNIPER

Warnings: Do not use if you suffer from any kidney disorders. Do not take if you are taking blood thinners.

Therapeutic Properties: Diuretic, antioxidant, analgesic, cicatrisant astringent and antiseptic.

LAVENDER

Warnings: May cause drowsiness.

Therapeutic Properties: Analgesic, antibiotic, anticonvulsive, antidepressant, antifungal, antiinfectious, anti-inflammatory, antirheumatic, antiseptic, antispasmodic, antivenous, antiviral, bactericidal, cicatrisant, decongestant, deodorant, detoxifying, disinfectant, restorative, sedative, relieves irritability and nervous tension (great for test anxiety), and tonic

True lavender (lavandula angustifolia) is the calming lavender. It can help restless babies, relieves insomnia, is great for burns, can be applied for insect bites and [burns, relieves premenstrual syndrome, can be effective against MRSA & tuberculosis.

Spike lavender (lavandula latifolia) is the stimulating lavender. It can be used for chest congestion, sprains, stiff joints, and muscular pain. Do not give to children under the age of 10 years.

LEMON BALM (MELISSA)

Warnings: Do not use lemon balm if you have any thyroid issues, are pregnant or nursing. May cause drowsiness.

Therapeutic Properties: Antidepressant, antihistaminic, antispasmodic, bactericidal, carminative, cordial, diaphoretic, emenagogue, febrifuge, hypotensive, nervine, sedative, stomachic, sudorific, and tonic. Melissa can also be used as an insect repellant and is a good remedy to treat shock.

LEMON VERBENA

Warnings: None found by author

Therapeutic Properties: Febrifuge, sedative, antispasmodic, stomachic, carminative.

LEMONGRASS

Warnings: Should not be taken during pregnancy or if you suspect you are pregnant.

Therapeutic Properties: Antioxidant, stomachic, sedative, fever reducer, anti-inflammatory, nervine, and immune booster.

LINDEN

Warnings: None found by author

Therapeutic Properties: sedative, anti-anxiety, decongestant, and nervine.

MAIDENHAIR FERN

Warnings: None found by author

Therapeutic Properties: Demulcent, emmenagogue, anticatarrhal, decongestant, hepatic.

MARJORAM

Warnings: Should not be used during pregnancy or breastfeeding. Should not be used during depression.

Therapeutic Properties: Analgesic, antiseptic, antispasmodic, aphrodisiac, antiviral, bactericidal, carminative, cephalic, cordial, diaphoretic, digestive, diuretic, emenagogue, expectorant, fungicidal, hypotensive, laxative, nervine, sedative, stomachic, vasodilator, and vulnerary. Good for insomnia blends, aids with cramps, great to use during cold and flu season.

MARSHMALLOW ROOT

Warnings: Not to be used with any other medication. Not to be used by diabetics.

Therapeutic Properties: Demulcent, diuretic, emollient, vulnerary, anti-inflammatory, antiasthmatic.

MILK THISTLE

Warnings: Can have severe side effects. Not to be taken with other medications. Can cause diarrhea. Violent actions have occurred in some people.

Therapeutic Properties: Anticatarrhal, anticarcinogenic, antidepressant.

MULLEIN

Warnings: Not to be taken internally.

Therapeutic Properties: Decongestant, emollient, astringent, digestive, sedative, anticatarrhal, anti-inflammatory, antiseptic, antibacterial, cephalic.

MUSTARD SEED

Warnings: None found by author

Therapeutic Properties: Rubefacient, stimulant, diuretic, emetic, carminative, tonic, circulation stimulant.

NUTMEG

Warnings: An overdose has been fatal in some people. Can have adverse effects such as nausea, seizures, and hallucinations. Do not take with any mental disorders, seizure disorder or neuralgic disorder. Not to be mixed with other medications.

Therapeutic Properties: Aromatic, stimulant, stomachic, digestive, carminative, anti-nausea.

OREGANO

Warnings: Should not be used if you are pregnant or suspect you are pregnant. Do not use in bathtub.

Therapeutic Properties: Analgesic, antiallergenic, antibacterial, antifungal, anti-inflammatory, antioxidant, antiparasitic, antiseptic, antispasmodic, antitoxic, antiviral, bactericidal, digestive, emenagogue, fungicidal, stimulant, tonic. Do not use during pregnancy, skin irritant.

OREGON GRAPE ROOT (poor man's goldenseal)

Warnings: Do not use while pregnant or nursing.

Therapeutic Properties: Antifungal, antimicrobial, and digestive.

PASSIONFLOWER

Warnings: Not to be taken with blood thinners. Not to be taken with sedatives.

Therapeutic Properties: Sedative hypnotic, antispasmodic, nervine, antianxiety, anti-hysteric, cephalic.

PEPPERMINT

Warnings: Should not be used if you are pregnant or suspect you are pregnant. Never put peppermint oil on neat or in the bath as it can cause skin irritation. Not to be used by small children. Peppermint cancels out any homeopathic remedies, so you should use one or the other.

Therapeutic Properties: Analgesic, anesthetic, antifungal, antiinfectious, anti-inflammatory, antiseptic, antigalactogogue, antiphlogistic, antispasmodic, astringent, carminative, cephalic, cholagogue, cordial, decongestant, digestive, emenagogue, expectorant, febrifuge, hepatic, invigorating, mucolytic, nervine, stimulant, stomachic, sudorific, vasoconstrictor and as a vermifuge.

PERIWINKLE

Warnings: None found by author

Therapeutic Properties: Laxative, tonic, astringent, anti-inflammatory, emollient, antiemetic.

PLEURISY ROOT

Warnings: Do not take if you are pregnant, nursing and not to be given to children.

Therapeutic Properties: Antispasmodic, diaphoretic, expectorant, tonic, carminative, cathartic, antirheumatic, anticatarrhal.

PLANTAIN

Warnings: Causes allergic reactions in some people.

Therapeutic Properties: Anti-inflammatory, febrifuge, styptic, diuretic, astringent, vulnerary, cephalic.

RASPBERRY LEAF

Warnings: Not to be used by pregnant women. Speeds labor and deliver.

Therapeutic Properties: Astringent, stimulant, vulnerary, stomachic, cooling, febrifuge.

RED CLOVER

Warnings: Not to be taken if you are pregnant, nursing, have any blood disorder or on blood thinners.

Therapeutic Properties: anti-asthmatic, anti-inflammatory, tonic, hormonal, and anti-cancer.

ROSE PETALS

Warnings: None found by author

Therapeutic Properties: Antidepressant, antiphlogistic, antiseptic, antispasmodic, antiviral, aphrodisiac, astringent, bactericidal, cholagogue, cicatrisant, depurative, emenagogue, haemostatic, hepatic, laxative, nervine, stomachic, and uterine oil.

ROSEHIPS

Warnings: None found by author

Therapeutic Properties: Laxative, diuretic, astringent, anti-inflammatory.

ROSEMARY

Warnings: Do not take if pregnant or nursing. Rosemary should not be used if you suffer from seizure disorder, epilepsy or high blood pressure. Children should not take rosemary younger than 4 years old.

Therapeutic Properties: Analgesic, antibacterial, anti-inflammatory, antirheumatic, antiseptic, astringent, antispasmodic, carminative, decongestant, disinfectant, diuretic, emenagogue, restorative, stimulant, and tonic.

SAGE

Warnings: If allergic, can cause mouth ulcers. Never use sage oil if you have high blood pressure or a seizure disorder.

Therapeutic Properties: Antibacterial, anticatarrhal, antifungal, antimicrobial, anti-inflammatory, antioxidant, antirheumatic, antiseptic, antispasmodic, cholagogue, choleretic, cicatrisant, depurative, digestive, disinfectant, emenagogue, expectorant, febrifuge, laxative, and stimulant.

SELF-HEAL

Warnings: Not to be used while pregnant or nursing

Therapeutic Properties: (summer savory) aromatic, carminative, expectorant, cordial, digestive; (winter savory) aromatic, stomachic, digestive.

SHEEP'S SORREL

Warnings: None found by author

Therapeutic Properties: Diuretic, diaphoretic, hepatic.

SKULLCAP

Warnings: Large amounts can cause adverse reactions. Do not take if you have diabetes, are pregnant, nursing, or with sedatives.

Therapeutic Properties: Antispasmodic, sedative, nervine, diuretic, tonic, antirheumatic.

SLIPPERY ELM

Warnings: May cause allergic reactions.

Therapeutic Properties: Demulcent, emollient, stomachic, antidiarrheal, digestive.

SPEARMINT

Warnings: Not to be taken by pregnant or breastfeeding women.

Therapeutic Properties: Antiseptic, antispasmodic, carminative, cephalic, emenagogue, expectorant, insecticide, nervine, restorative, stimulating, and tonic.

ST. JOHN'S WORT

Warnings: Can be phototoxic after prolonged usage. Do not take with other antidepressants. Do not take if you have any mental disorders.

Therapeutic Properties: Immunostimulant, astringent, antiviral, vermifuge, antidepressant, cooling, anti-inflammatory, antibacterial.

TARRAGON

Warnings: Persons with a history of cancer should not take tarragon. Do not take when pregnant or nursing.

Therapeutic Properties: Anti-inflammatory, antirheumatic, antiseptic, antispasmodic, aperitif, circulatory agent, digestive, deodorant, emenagogue, stimulant and a vermifuge. Tarragon can also be used to stimulate the immune system and for mental stimulation.

THYME

Warnings: Should not be used on children or by women who are pregnant or suspect that they are pregnant, or breast-feeding. Thyme should not be used in baths, as it can be a skin irritant. Do not diffuse. Persons with high blood pressure should never use thyme.

Therapeutic Properties: Carminative, digestive, bechic, antimicrobial, cardiac, antirheumatic, diuretic, vulnerary, antispasmodic, cicatrisant, expectorant, diaphoretic, anticatarrhal, astringent, bactericidal, antiseptic, cephalic, insecticide, hypertensive, tonic, vermifugal and antidepressant.

TURMERIC

Warnings: Not to be used if pregnant, nursing, have gallbladder or liver issues. May cause contact dermatitis.

Therapeutic Properties: Aromatic, stimulant, anti-inflammatory, immune stimulant.

UVA URSI

Warnings: Do not use if pregnant or nursing or suffer from heart disease.

Therapeutic Properties: Antiseptic, diuretic, antibacterial, urinary.

VALERIAN

Warnings: Large amounts can cause adverse reactions. Do not take with other medications. Not enough information known to be ensured of its safety during pregnancy or breastfeeding. May cause drowsiness.

Therapeutic Properties: Aromatic, stimulant, analgesic,

calming, nervine, tonic, antispasmodic, stomachic, cicatrisant, sedative, tranquilizing.

VIOLET

Warnings: Not to be used while pregnant or nursing.

Therapeutic Properties: Aromatic, laxative, anti-inflammatory, sedative, cephalic.

WHITE WILLOW BARK

Warnings: Not to be taken by children. Can cause stomach issues or allergic reactions. Not to be taken with other medications.

Therapeutic Properties: Analgesic, tonic, stimulant, astringent, vermifuge.

WILD CHERRY BARK

Warnings: Do not take if pregnant or nursing. Contains cyanide. Overdose is possible.

Therapeutic Properties: Astringent, tonic, sedative, anticatarrhal, expectorant, decongestant.

WILD LETTUCE

Warnings: None found by author

Therapeutic Properties: Sedative, nervine, hypnotic, antispasmodic.

WITCH HAZEL

Warnings: Use externally only. Dilute for children.

Therapeutic Properties: Astringent, tonic, sedative, styptic, antibruising, anti-inflammatory, antitumor, antiseptic.

WORMWOOD

Warnings: Can cause epileptic seizures and liver damage. Not to be taken internally. Not to be used by pregnant or nursing women.

Therapeutic Properties: Aromatic, tonic, nervine, stomachic, febrifuge, carminative, digestive, nervine, antiemetic.

YARROW

Warnings: If you have hay fever, you may be allergic to yarrow. Should not be used if you are, or suspect you are pregnant or are breast-feeding. May cause headaches.

Therapeutic Properties: Diaphoretic, antiseptic, antispasmodic, hypotensive, diaphoretic, emenagogue, digestive, astringent, anti-inflammatory, diuretic, cicatrisant, antiseptic, anticatarrhal, carminative, antirheumatic, haemostatic, emenagogue, hepatic, stimulant, hypotensive, stomachic and tonic.

YELLOW DOCK

Warnings: Overdoses have resulted in death. Not to be taken by children, pregnant or nursing women, persons with any diseases or with any other medications.

Therapeutic Properties: Laxative, tonic, antirheumatic, astringent, stomachic, emollient, cytophylactic, anticarcinogenic.

ESSENTIAL OIL THERAPEUTIC PROPERTIES AND WARNINGS

ALOE VERA OIL

Warnings: No warnings discovered by this author. Please complete your own research before using this oil.

Therapeutic Properties: Antibacterial, cicatrisant, emollient, analgesic, anti-inflammatory, antifungal, antiviral, astringent, emollient, cytophylactic, vulnerary, anti-irritant, antioxidant, and diuretic.

ANGELICA OIL

Warnings: Do not use if you are pregnant, nursing, or think you may be pregnant. Do not use if you have diabetes, epilepsy, or seizures, or with children. This oil is phototoxic, and therefore should not be used before prolonged sun exposure.

Therapeutic Properties: Febrifuge, hepatic, nervine, stimulant, stomachic, tonic, antispasmodic, carminative, holy, ritualistic, depurative, diaphoretic, digestive, diuretic, emenagogue, expectorant.

ANISE OIL

Warnings: Anise oil should not be used for prolonged periods of time. Do not use if you are pregnant, nursing, or think you may be pregnant.

Therapeutic Properties: Antiepileptic, antirheumatic, antiseptic, anti-spasmodic, aperient, carminative, cordial, decongestant, digestive, expectorant, culinary, insecticide, sedative, stimulant, anti-hysteric, respiratory, and vermifuge.

ARNICA OIL

Warnings: Arnica oil should never be taken internally or applied to an open wound. Always use a carrier oil (such as jojoba, sesame, grapeseed or your preference) with arnica oil. A patch test should be used with arnica oil as it is known for causing skin issues and allergies in certain people.

Therapeutic Properties: Analgesic, Anti-bruising, anti-inflammatory and anti-arthritic.

BASIL OIL

Warnings: Always use a carrier oil (such as jojoba, sesame, grapeseed or your preference) with basil oil as it can burn the skin. Do not use in bathwater as it can burn the skin. Do not use if you have epilepsy, seizures, or are pregnant or nursing.

Therapeutic Properties: Analgesic, culinary, antibacterial, immune boosting, antibiotic, antidepressant, relaxant, rituals, holy, anti-infectious, anti-inflammatory, antiseptic, anti-spasmodic, antiviral, carminative, digestive tonic, emenagogue, ophthalmic, calming, intestinal, carminative, earaches, restorative, general stimulant, stomachic.

BAY OIL

Warnings: Use sparingly for short durations of time.

Therapeutic Properties: antiseptic, emmenagogue, sedative, febrifuge, antibiotic, anti-neuralgic, aperitif, anti-spasmodic, insecticide and stomachic.

BENZOIN

Warnings: Should not be used in bathwater or in a diffuser as it is very thick and sticky and will adhere to skin. Always use a carrier oil (such as jojoba, sesame, grapeseed or your preference) to help dilute the benzoin. Do not use on children.

Therapeutic Properties: Antidepressant, anti-inflammatory, deodorant, analgesic, calming, antirheumatic, antiseptic, astringent, carminative, cordial, disinfectant, diuretic, euphoric, relaxant, expectorant, sedative, vulnerary, warming.

BERGAMOT OIL

Warnings: Do not use if you are pregnant, nursing, or think you may be pregnant. This oil is phototoxic, and therefore should not be used before prolonged sun exposure. Always dilute with a carrier oil (such as jojoba, sesame, grapeseed or your preference) before applying topically.

Therapeutic Properties: Analgesic, uplifting, aromatic, antibiotic, antianxiety, weight reduction, antidepressant, antiseptic, antispasmodic, cicatrisant, deodorant, digestive, disinfectant, febrifuge, vulnerary, vermifuge.

BIRCH OIL

Warnings: Birch oil is very potent. Always dilute with a carrier oil (such as jojoba, sesame, grapeseed or your preference) before applying topically. Birch oil has had some severe allergies associated with its usage. Ensure you are not suffering any side effects with a patch test before using birch oil. Do not use if you are pregnant, nursing, or think you may be pregnant.

Therapeutic Properties: Analgesic, aromatic, antiarthritic, antidepressant, cicatrisant, antibacterial, antifungal, anti-inflammatory, antirheumatic, antiarthritic, antiseptic, antispasmodic, astringent, disinfectant, depurative, diuretic, febrifuge, germicide, insecticide, tonic, stimulant, and detoxifier.

BLACK PEPPER OIL

Warnings: Do not use black pepper oil if you have any kidney issues as it can cause kidney damage.

Therapeutic Properties: Analgesic, respiratory, antiarthritic, antibacterial, anticatarrhal, culinary, anti-inflammatory, antioxidant, antirheumatic, anti-spasmodic, warming, aperient, carminative, digestive, diaphoretic, antiseptic, and expectorant.

BLUE CYPRESS OIL (see cypress oil)

BORAGE SEED OIL

Warnings: Borage seed oil can cause thinning of the blood. Do not take if you have upcoming tattoos or surgeries. Do not take borage seed oil if you have any liver issues.

Therapeutic Properties: Anti-inflammatory, diuretic, demulcent, emollient, cicatrisant, febrifuge, anticatarrhal, antidepressant, antirheumatic, hormonal, purifier, antiarthritic, antiulcer, and diuretic.

CAJUPUT OIL

Warnings: Please check with your physician before beginning a regimen of mixing cajuput oil with other medications. Do not use on children.

Therapeutic Properties: Analgesic, antineuralgic, antiseptic, antispasmodic, bactericide, carminative, cosmetic, decongestant, emenagogue, cosmetic, antineuralgic, expectorant, febrifuge, stimulant, tonic, sudorific, vermifuge, insecticide, respiratory, antifungal, diaphoretic, vulnerary, and antioxidant.

CALENDULA OIL

Warnings: Do not use if you are pregnant, nursing, or think

you may be pregnant.

Therapeutic Properties: Antispasmodic, cicatrisant, emenagogue, antipyretic, anti-inflammatory, vulnerary, menstrual cramps, cancer, stomach, antiulcer, antibruising, tonic, sudorific, anti-itch.

CAMPHOR OIL

Warning: Do not use on open wounds or mucus membranes. Do not heat camphor oil or use on children.

Therapeutic Properties: Stimulant, anesthetic, anti-inflammatory, antineuralgic, antispasmodic, antiseptic, decongestant, disinfectant, insecticide, nervine, antianxiety and sedative.

CARDAMOM OIL

Warnings: Always conduct a patch test before beginning a new oil. Cardamom has caused skin issues in some people.

Therapeutic Properties: Antimicrobial, carminative, antiseptic, antispasmodic, aphrodisiac, astringent, digestive, diuretic, stomachic, antioxidant, expectorant, and stimulant.

CASSIA OIL

Warnings: Cassia oil should always be mixed with a carrier oil (such as jojoba, sesame, grapeseed or your preference) before usage as it can cause burns due to its potency.

Therapeutic Properties: Anti-diarrheal, aromatic, antidepressant, warming, astringent, antiemetic, antigalactogogue, antiviral, immune booster, antimicrobial, antirheumatic, antiarthritic, astringent, carminative, circulatory, emenagogue, culinary, febrifuge, stimulant, digestive, and uplifting.

CEDARWOOD OIL

Warnings: Do not use on children. Cedarwood oil can terminate a pregnancy. Do not use if you are pregnant, nursing, or think you may be pregnant or are trying to conceive.

Therapeutic Properties: Antiseborrhoeic, digestive, antirheumatic, antiseptic, aromatic, antispasmodic, astringent, diuretic, grounding, emmenagogue, comforting, expectorant, fungicide, insecticidal, sedative, and tonic.

CHAMOMILE OIL

Warnings: Chamomile oil can irritate the skin. Do not use if you are pregnant, nursing, or think you may be pregnant.

Therapeutic Properties: Analgesic, aromatic, antiallergenic, antibiotic, antidepressant, antifungal, antiinfectious, comforting, anti-inflammatory, antimicrobial, antineuralgic, antiphlogistic, antiseptic, antispasmodic, bactericidal, carminative, cholagogue, cicatrisant, cooling, deodorant, digestive, emmenagogue, febrifuge, hepatic, nervine, sedative, sudorific, stomachic, tonic, vermifuge, vulnerary, and warming.

GERMAN CHAMOMILE (Matricaria Recutita) Anti-inflammatory, analgesic, anti-allergenic, antispasmodic, antibacterial, carminative, digestive, fungicidal, nervine, and sedative, antiseptic, anticatarrhal.

ROMAN CHAMOMILE (Anthemus Nobilis) Anti-inflammatory, antispasmodic, antiseptic, antidiuretic, antitumor, aromatic, antimicrobial, sedative, antibiotic, antineuralgic, cholagogue, digestive, bactericidal, carminative, antiphlogistic, hepatic, and tonic.

CILANTRO OIL

Warnings: No warnings discovered by this author. Please complete your own research before using this oil.

Therapeutic Properties: Analgesic, antispasmodic, fungicidal, depurative, stomachic and stomachic.

CINNAMON BARK OIL

Warnings: Cinnamon bark oil should not be used by those undergoing cancer treatments such as chemotherapy or radiation. This oil should always be diluted with a carrier oil (such as jojoba, sesame, grapeseed or your preference) as it can cause significant burns to the skin if undiluted. Do not use if you are pregnant, nursing, or think you may be pregnant.

Therapeutic Properties: Antibacterial, analgesic, digestive, culinary, anticlotting, antifungal, uplifting, antimicrobial, antioxidant, hypotensive, anticarcinogenic, insecticide, astringent, carminative, cooling, stimulating, and aromatic.

CITRUS OILS

Warnings: These oils are phototoxic, and therefore should not be used before prolonged sun exposure.

Therapeutic Properties: Antitoxic, culinary, uplifting, germicidal, antiviral, antibacterial, detoxifying, aromatic, astringent, and circulatory.

CLARY SAGE OIL

Warnings: Do not use with low blood pressure, or if you are hypoglycemic. Can cause drowsiness, so it's better to not drive or operate heavy machinery while using this oil. Do not use if you are pregnant, trying to get pregnant, nursing, or think you may be pregnant.

Therapeutic Properties: Anticonvulsive, antidepressant, aromatic, antispasmodic, opthalmic, antiseptic, perfumery, aphrodisiac, astringent, bactericidal, restorative, carminative, deodorant, digestive, emenagogue, euphoric, hypotensive, hormones, nervine, sedative, stomachic, tonic, calming, soothing, uterine, and vulnerary.

CLEMATIS OIL

Warnings: Do not ingest internally.

Therapeutic Properties: Varicose veins, stomachic, nervine, antispasmodic, antisyphilis, vulnerary, antiulcer, vulnerary and cicatrisant.

CLOVE OIL

Warnings: A natural blood thinner, do not take if you are taking blood thinners or are scheduled for an upcoming tattoo or surgery. Clove oil is very thick and strong, do not use in diffuser or in baths. Always dilute with a carrier oil (such as jojoba, sesame, grapeseed or your preference). Do not use if you are pregnant, nursing, or think you may be pregnant.

Therapeutic Properties: Analgesic, carminative, aromatic, antifungal, anti-inflammatory, bactericidal, antimicrobial, antirheumatic, antiseptic, antiviral, anesthetic, insecticide, aphrodisiac, stimulant, and culinary.

COMFREY OIL

Warnings: Do not take internally. Do not take if you have a liver disease, or a serious disease such as cancer. Do not use if you are pregnant, nursing, or think you may be pregnant.

Therapeutic Properties: Anti-inflammatory, antirheumatic, antiulcer, heavy menstrual periods, diarrhea, vulnerary, persistent cough, respiratory, antibronchitis, and vulnerary.

CORIANDER OIL

Warnings: Do not take if you have any kidney issues or if you are pregnant, nursing, or think you may be pregnant.

Therapeutic Properties: Analgesic, culinary, aphrodisiac, antispasmodic, carminative, depurative, deodorant, digestive, fungicide, lipolytic, aromatic, stimulant, stomachic, diarrhea, flatulence, loss of appetite, upset stomach, stomach spasms, nausea, hernia, hemorrhoids, and antirheumatic.

COSMOS OIL

Warnings: No warnings discovered by this author. Please complete your own research before using this oil.

Therapeutic Properties: Insecticidal, antibacterial, antioxidant, and aromatic.

CYPRESS OIL

Warnings: Do not use on varicose veins. Do not use if you are pregnant, nursing, or think you may be pregnant.

Therapeutic Properties: Antiinfectious, anti-inflammatory, hormone issues, antiparasitic, antirheumatic, antiseptic, antispasmodic, astringent, decongestant, deodorant, diuretic, restorative, vasoconstrictor.

DILL OIL

Warnings: No warnings discovered by this author. Please complete your own research before using this oil.

Therapeutic Properties: Antispasmodic, antioxidant, antimicrobial, carminative, digestive, disinfectant, galactogogue, culinary, antiarthritic, sedative, stomachic, and sudorific.

ECHINACEA OIL

Warnings: No warnings discovered by this author. Please complete your own research before using this oil.

Therapeutic Properties: Antibiotic, analgesic, antirheumatic, urinary, antibacterial, antiviral, respiratory, antiinfectious, anti-inflammatory, anti-allergen, immune booster, and antioxidant.

EUCALYPTUS OIL

Warnings: Eucalyptus can trigger asthma attacks and should never be used in conjunction with other medications, on the face, on children, or by persons with high blood pressure.

Therapeutic Properties: Analgesic, aromatic, antibacterial, antifungal, perfumery, anti-inflammatory, antimicrobial, antiseptic, antispasmodic, antiviral, bactericidal, decongestant, deodorant, diuretic, expectorant, mucolytic, stimulating, vulnerary, and tonic.

FENNEL OIL

Warnings: Fennel oil should not be used if you have a disorder such as seizures, cancer, kidney issues, or hormone problems. Do not use if you are pregnant, nursing, or think you may be pregnant.

Therapeutic Properties: Anti-inflammatory, antidepressant, antiemetic, diaphoretic, analgesic, opthalmic, antiseptic, antispasmodic, digestive, diuretic, stimulant, rubefacient, laxative, and antibruising.

FIR OIL

Warnings: Do not use if you are pregnant, nursing, or think

you may be pregnant.

Therapeutic Properties: Analgesic, antibacterial, anti-inflammatory, antiinfectious, antioxidant, detoxifier, respiratory, aromatic, grounding, calming, warming, deodorant, and antiseptic.

FRANKINCENSE OIL

Warnings: Do not use if you are pregnant, nursing, or think you may be pregnant, especially during the first trimester of pregnancy.

Therapeutic Properties: Analgesic, spiritual, grounding, antiasthmatic, anti-inflammatory, antiseptic, astringent, carminative, cicatrisant, cytophylactic, digestive, disinfectant, holy, ritualistic, diuretic, emenagogue, expectorant, sedative, tonic, uterine, uplifting, calming, and vulnerary.

GARLIC OIL

Warnings: Do not give garlic oil to babies. Do not use if you are pregnant, nursing, or think you may be pregnant.

Therapeutic Properties: Antibacterial, antiviral, antidandruff, antiseptic, anti-hypertensive, culinary, detoxifier, vasodilator, hypotensive, antioxidant, anticarcinogenic, antifungal, carminative, antimicrobial, anticatarrhal, anticarcinogenic, and expectorant.

GERANIUM OIL

Warnings: Do not use if you are pregnant, nursing, or think you may be pregnant. Do not use if you have low blood sugar or have skin issues. May cause insomnia.

Therapeutic Properties: Analgesic, antibacterial, antidepressant, antifungal, antianxiety, aromatic, anti-inflammatory, antiseptic, astringent, bactericidal, culinary, deodorant, hemostatic, cicatrisant, cytophylactic, diuretic, styptic, tonic, vermifuge, and vulnerary.

GINGER OIL

Warnings: Do not use ginger oil if you are on blood thinners, have sensitive skin, or have gallstones.

Therapeutic Properties: Analgesic, antiemetic, antiseptic, antispasmodic, anti-inflammatory, bactericidal, carminative, cephalic, culinary, expectorant, febrifuge, laxative, rubefacient, stimulant, stomachic, sudorific, tonic, and antioxidant.

GINGKO BILOBA OIL

Warnings: No warnings discovered by this author. Please complete your own research before using this oil.

Therapeutic Properties: Antioxidant, antiinfectious, memory booster, antiasthmatic, stimulant, anti-inflammatory, antidepressant, decongestant, energizer, circulatory, antioxidant, and nervine.

GINSENG OIL

Warnings: No warnings discovered by this author. Please complete your own research before using this oil.

Therapeutic Properties: Anti-inflammatory, enhances circulation, aphrodisiac, tonic, vasodilator, stimulant, antianxiety, immune booster, antioxidant, appetite suppressant, and aphrodisiac.

GRAPEFRUIT OIL

Warnings: This oil is phototoxic, and therefore should not be used before

Prolonged sun exposure. Do not use if you have a skin condition as it can irritate the skin.

Therapeutic Properties: Antidepressant, culinary, antiseptic, antioxidant, aperitif, energizer, astringent, diuretic, disinfectant, lymphatic, stimulant, appetite reduction, antianxiety, tonic, and aromatic.

HELICHRYSUM OIL (immortelle, everlasting)

Warnings: Do not use with blood thinners or with children. Do not use if you are pregnant, nursing, or think you may be pregnant.

Therapeutic Properties: Antiallergenic, antibruising, anticoagulant, antidepressant, anti-inflammatory, antiseptic, antispasmodic, analgesic, antibruising, anticoagulant, antimicrobial, antiviral, antitussive, cicatrisant, antifungal, hepatic, holy, ritualistic, expectorant, and tonic.

HIBISCUS OIL

Warnings: Do not use if you are pregnant, nursing, or think you may be pregnant.

Therapeutic Properties: Antiallergenic, hypertensive, anticoagulant, antihaematomic, anti-inflammatory, antimicrobial, immune booster, antiphlogistic, antiseptic, weight reduction, antitussive, aromatic, dye, cholagogue, cicatrisant, cytophylactic, diuretic, emollient, expectorant, febrifuge, fungicidal, hepatic, nervine, splenic, and anticarcinogenic.

HOLLY OIL

Warnings: No warnings discovered by this author. Please complete your own research before using this oil.

Therapeutic Properties: Hypertensive, antirheumatic, digestive, circulation, protection, and purgative.

HONEYSUCKLE OIL

Warnings: No warnings discovered by this author. Please complete your own research before using this oil.

Therapeutic Properties: Antibacterial, culinary, perfumery, antifungal, aromatic, and enhances intuition.

HYSSOP OIL

Warnings: Do not use if you are pregnant, nursing, or think

you may be pregnant. Do not use if you suffer from a seizure disorder or high blood pressure. Do not mix with other medications.

Therapeutic Properties: Antirheumatic, antiseptic, antispasmodic, antiarthritic, aromatic, astringent, antibruising, antiinfectious, carminative, cicatrisant, digestive, diuretic, emenagogue, expectorant, febrifuge, hypertensive, nervine, stimulant, sudorific, tonic, vermifuge, vulnerary, holy, and rituals.

JASMINE OIL

Warnings: Do not use if you are pregnant, nursing, or think you may be pregnant.

Therapeutic Properties: Antidepressant, perfumery, rituals, antiseptic, antispasmodic, aphrodisiac, antianxiety, cicatrisant, emenagogue, expectorant, galactogogue, aromatic, parturient, respiratory, sedative, uterine, and spiritual.

JUNIPER BERRY OIL

Warning: Do not take for extended periods of time. Do not take if you have kidney issues. Do not mix with other medications. Do not use if you are pregnant, nursing, or think you may be pregnant.

Therapeutic Properties: Antirheumatic, antiseptic, antispasmodic, antitoxic, astringent, carminative, antifatigue, energizer, circulatory stimulant, diuretic, depurative, sudorific, depurative, stimulating, stomachic, rubefacient, vulnerary, tonic, antiinfectious, anti-inflammatory, and detoxifying.

LAVENDER OIL

Warnings: No warnings discovered by this author. Please complete your own research before using this oil.

Therapeutic Properties: Analgesic, antimicrobial, antibiotic, anticonvulsive, hypotensive, antidepressant, antifungal, antianxiety, antiinfectious, anti-inflammatory, aromatic, antirheumatic, antiseptic, antispasmodic, antivenous, antiviral, bactericidal, calming, cicatrisant, decongestant, deodorant, detoxifying, disinfectant, restorative, sedative, nervine, tranquilizing, tonic, and perfumery.

TRUE LAVENDER (Lavandula angustifolia) calming, holy, antidepressant, analgesic, spiritual, vulnerary, hormonal, and rituals.

SPIKE LAVENDER (Lavandula latifolia) Stimulant, aromatic, antiarthritic, insecticidal, decongestant and expectorant, analgesic, and perfumery.

LAVANDIN (Lavandula x intermedia) Calming, antidepressant, cicatrisant, expectorant, antiinfectious, sedative, and nervine.

LEMON OIL

Warnings: This oil is phototoxic, and therefore should not be used before prolonged sun exposure. Do not use if you are pregnant, nursing, or think you may be pregnant. Can cause skin irritation.

Therapeutic Properties: Antispasmodic, uplifting, astringent, aromatic, culinary, germicidal, detoxifier, tonic, and immune booster.

LEMON BALM OIL (see melissa)

Warnings: Do not take if you have thyroid issues. Do not use if you are pregnant, nursing, or think you may be pregnant. May cause drowsiness.

Therapeutic Properties: Antibacterial, antidepressant, antihistaminic, antispasmodic, bactericidal, bronchial, carminative, cordial, diaphoretic, emenagogue, febrifuge, hypotensive, nervine, sedative, stomachic, sudorific, insect repellant, vulnerary, and tonic.

LEMON THYME OIL

Warnings: Do not use if you are pregnant, nursing, or think you may be pregnant.

Therapeutic Properties: Decongestant, relaxant, antispasmodic, antiaging, immune boosting, decongestant, antiasthmatic, calming, antianxiety, aromatic, and culinary.

LEMONGRASS OIL

Warnings: Do not use if you are pregnant, nursing, or think you may be pregnant.

Therapeutic Properties: Aromatic, analgesic, culinary, antipyretic, anti-inflammatory, calming, febrifuge, immune boosting, astringent, fungicidal, bactericidal, antidepressant, uplifting, aromatic, antioxidant, mood enhancer, stomachic, sedative, and nervine.

LIME OIL

Warnings: Do not use if you are pregnant, nursing, or think you may be pregnant. This oil is phototoxic, and therefore should not be used before prolonged sun exposure.

Therapeutic Properties: Antiseptic, antiviral, aperitif, astringent, aromatic, antiinfectious, bactericidal, disinfectant, febrifuge, hemostatic, respiratory, restorative, tonic, and culinary.

LINDEN BLOSSOM OIL

Warnings: No warnings discovered by this author. Please complete your own research before using this oil.

Therapeutic Properties: Diuretic, immune booster, anticancer, calming, antianxiety, anti-inflammatory, hypertensive, and expectorant.

LOTUS OIL

Warnings: Not enough known about use during pregnancy. Avoid if pregnant or nursing. No other warnings discovered by this author.

Therapeutic Properties: Aromatic, astringent, emmenagogue, expectorant, sedative, aphrodisiac, hypotensive, aromatic, vasodilator, calming, chakras, meditative, holy, ritualistic, tranquilizing, and hypnotic.

MANDARIN OIL

Warnings: This oil is phototoxic, and therefore should not be used before prolonged sun exposure.

Therapeutic Properties: Antibacterial, antiseptic, antispasmodic, aromatic, balancing, calming, antiviral, bactericidal, circulatory, cytophylactic, depurative, digestive, expectorant, hepatic, nervine, relaxant, sedative, stomachic, and a tonic.

MANUKA OIL

Warnings: No warnings discovered by this author. Please complete your own research before using this oil.

Therapeutic Properties: Antiallergenic, antibacterial, antidandruff, antianxiety, calming, antifungal, anti-inflammatory, antihistaminic, cicatrisant, cytophylactic, deodorant, vulnerary, and nervine.

MARJORAM OIL

Warnings: Do not use if you are taking blood thinners or suffer from depression. Do not use if you are pregnant, nursing, or think you may be pregnant.

Therapeutic Properties: Analgesic, antiseptic, antispasmodic, aphrodisiac, antiviral, bactericidal, carminative, cephalic, cordial, diaphoretic, digestive, diuretic, culinary, emenagogue, expectorant, tranquilizing, fungicidal, hypotensive, laxative, nervine, sedative, spiritual, holy, ritualistic, stomachic, vasodilator, and vulnerary.

MELALEUCA OIL (tea tree oil)

Warnings: No warnings discovered by this author. Please complete your own research before using this oil.

Therapeutic Properties: Antibacterial, antibiotic, antifungal, antiinfectious, anti-inflammatory, antimicrobial, antiparasitic, antiseptic, antiviral, balsamic, cicatrisant, decongestant, emollient, expectorant, anti-itch, fungicide, immune stimulant, respiratory, insecticide, stimulant, antiallergenic, sudorific, vulnerary, vaginal infections, dental, and vasodilator.

MELISSA OIL (lemon balm oil)

Warnings: Do not take if you have thyroid issues. Do not use if you are pregnant, nursing, or think you may be pregnant. May cause drowsiness.

Therapeutic Properties: Antibacterial, antidepressant, antihistaminic, antispasmodic, bactericidal, bronchial, carminative, cordial, diaphoretic, emenagogue, febrifuge, hypotensive, nervine, sedative, stomachic, sudorific, insect repellant, vulnerary, and tonic.

MYRRH OIL

Warnings: Do not use if you are pregnant, nursing, or think you may be pregnant.

Therapeutic Properties: Analgesic, antibacterial, anticatarrhal, antifungal, anti-inflammatory, antimicrobial, antiseptic, antispasmodic, astringent, carminative, cicatrisant, circulatory, diaphoretic, emollient, expectorant, holy, rituals, immune stimulant, mucolytic, revitalizing, sedative, stimulant, stomachic, vulnerary, and tonic.

MYRTLE OIL

Warnings: Do not use internally or with children or any pulmonary issues. Do not use if you are pregnant, nursing, or think you may be pregnant.

Therapeutic Properties: Antiseptic, antimicrobial, anti-inflammatory, nervine, uplifting, astringent, deodorant, digestive, expectorant, respiratory, sedative.

NEEM OIL

Warnings: Do not use internally or with children or any pulmonary issues. Do not use if you are pregnant, nursing, or think you may be pregnant. Do not use if you have autoimmune disorders, are a child, have multiple sclerosis or rheumatoid arthritis, or suffer from any liver issues.

Therapeutic Properties: Anti-inflammatory, detoxifier, antiparasitic, antiulcer, antifungal, antibacterial, antiviral, antioxidant, anticarcinogenic, and dental.

NEROLI OIL

Warnings: Neroli can be a skin irritant in some people. Do not use on children.

Therapeutic Properties: Antidepressant, antiseptic, aromatic, antispasmodic, antiinfectious, aphrodisiac, antianxiety, bactericidal, cordial, carminative, cicatrisant, cephalic, cytophylactic, deodorant, disinfectant, digestive, emollient, sedative, and a tonic.

NIAOULI OIL

Warnings: No warnings discovered by this author. Please complete your own research before using this oil.

Therapeutic Properties: Analgesic, antirheumatic, antiseptic, antimicrobial, antimalarial, bactericidal, balsamic, cicatrisant, decongestant, expectorant, febrifuge, insecticide, stimulant, vermifuge, urinary, respiratory, anti-inflammatory, and vulnerary.

ORANGE OIL

Warnings: This oil is phototoxic, and therefore should not be used before prolonged sun exposure.

Therapeutic Properties: Anti-inflammatory, antidepressant, antispasmodic, antimicrobial, antibacterial, aromatic, culinary, antiseptic, aphrodisiac, carminative, cholagogue, diuretic, immune stimulant, tonic, and sedative.

OREGANO OIL

Warnings: Do not apply directly to skin, such as in the bathtub, as it can cause rashes or burns on skin. Always dilute oregano oil with a carrier oil (such as jojoba, sesame, grapeseed or your preference). Do not use if you are pregnant, nursing, or think you may be pregnant.

Therapeutic Properties: Analgesic, antiallergenic, antibacterial, antifungal, anti-inflammatory, antioxidant, antiparasitic, antiseptic, antispasmodic, antitoxic, antiviral, bactericidal, culinary, disinfectant, digestive, antiinfectious, anticarcinogenic, emenagogue, antiarthritic, respiratory, fungicidal, stimulant, tonic.

OREGON GRAPE ROOT OIL

Warnings: Do not use if you are pregnant, nursing, or think you may be pregnant.

Therapeutic Properties: Aromatic, antifungal, digestive, spiritual, cleansing, detoxifying, antiulcer, stomachic, antiinfectious, skin issues, and antimicrobial.

PALMAROSA OIL

Warnings: No warnings discovered by this author. Please complete your own research before using this oil.

Therapeutic Properties: Antiseptic, antiviral, bactericidal, cytophylactic, skin issues, antianxiety, digestive, febrifuge, nervine, antirheumatic, antiarthritic, and hydration balm.

PATCHOULI OIL

Warnings: Patchouli oil should not be taken by persons with any eating disorders.

Therapeutic Properties: Antidepressant, anti-inflammatory, antimicrobial, antiphlogistic, antiseptic, aphrodisiac, astringent, bactericidal, aromatic, cicatrisant, fixative, cytophylactic, deodorant, diuretic, emollient, febrifuge, calming, grounding, fungicide, insecticide, nervine, sedative, and a tonic.

PEPPERMINT OIL

Warning: Peppermint oil can cause skin irritation, so do not use in the bath. Never use peppermint oil with prescribed medications. Do not use if you are pregnant, nursing, or think you may be pregnant.

Therapeutic Properties: Analgesic, anesthetic, antifungal, antiinfections, anti-inflammatory, antiseptic, antigalactogogue, antiphlogistic, antispasmodic, astringent, carminative, cephalic, cholagogue, cordial, decongestant, digestive, emollient, emenagogue, expectorant, febrifuge, hepatic, culinary, invigorating, mucolytic, cicatrisant, nervine, stimulant, stomachic, sudorific, aromatic, vasoconstrictor, vermifuge, nervousness, vertigo, respiratory problems, and digestion.

PERU BALSAM OIL

Warnings: Do not use if you are pregnant, nursing, or think you may be pregnant. Do not use if you suffer from allergies, or kidney issues. Do not take internally.

Therapeutic Properties: Aromatic, antifungal, vulnerary, anti-inflammatory, calming, grounding, respiratory, aromatic, antiparasitic, antiinfectious, and antiseptic.

PETITGRAIN OIL

Warnings: No warnings discovered by this author. Please complete your own research before using this oil.

Therapeutic Properties: Antiseptic, antispasmodic, antidepressant, aromatic, balancing, calming, cosmetic, cicatrisant, uplifting, deodorant, nervine, and sedative.

PINE OIL

Warnings: Do not use if you have sensitive skin as pine oil can irritate skin. Do not use if you have high blood pressure. Do not use if you are pregnant, nursing, or think you may be pregnant.

Therapeutic Properties: Antirheumatic, antibacterial, analgesic, diuretic, energizing, antiseptic, aromatic, culinary, rubefacient, relaxant, boosts metabolism, depurative, antioxidant, urinary, and decongestant.

PINK GRAPEFRUIT OIL

Warnings: No warnings discovered by this author. Please complete your own research before using this oil.

Therapeutic Properties: Energizer, Weight control, antioxidant, anticarcinogenic, antiseptic, detoxifier, weight reduction, purifier, and tonic.

POPPY OIL

Warnings: No warnings discovered by this author. Please complete your own research before using this oil.

Therapeutic Properties: Sedative, astringent, expectorant, diaphoretic, antispasmodic, analgesic, hypnotic, and anticarcinogenic.

RAVENSARA OIL

Warnings: No warnings discovered by this author. Please complete your own research before using this oil.

Therapeutic Properties: Analgesic, antioxidant, antiallergenic, aromatic, antibacterial, anti-inflammatory, antimicrobial, antidepressant, antifungal, cicatrisant, antiseptic, aromatic, antiperspirant, antispasmodic, antiviral, aphrodisiac, disinfectant, carminative, diuretic, antitumor, expectorant, relaxant, nervine, and tonic.

ROMAN CHAMOMILE OIL (chamomile oil)

Warnings: Chamomile oil can irritate the skin. Do not use if you are pregnant, nursing, or think you may be pregnant.

Therapeutic Properties: Anti-inflammatory, antispasmodic, antiseptic, antidiuretic, antitumor, aromatic, antimicrobial, sedative, antibiotic, antineuralgic, cholagogue, digestive, bactericidal, carminative, antiphlogistic, hepatic, and tonic.

ROSE OIL

Warnings: Do not use if you are pregnant, nursing, or think you may be pregnant.

Therapeutic Properties: Antidepressant, culinary, antiphlogistic, antiseptic, antispasmodic, antiviral, aphrodisiac, astringent, bactericidal, cholagogue, cicatrisant, depurative, emenagogue, hemostatic, hepatic, anticarcinogenic, aromatic, antiarthritic, rituals, laxative, nervine, stomachic, and uterine tonic.

ROSEMARY oil

Warnings: Do not use if you have seizures, high blood pressure, epilepsy, or are trying to get pregnant. Do not use if you are pregnant, nursing, or think you may be pregnant. Do not use on children.

Therapeutic Properties: Analgesic, culinary, antibacterial, anti-inflammatory, digestive, memory enhancer, antirheumatic, aromatic, antiseptic, circulatory, astringent, antispasmodic, carminative, antiaging, anticarcinogenic, immunity booster, decongestant, antioxidant, disinfectant, diuretic, restorative, stimulant, and tonic.

SAGE OIL

Warnings: Not safe to use if you suffer from high blood pressure or any type of seizures.

Therapeutic Properties: Antibacterial, antifungal, antimicrobial, focus, anti-inflammatory, antioxidant, antiseptic, antispasmodic, cholagogue, choleretic, cicatrisant, immune booster, antiaging, depurative, culinary, aromatic, positivity, digestive, disinfectant, emenagogue, expectorant, febrifuge, laxative, and stimulant.

SANDALWOOD OIL

Warnings: Do not use if you have any kidney issues. Can cause allergic skin reactions, so a patch test should be completed before using.

Therapeutic Properties: Antifungal, anti-inflammatory, grounding, antiseptic, antiphlogistic, antispasmodic, aphrodisiac, astringent, calming, memory enhancer, cicatrisant, mental clarity, carminative, decongestant, diuretic, relaxing, disinfectant, emollient, expectorant, harmonizing, hypotensive, insecticide, memory booster, sedative, and tonic.

SESAME OIL

Warnings: No warnings discovered by this author. Please complete your own research before using this oil.

Therapeutic Properties: Grounding, digestive, cosmetic, anticarcinogenic, antirheumatic, culinary, anti-inflammatory, antiaging, antifungal, antianxiety, antidepressant, purifying, and antioxidant.

SPEARMINT OIL

Warning: Do not take internally. Do not use if you are pregnant, nursing, or think you may be pregnant.

Therapeutic Properties: Antiseptic, antispasmodic, aromatic, carminative, cephalic, antianxiety, emenagogue, stomachic, expectorant, circulatory, antifatigue, insecticide, respiratory, hormonal, nervine, culinary, restorative, immune boosting, antibacterial, stimulating, calming, relaxing, and tonic.

SPIKENARD OIL

Warnings: Do not use if you are pregnant, nursing, or think you may be pregnant.

Therapeutic Properties: Antibacterial, meditative, antibiotic, deodorant, digestive, respiratory, antioxidant, antianxiety, vasoconstrictor, antidepressant, antifungal, holy, anti-inflammatory, grounding, spiritual, deodorant, laxative, sedative, rituals, and uterine.

SPRUCE OIL

Warnings: Do not use if you are pregnant, nursing, or think you may be pregnant. Do not take if you suffer from any type of heart condition or asthma.

Therapeutic Properties: Anti-infectious, anti-inflammatory, antispasmodic, expectorant, immune system stimulant, respiratory, aromatic, grounding, vulnerary, antiarthritic, antirheumatic, antimicrobial, mentally invigorating, grounding, strengthen nervous system, and disinfectant.

ST. JOHN'S WORT OIL

Warnings: Do not mix with other medications unless under supervision of your prescribing doctor. Watch for side effects. Perform a patch test before using. This oil is phototoxic, and therefore should not be used before prolonged sun exposure.

Therapeutic Properties: Anti-inflammatory, antioxidant, astringent, hormonal, antidepressant, antianxiety, antiarthritic, decongestant, antineuralgic, antirheumatic, cicatrisant, vermifuge, immunostimulant, and cooling.

SWEET ORANGE OIL

Warnings: Use caution when giving to children and do not use for long periods of time. This oil is phototoxic, and therefore should not be used before prolonged sun exposure.

Therapeutic Properties: Aromatic, anticarcinogenic, detoxifying, energizing, tonic, circulative, stomachic, digestive, anticoagulant, culinary, antidepressant, anti-inflammatory, antiseptic, carminative, cicatrisant, restorative, relaxing, antianxiety, cholagogue, antimicrobial, germicidal, digestive, diuretic, and antispasmodic.

TANGERINE OIL

Warnings: This oil is phototoxic, and therefore should not be used before prolonged sun exposure.

Therapeutic Properties: Antiseptic, antispasmodic, cytophylactic, restorative, anticarcinogenic, calming, antibacterial, aromatic, culinary, depurative, sedative, stomachic, antiulcer, weight reduction, antifungal, antiinfectious, vulnerary, and tonic.

TARRAGON OIL

Warnings: Do not use if you are pregnant, nursing, or think you may be pregnant.

Therapeutic Properties: Anti-inflammatory, antirheumatic, detoxifying, stomachic, hormonal, antiseptic, antispasmodic, aperitif, balancing, aromatic, circulatory agent, digestive, deodorant, emenagogue, antifatigue, stimulant, and a vermifuge.

TEA TREE OIL (melaleuca)

Warnings: No warnings discovered by this author. Please complete your own research before using this oil.

Therapeutic Properties: Antibacterial, antibiotic, antifungal, antiinfectious, anti-inflammatory, antimicrobial, antiparasitic, antiseptic, antiviral, balsamic, cicatrisant, decongestant, emollient, expectorant, anti-itch, fungicide, immune stimulant, respiratory, insecticide, stimulant, antiallergenic, sudorific, vulnerary, vaginal infections, dental, and vasodilator.

THYME OIL

Warnings: Do not use in the bathtub as it will cling to skin and burn. This oil is too thick to use in a diffuser and my harm your diffuser. Do not use on children. Do not use if you have high blood pressure. Do not use if you are pregnant, nursing, or think you may be pregnant.

Therapeutic Properties: Antimicrobial, antirheumatic, antiseptic, antispasmodic, bactericidal, bechic, perfumery, cardiac, carminative, anti-inflammatory, antiinfectious, cicatrisant, restorative, diuretic, aromatic, emenagogue, expectorant, hypertensive, insecticide, stimulant, bronchial, digestive, tonic, culinary, immunostimulant, and vermifugal.

VALERIAN OIL

Warnings: This oil does not have enough evidence to present as safe to use during pregnancy or breastfeeding or trying to conceive. I would advise to not use during those times. Do not combine with other medications.

Therapeutic Properties: Analgesic, antianxiety, antidepressant, antispasmodic, rituals, hormonal, tranquilizing, stomachic, nervine, positivity, cicatrisant, calming and sedative.

VANILLA OIL

Warnings: No warnings discovered by this author. Please complete your own research before using this oil.

Therapeutic Properties: Aromatic, anticarcinogenic, tranquilizing, antidepressant, antioxidant, aphrodisiac, culinary, sedative, febrifuge, relaxant, hormonal, and febrifuge.

VETIVER OIL

Warnings: Do not take consistently for long periods of time.

Therapeutic Properties: Anticarcinogenic, antidepressant, cicatrisant, antioxidant, aphrodisiac, febrifuge, sedative, antiseptic, anti-inflammatory, cooling, relaxant, calming, and tranquilizing.

VITAMIN E OIL

Warnings: Do not ingest internally

Therapeutic Properties: Preservative, emollient, antiaging, antifatigue, antiarthritic, culinary, anticarcinogenic, antiperspirant, cicatrisant, and antioxidant.

WHEAT GERM OIL

Warnings: No warnings discovered by this author. Please complete your own research before using this oil. Do not use if you are a celiac.

Therapeutic Properties: Antiaging, emollient, bactericidal, cell regenerator, and antioxidant.

WHITE FIR OIL

Warnings: No warnings discovered by this author. Please complete your own research before using this oil.

Therapeutic Properties: Aromatic, expectorant, antiinfectious, respiratory, weight reduction, anticancer, antioxidant, detoxifying, anti-inflammatory, antirheumatic, antiseptic, analgesic, rituals, spiritual, antiaging, cardiovascular, and antirheumatic.

WILD ORANGE OIL

Warnings: No warnings discovered by this author. Please complete your own research before using this oil.

Therapeutic Properties: Aromatic, cleanser, antimicrobial, energizer, febrifuge, depurative, hypotensive, stomachic, diuretic, digestive, culinary, cicatrisant, purifying, uplifting, antioxidant, immune booster, antiseptic, antirheumatic, and carminative.

WINTERGREEN OIL

Warnings: There are many warnings about wintergreen oil. It is a very effective arthritis pain reliever, but do not use for extended periods of time. Ensure through your physician that it is safe to use wintergreen oil with your prescribed medications. Watch for side effects. Do not give to children. Do not use if you are pregnant, nursing, or think you may be pregnant.

Therapeutic Properties: Analgesic, anodyne, antiarthritic, calming, antirheumatic, antispasmodic, antiseptic, diuretic, aromatic, astringent, carminative, diuretic, culinary, spiritual, warming, stress reduction, emenagogue, and stimulant.

YARROW OIL

Warnings: Has been known to cause headaches in some people. Do not use if you are pregnant, nursing, or think you may be pregnant.

Therapeutic Properties: Anti-inflammatory, febrifuge, antirheumatic, antiseptic, vulnerary, antispasmodic, astringent, carminative, nervine, cicatrisant, circulative, diaphoretic, digestive, expectorant, haemostatic, hypotensive, stomachic, styptic, and tonic.

YLANG-YLANG OIL

Warnings: Do not use if you are on blood thinners or have high blood pressure. May cause headaches, watch for side effects. Can cause skin allergies in some people. Do not use if you are pregnant, nursing, or think you may be pregnant.

Therapeutic Properties: Antidepressant, antiinfectious, aromatic, meditative, antiseborrhoeic, antiseptic, aphrodisiac, cicatrisant, relaxant, calming, balance, euphoric, hypotensive, hormonal, tranquilizing, nervine, sedative, and tonic.

CONDITIONS AND RECIPES

These conditions are mental, physical, spiritual, emotional, wants, needs and desires. Our brains and our thoughts, they are everything. Think of your thoughts as a warning guide that something is wrong in your body. When you start feeling depressed or anxious, you might think it is for no reason, but in actuality, it is probably your body saying "Warning! Warning! Change something now!" When our thoughts are out of balance, we lose sight of what is important in our lives. We begin experiencing emotional upheaval, physical illnesses, social decline and scattered, chaotic, negative thoughts. By choosing to help yourself naturally, you are taking the best route to healing your brain, getting grounded and building your cornerstone of faith.

This alphabetical guide can help you to easily locate what condition you may currently be experiencing and provide you with numerous ways to deal with that particular desire; either Ayurveda, herbs, essential oils or alternative healing methods. You may choose to practice one healing modality or try all of them until you get the results you desire. The choice is yours. That is what is so amazing about *ALTERNATIVE HEALING METHODS FOR*

EMOTIONAL AND SPIRITUAL NEEDS. **<u>YOU</u>** have a choice in what type of natural healing you want to incorporate into your life.

ABUNDANCE

Love? Money? Good health? Chocolate? What is it that we desire the most? Everyone has different ideas of what they could use more of in their lives. These recipes have been handed down for generations and have been used to bring about an abundance of wealth, love and happiness to the intended. Have fun and let me know which ones' work for you!

AYURVEDA: **Ayurvedic Flower Offering**

In Ayurveda, a flower offering is the perfect choice for bringing abundance into your life. Choose flowers that are bright and colorful to you. Picking wildflowers while saying thanks of gratitude is the optimal flower offering. But purchasing flowers will work if you have the right intentions. Put the flowers in a vase, or planter, and place in the "front" of your home, near the front door. This should bring blessings and abundance to your doorstep.

HERBS: Herbal Abundance Sachet

This recipe has been used for hundreds, if not thousands, of years to bring abundance into the home, or wherever you place it. While making this sachet, think about that which you wish to be abundant, whether it be health, love, wealth or happiness.

Yield: 4 Sachets

1/8 cup dried oregano leaves

1/8 cup dried calendula flowers

¼ cup dried spearmint leaves

4- 3x6 inch rectangles of fabric

4- 4-inch pieces of ribbon

Dry the herbs until no moisture present to prevent mildewing. Crunch the herbs in a bowl with your fingers until crumbly. Do not crunch so much as to make a powder of them. Next, fold the material until it forms a square with the printed sides facing each other. Sew the edges of two of the sides together, until you have a pocket formed. Turn the material right sides out. Place the herbs inside the pocket, then continue sewing until it is closed. You may fashion a loop out of a scrap of material or ribbon and attach to one corner of your sachet for hanging purposes. Set the sachet in a spot where you will be meditating or doing most of your thinking. I place mine on my desk by my computer. Each day give it a few squeezes with your fingers to release a new round of aromas. When you smell the beautiful fragrance, remind yourself to say a prayer of gratitude for your desires. List your desires in your mind. When not in use, you can store in a zip lock bag to retain the fragrances. I use mine for a month or two before I can no longer detect any smells.

ESSENTIAL OIL: Wealth/Health Oil Spray

This spray is used on my body when I am trying to attract wealth and health. I don't know if it's a coincidence, but good things happen when I wear this. You can use this as a room spray, for your car, office, or body.

Yield: 4 Ounces

5 drops frankincense oil

5 drops myrrh oil

5 drops orange oil

5 drops spruce oil

5 drops vitamin E oil

4 ounces water

Using a funnel, pour all of the ingredients into a spray bottle. Label and date bottle. Oils and water separate, so you will need to shake very well before each usage. Spray the area lightly as desired. Ensure that you do not get spray into eyes, ears, mouth, open wounds, or other sensitive areas. Store spray bottle in a dark, cool area for up to 6 months.

***ALTERNATIVE REMEDY:* Alternative Tips to Attract Good Things**

- *Give, Give, Give. Giving to others always brings goodness back to you ten-fold. You may not think you have much, but you can always give something, even if it is your time.*
- *Do not live in the past, it leads to depression. Do not live in the future, it brings anxiety. Live in the present moment and be thankful.*
- *Gratitude. I feel my entire existence is based on gratitude. I thank God numerous times daily for, not only what I have, but for what I have yet to receive.*
- *Meditate and pray for what you need. Always use positive phrases and think positive thoughts about what you desire. It will come to you.*

ADDICTIONS

Withdrawing from addictions can sometimes lead dire consequences and withdrawal symptoms. Ensure through your physician that abruptly ending your addiction will not cause additional harm. The brain and the body can become dependent on certain chemicals, foods or behaviors to feel normal. The problem is that the substance can cause detrimental consequences to us; emotionally and physically. Deciding to end a bad behavior or an addiction can sometimes be the hardest part of the withdrawal process. The first step is, indeed, the hardest. These herbal, aromatherapy, Ayurvedic and home remedies can help you with that decision.

AYURVEDA: **Ayurvedic Addiction Habits**

To stop harmful addictions, they must be replaced with healthy habits. I found that tobacco withdrawal was the hardest thing I had to overcome in my life. Ten years later I continue occasionally to fight the urge to smoke. I can do this successfully by getting back to nature. I walk outside, work in my herb garden or begin outdoor projects. There is a myriad of natural remedies that will not only make you healthier, happier and more fit, but will stop urges and cravings when you give up something that has become an addiction. Some of these natural remedies include:

Meditation – *Meditation should be completed in a quiet, peaceful area. Low music may be played. Try to find an area free of negativity and distractions.*

- *Sit on a pillow, folded towel, or a rug. Cross your legs comfortably. Sit erect, but not stiffly.*
- *Closing your eyes, think of peaceful things that make you happy. Controlling the mind is difficult and you may find your thoughts returning again and again to negativity. Just tell those negative thoughts to go away and replace them with happy thoughts.*
- *Breathe. Each time your thoughts return to you, direct your thoughts to your breathing patterns. Try to completely empty the lungs of air with deep, slow, inhales and exhales. Continuously return your thoughts to your breathing.*
- *For 5-30 minutes, sit in silence, or softly changing a mantra, and give your mind the positivity it needs to get you through another hectic day. You will find each day becoming easier, and your thoughts beginning to reflect the positivity you focus on each time you meditate. Problem solving, spirituality, communication, love, social interaction and peace all become deeply affected by meditating.*

Nutrition – *Studies have shown that eating sensibly will remove enzymes, antibodies and brain chemicals that are out of balance, thereby relieving many of the physical and mental cravings and illnesses that accompany withdrawal from addictions. Eating sensibly includes: eating organic when possible; choosing wisely when eating fats, starches, sugar, salt, caffeine, carbs and dairy; eating more often with smaller portions, eating as many fruits and vegetables as possible; no soft drinks or junk food. Your body will respond in ways you never thought possible. Detoxing the junk out of your system will not only have you feeling great but will increase your ability to fight your addictions ten-fold.*

Exercise – *Any type of exercise is good exercise. Whether it be yoga, jumping jacks, walking, swimming, biking, gardening, housecleaning, or anything that gets your body moving. Exercise helps to release endorphins, which will lift you out of that fog that accompanies addiction, and have you living life to the fullest.*

Acupuncture – *Ayervedic studies show that numerous people in the Eastern part of the world have overcome addictions by the simple method of acupuncture. Acupuncture releases chemicals from the brain that stimulate our immune system enabling us to fight off unwanted diseases, toxins, and emotions. Give this a try to see if acupuncture will be right for you.*

HERBS: **Flower Tea**

Chamomile and dandelion both contain properties to help with curbing addictions and cravings. A few of the therapeutic properties in these herbs include analgesic, antidepressant, anti-inflammatory, antispasmodic, carminative, nervine, sedative, tonic and diuretic agents. These properties can help with anxiety, cramps, cravings, nervousness, sleeplessness and a host of other unwanted side effects.

Yield: 1 Cup

1 teaspoon chamomile

1 teaspoon dandelion

Boil one cup of water. In a tea ball or other tea strainer, add the herbs, seeds or stems. Place the tea ball in the cup or place the herbs directly into the cup. Slowly pour the boiling water over the herbs. Cover cup tightly and let steep for 6-10 minutes. Remove tea ball or strain the tea. Add honey, sugar, or sweetener if desired. Drink when at comfortable temperature. Discard herbs.

ESSENTIAL OIL: **Breath of New Beginnings Oil**

These essential oils contain the components needed to calm that rampaging mind during addiction withdrawal. When your brain tries to tell you that you need that habit, fire back with a breath of positive oils.

Yield: 1 Application

2 drops melissa

or

2 drops clary sage

Slowly drop the essential oil drops onto the palm of your hand, a tissue, or an essential oil inhaler. Using your thumb and forefinger, cover one nostril while inhaling deeply the aromas with your open nostril. Repeat process on other side. Reapply several times daily.

***ALTERNATIVE REMEDY:* Alternative Detox Infusion**

These herbs contain therapeutic properties that work on detoxing the body. Drink slowly throughout the day for an overall feeling of wellness.

Yield: 1 Pint

2 – teaspoons peppermint leaves

1 – teaspoon gingko chopped

1-pint water

Steep the leafy or flowery parts of the herb in one pint of boiling water (remove from heat) for 15-30 minutes. Strain and sweeten with honey or sweetener of choice. Discard herbs. Drink by teaspoonful throughout the day.

ANGER

There are a host of chemical reactions that occur throughout our body during a fit of anger. We are affected from the brain to the digestive system and havoc reigns supreme when we let our anger get the best of us. Learning to control anger and remain calm is a very spiritual experience. These tips and recipes can help you to control your own anger or calm down a family member who may be experiencing bouts of anger and rage. These recipes have been used world-wide, for centuries. Try some the next time you feel yourself getting out of control and rid yourself of the physical and mental horror and repercussions of uncontrollable anger.

***AYURVEDA:* Ayurvedic Sheetali Pranayama**

Pranayama is the Ayervedic word for breathing exercises. This breathing exercise expels heat from the body and introduces cool air throughout our system. Try it, right now. You can do it anywhere at any time. This pranayama exercise also cools the pitta element in our body and brings pitta back into balance, while calming the mind, spirit and soul.

- *Sheetali: roll your tongue into a tube shape. Breathe in through your tongue tube (notice how cool the air is going in), and then breathe out through your nose (this is the hot air). Do this for 5 minutes and your whole body will be cooler, calmer, and you will find that during those 5 minutes your anger has decreased significantly.*

HERBS: **Anger Cooling Herbal Tea**

Cooling herbs help to relieve some of the pitta heat of an angry person. If you are prone to fits of anger, stay away from "heated foods" like hot spices and peppers. Try these herbs that have cooling and healing properties such as cephalic, vasoconstrictor and nervine components to help even out your moods and reactions to various situations.

Yield: 1 Cup

1 teaspoon cilantro leaves

1 teaspoon spearmint

1 cup water

Boil one cup of water. In a tea ball or other tea strainer, add the herbs, seeds or stems. Place the tea ball in the cup or place the herbs directly into the cup. Slowly pour the boiling water over the herbs. Cover cup tightly and let steep for 6-10 minutes. Remove tea ball or strain the tea. Add honey, sugar, or sweetener if desired. Drink when at comfortable temperature.

Discard herbs.

ESSENTIAL OIL: *Anger Diffuser*

If you are expecting someone to come into your work or home with anger issues or negativity, this is the diffuser to run, and they won't even know why they feel so calm. The healing properties in this blend contain antidepressant, aphrodisiac, euphoric, hypotensive, nervine and sedative elements.

Yield: 1 Application

4 drops ylang-ylang oil

4 drops bergamot oil

Water

Each diffuser has different amounts of water and oils that can be used for that particular diffuser. Adjust the recipes according to your diffuser. Add the water, then add the oils and run your diffuser for the desired effect.

ALTERNATIVE REMEDY: Anger Color Therapy Session

Colors have been used for a long time to help people control their emotions, or to bring about feelings and emotions that you do desire. There are so many techniques people have used to control anger issues, but using color is a quick, free, and easy way to calm yourself down. I have listed below the colors used for anger therapy. Try sitting in a room with the walls painted one of these colors, meditate on these colors, or wear these colors. It helps if you look at them and try to breathe long and slow breaths while saying affirmative messages to yourself. The colors you can use for anger therapy are:

Blue, magenta, pink and white

ANSWERS

(Divinations)

Questions about our future, questions about our loved ones, questions about our impending health, and questions about our financial security plague all of us every day. For eons, people have turned to natural methods to find the answers to life's daily questions. These recipes have been handed down for generations and may allow you to find the answers within yourself that you are seeking.

***AYURVEDA:* Ayerveda Mind Expanders**

- *Rise before 6:00 am each day. Do not sleep late in the morning as extended sleep fogs your brain and makes it hard to focus.*
- *Drink an entire bottle of water on rising. Thin the blood and get it pumping to your brain.*
- *Meditate and pray to clear the mind of negativity and bring positive forces into your life.*

- *Include saffron in your diet.*
- *Conduct a yoga routine daily to clear mind and bring focus, peace and harmony to your thoughts.*
- *Massage your temples and neck with essential oils.*

***HERBS:* Answers for Me Herbal Tea**

These two herbs are used in many different cultures to expand one's mind and open up the soul to receive answers from God.

Yield: 1 Cup

1 teaspoon rose petals

1 teaspoon lemongrass

1 cup water

sweetener

Boil one cup of water. In a tea ball or other tea strainer, add the herbs, seeds or stems. Place the tea ball in the cup or place the herbs directly into the cup. Slowly pour the boiling water over the herbs. Cover cup tightly and let steep for 6-10 minutes. Remove tea ball or strain the tea. Add honey, sugar, or sweetener if desired. Drink when at comfortable temperature. Discard herbs.

***ESSENTIAL OIL:* Send Me a Sign Rub**

The oils included in this blend are known to purify the soul, clear the mind of any negativity, and open the thoughts to higher powers to receive answers to innermost secret wonderings and inquiries.

Yield: ½ Ounce

4 drops rose oil

3 drops sandalwood oil

3 drops angelica oil

2 drops frankincense oil

½ ounce carrier oil (sesame or coconut oil is preferred)

Using a bowl or a jar, combine the ingredients together using a whisk or a fork. Using your fingertips, spread the rub onto the temples, chest, back, neck or soles of feet, ensuring that you do not get into eyes, ears, mouth, open wounds, genitals, mucus membranes, or other sensitive areas. You may cover area with light gauze or old clothing to prevent staining furniture. Leave mixture on until you are ready to reapply. Store remainder in a dark colored jar, in a cool, dark area for up to one year.

***ALTERNATIVE REMEDY:* Alternative Balancing Crown Chakra**

The crown chakra (sahasrara) at the top of our head is thought to control spiritual matters. When this chakra is out of balance, it may be difficult to focus, pray, or get answers to the questions that you seek. We can help to bring this chakra into balance with meditation and visualization.

- *Sit comfortably in a cross-legged position. You may use pillows to support your knees or back. Lay your hands in your lap, palms up, and fingers touching.*
- *Breathe deeply in through your mouth, and out of your nose. Continue breathing while trying to rid your thoughts of any negativity. Instead, focus on the questions you have about your future, relationships, or career.*
- *Visualize the most optimal outcome for yourself. You should attempt to have at least 10 – 20 minutes of visualization practice. Visualize the steps it would take to reach that perfect outcome. The answers you seek will come to you throughout this process.*

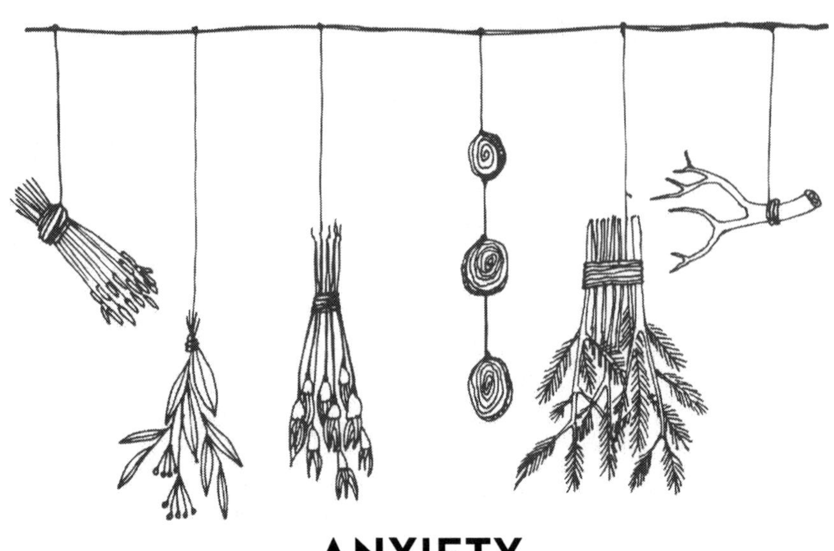

ANXIETY

The pulse pounds, negative thoughts take over the brain and sadness and fear are the emotions that pour out like sweat. Anxiety is no joke. Jobs, friends and families suffer and are often destroyed as a result of a life filled to the brim with anxiety. I will ask myself "what's the worst that could happen?" I envision the worst possible scenario, the steps I would take to overcome the worst possible outcome and slowly bring myself out of my anxious state. There are several techniques, tips, and recipes from various cultures and time periods that work to give you your life back and end the negativity and fear that surrounds you. Therapy and medical intervention should be sought if anxiety is affecting serious areas of your life.

AYURVEDA: Anti-Anxiety Treatments

Ayerveda believes in the holistic approach to healing a person suffering from anxiety. This involves the body, mind, diet, thoughts and spirit. Working on all of these areas will not only decrease your anxiety, but also have you living a happier more fulfilling lifestyle. Try one of more of the following techniques to curb anxiety, fear and paranoia.

- *Inhalation Therapy – try alternate nostril breathing. Sit comfortably, bring the right thumb up and place it on right side of right nostril, palm facing the mouth, and close the nostril. Close the eyes and breathe deeply through the left nostril five times. Repeat entire sequence on left side.*

- *Decrease vata in the body. The vata diet consists of heavy, grounding foods. This adds substance to the soul and body and thoughts will not run rampant like the air. Eat several small meals and avoid getting full. Included in this diet are brown rice, herbal teas, small amount of wine, carrots, nuts, radishes, potatoes, dairy, tomatoes, corn, ghee and peas. Avoid light airy foods such as cauliflower, sugar, broccoli, cucumber, asparagus, lettuce and onions.*

- *Meditation – calming the mind is the number one concern for overly anxious type people. Meditation teaches us how to calm the mind and enjoy our surroundings. Start off meditating 5 – 10 minutes each day. Concentrate on your breathing and try to banish any negative thoughts.*

- *Praying – I use mala beads to get in tune with my spiritual side. I finger each bead as I say a prayer of thanks for the gifts I have received and say a prayer of thanks for those gifts I have not yet received.... I but will! If you name what you want/need, and know what you want, be grateful for that thing, then it is already yours.*

- *Yoga – Yoga can help to ground you physically and mentally. I believe yoga to be more powerful than any over the counter anxiety medication. Yoga helps us inside and out, and we feel, through conquering poses, that we can conquer anything at all! Gorilla pose is excellent as a grounding technique. Fold forward and place your fingers under your feet, palms up. Press into your fingers with your feet and hold position for 10 breaths. Rise slowly when done.*

***HERBS:* Chamomile Tea**

This recipe is thousands of years old and is proven to be an effective and therapeutic calming agent with its antianxiety and sedative properties.

Yield: 1 Cup

2 teaspoons chamomile

1 cup water

Sweetener (if desired)

Boil one cup of water. In a tea ball or other tea strainer, add the herbs, seeds or stems. Place the tea ball in the cup or place the herbs directly into the cup. Slowly pour the boiling water over the herbs. Cover cup tightly and let steep for 6-10 minutes. Remove tea ball or strain the tea. Add honey, sugar, or sweetener if desired. Drink when at comfortable temperature.

Discard herbs.

ESSENTIAL OIL: Antianxiety Powder

Sleeping when you are anxious about something is an almost impossible task. The therapeutic properties in these oils will have you resting and relaxing in the most luxurious manner.

Yield: ¼ Cup

3 drops clary sage oil

3 drops ylang-ylang oil

3 drops rose oil

¼ cup cornstarch

Combine all ingredients into a large bowl. Stir well with a whisk until all clumps disappear. Let sit in open air for 12-24 hours. Poke several holes in mason jar lids using nail and hammer. Spoon the powder mixture into the mason jars and cover with lid and ring. Use this lid as a shaker and shake the ingredients into pillowcases, and under sheets on bed. The oils will be mild, but have a soothing, calming effect on the person sleeping on them all night. I like to get a piece of plastic wrap, remove the mason jar ring, and place the plastic wrap over the top of the jar, and replace the ring. This will keep the powder from accidently spilling out when not in use. Store in a cool, dark area for up to one year.

ALTERNATIVE REMEDY: Ayervedic Scalp Rub

This recipe is used in India as a way to decrease anxiety and bring calm, relief and peace to a person. Brahmi has powerful antianxiety properties.

Yield: 1 Ounce

1 teaspoon brahmi

1-ounce carrier oil

Using a bowl or a jar, combine the ingredients together using a whisk or a fork. Using your fingertips, spread the rub onto an area such as neck, temples or back, ensuring that you do not get into eyes, ears, mouth, open wounds, genitals, mucus membranes, or other sensitive areas. You may cover area with light gauze or old clothing to prevent staining furniture. Leave mixture on until you are ready to reapply. Store remainder in a dark colored jar, in a cool, dark area for up to one month.

***ALTERNATIVE REMEDY #2:* Spicy Antianxiety Drink**

The calming ingredients in this blend will have you feeling wonderful very quickly. Nutmeg is a stimulant, carminative and digestive spice and the honey has antianxiety properties, working together they reduce anxiety. The vitamins and minerals in this drink will give you energy and help you to focus on what's important to you and not worry about every little thing.

Yield: 1 Cup

1 cup orange juice

1 tablespoon honey

1 tablespoon nutmeg

Mix the ingredients together with a whisk or spoon, in a tall glass. You may chill with ice. Drink slowly over the course of 30 minutes.

APHRODISIAC

Ahhhh, the nectar of the Gods. An aphrodisiac affects the areas of the brain that produce sexual arousal and feelings of intimacy. When you want to bring romance and love into your life, aphrodisiacs are a "cheat" way to lure in that partner that is not feeling the love at the moment. Aphrodisiacs have been used since the beginning of time to bring love and happiness into our lives. We use them often without even realizing what we're doing. Lighting candles, wearing perfume, dressing provocatively, smiling, all are forms of aphrodisiacs. Here are a few more well-known aphrodisiacs that you can add to your list of "getting what I want."

***AYURVEDA:* Swadhisthana Chakra Healing**

Our sexual chakra is the second or sacral chakra, located right under our navel. Our sexuality stems from this chakra. If you hare having issues in your sex life, this may be the root of the problem. To increase your sexual feelings, and relieve feelings of shame, distrust, resentment and anger that often stand in the way of opening up sexually, you can use the following guidelines to clear your sacral chakra and improve your sex life:

- *Use the color orange, such as an orange candle, orange pillows, or orange clothing.*
- *Increase consumption of sensually tasting foods, such as strawberries, oysters, honey and chocolate.*
- *Relax in water as often as possible. Listen to recordings of water and ocean sounds. Buy a small desktop fountain and relax in its sound and beauty. Water is thought to embody the wavelengths of the brain that are connected to our sexuality.*
- *Walking in the moonlight is a good way to clear the sacral chakra and open the mind to sexual encounters.*
- *Take a long, slow, luxurious bath in warm water with sea salt and 1 -tablespoon of baking soda.*

ESSENTIAL OIL: Love Massage

Who can say "no" to a massage? Use this rub with these oils that are known far and wide for their aphrodisiacal properties and your partner won't know what hit him or her. This heady aroma along with the massage will open a person's desires and bring feelings of sexuality out into the open.

Yield: 2 Applications

3 drops rose

4 drops ylang-ylang

5 drops patchouli oil

2 tablespoons carrier oil

In a bowl or a jar, combine the ingredients together using a whisk or a fork. With your fingertips, spread the rub onto the chest, pulse points or back area, ensuring that you do not get into eyes, ears, mouth, open wounds, genitals, mucus membranes, or other sensitive areas. You may cover area with light gauze or old clothing to prevent staining furniture. Leave mixture on until you are ready to reapply. Store remainder in a dark colored jar, in a cool, dark area for up to one year.

***HERBS:* Aphrodisiac Honey**

Honey and these herbs have been proven to be powerful aphrodisiacs. This little gem can be served to your partner and they will have no idea why they suddenly want to get lovey dovey. Serve warm on toast or biscuits.

Yield: 1 Cup

1 cup honey

2 teaspoons peppermint leaves

2 teaspoons echinacea

Place all of the ingredients into a double boiler on very low until honey is very warm. Stir constantly. Remove from heat, cover and steep 1 – 6 hours. Strain through cheesecloth and jar and label. Store remainder in a jar with a tight-fitting lid in a cool, dark area for up to one year.

***ALTERNATIVE REMEDY*: Aphrodisiac Diet**

Foods have been long known to pique one's interest in a lover. Making a meal using ingredients that have been known for thousands of years to increase the libido is fun and easy. There are so many foods, herbs, drinks and spices to use, that it is hard to just choose a few. This list includes many of the foods used around the world to add love and lust to just about any atmosphere.

Oysters, Chocolate, Strawberries, Pistachios, Chilis, Asparagus, Champagne, Celery, Garlic, Ginseng, Peaches, Saffron, Figs, Avocados, Bananas, Pomegranates, Nuts, Wine, Fish, Honey

BALANCE

(Life)

Finding balance in your life can be a full-time job. And it should be! Balance is fleeting and requires the spiritual, mental, emotional, financial, familial and physical sides of ourselves to correlate and work in harmony. Getting all areas of our lives, which are often in chaos, to blend and flow smoothly is hard to accomplish. These recipes and tips can assist us on the journey to harmony and balance in our lives.

AYURVEDA: Life Balancing Yoga

There are many poses (asanas) in yoga that will help to bring balance to your life. Try some of these simple poses yourself. Notice how you are feeling before you start this routine, and how you feel after you are done. You will feel calmer, stronger, and more in control of your life.

- *Chair Flow—stand with your feet about six inches apart. Extend your arms straight out in front of your body.*

Tighten your abdominal muscles and slowly lower your body as if you are sitting in a chair. Tuck your tailbone in, raise your arms slightly and breathe in and out deeply, 3 times. Move back into a standing position and raise your arms over your head (mountain pose.) Repeat 10 times.

- *Downward Dog—Kneel on all fours on a soft yoga or Pilates mat. Slowly straighten your legs until your hips are high in the air. Keep your head down between your arms. Push back with your hands until there is a straight line from your feet to your hips. Hang your head softly and shake your head yes, and no, relieving tension in your neck. Take 3 deep breaths in down dog position. Slowly come back down onto your hands and knees. Repeat twice.*
- *Corpse Pose—Lay on your yoga mat with your arms down by your side. Place your palms up. Make sure your shoulders are flat on the floor. Start by slowly moving your head from side to side slowly, to release any tension that may have built up in your neck. Lay motionless on the floor, with your eyes closed, concentrating on slowly breathing in and out. Stay in this position for 5 minutes.*

***HERBS*: Balancing Blend**

There are many herbs that can help to bring balance to our body, spirit, mind and soul. These include ginger, cardamom, lemon peel, chamomile, lemon balm, lavender and clary sage. These herbs have calming and uplifting properties that will help to balance your mind and body giving you the peace you need. Try a combination of one or more of these herbs in teas and choose the one you like best and that you feel brings balance to your life.

Yield: 1 Cup

1 teaspoon lemon balm leaves (or any of the above herbs)

1 teaspoon lavender flowers (or any of the above herbs)

1 cup water

Sweetener

Boil one cup of water. In a tea ball or other tea strainer, add the herbs, seeds or stems. Place the tea ball in the cup or place the herbs directly into the cup. Slowly pour the boiling water over the herbs. Cover cup tightly and let steep for 6-10 minutes. Remove tea ball or strain the tea. Add honey, sugar, or sweetener if desired. Drink when at comfortable temperature. Discard herbs.

***ESSENTIAL OILS:* Balancing Diffuser**

Changing the air that we breathe is a simple, yet effective way to calm the mind, bring contentment to the body and uplift the spirit. Incorporating all of the things we need for a balanced, loving life. These essential oils have the components needed to help you bring your life, body, spirit and soul into balance. Great to use during meditation, prayer or just trying to wind down after a long, hard day.

Yield: *1 Application*

3 drops ylang-ylang oil

3 drops melissa oil

2 drops clary sage oil

Water

Each diffuser has different amounts of water and oils that can be used for that particular diffuser. Adjust the recipes according to your diffuser. Add the water, then add the oils and run your diffuser for the desired effect.

ALTERNATIVE REMEDY: **Life Balance**

- *Relax; try to find a small part of your day that is just for you to do nothing. Don't watch TV, don't eat, don't be distracted by outside influences or in any way engage with other people or social media. Meditation and prayer are great activities to do that will have you focusing on yourself and what is good for you. Twenty minutes a day can make all the difference in the world.*

- *No negativity; when you are around people who gossip, talk down to you or otherwise fill your space with negativity, it cannot help but to affect you. Try to avoid situations where you have to interact with these types of people. Surround yourself with positive people who will uplift you and show you support and love.*

- *Move; get yourself off of that couch and into a more physical frame of mind. You can clean, organize, walk, enjoy your family, just get up and go. Working on our physical selves will help to balance all parts of ourselves. Getting out into nature is one of the quickest, most effective ways to bring balance to our body, spirit and soul.*

- *Read uplifting and positive books. Try to read a chapter a day, and then journal how you can bring the lessons from that day into your life. Don't stop there...actually try incorporating the lessons you have learned into your life each day. You will be surprised at how much you can learn from these books and how much better your life, attitude and spiritual growth will become.*

BIPOLAR

So much more is known about bipolar disorders than was known even a decade ago. Bipolar runs in my family and I have spent my life watching people spend all their money in ten minutes of mania, to be followed by ten days of depression that was sometimes suicidal stemming from financial despair. Bipolar disorder is no joke. So many medications are on the market today to assist with leveling out the chemicals in the brain that run rampant with this disorder. Mental health practitioners are well versed with techniques to help someone suffering from bipolar disorder. These mood-altering recipes have been used forever in calming the mind, spirit and soul, and they work wonders on many people suffering with this potentially horrid disorder

***AYERVEDA:* Remedies for Bipolar**

An imbalance of the doshas is thought to be responsible for bipolar disorder. The remedies make sense and it seems that a person suffering from bipolar could use a few of these grounding practices in their lives.

- *Color therapy—surround yourself with yellows, greens, browns, golds, violets and earth tone colors for balancing and grounding.*

- *Diet—warm heavy foods are known to ground and calm a person with bipolar disorder.*

- *Yoga—slow poses and movements will help to calm and center one. Developing a practice to do every day adds a sense of routine, which is very important for stabilizing moods. Doing yoga, meditation, praying or exercise outside in the midst of nature really helps persons with bipolar.*

- *Meditate—sit cross-legged and close your eyes. Empty the mind, which is very difficult for this type of illness, and concentrate on your breathing. Start out with five minutes a day and increase to twenty minutes per day over time. Learning how to meditate is probably the single most important lesson for someone with bipolar disorder and can bring about miraculous results.*

- *Gratitude—be grateful daily for the things you have, and more importantly, be grateful for those things which you have yet to receive. If you give thanks for the future you desire, show belief that you will achieve your dreams, work on baby steps to achieve your goal and thank your provider for allowing you to have that which you do not yet have...it will be yours. If you can CONCEIVE it, and you BELIEVE it, you will ACHIEVE it!*

HERBS: Bi-polar Tea

This tea has a leveling effect on the moods, making one calm, but content. Go from having two extreme moods to just one happy, calm mood.

Yield: *1 Cup*

1 teaspoon bee balm

1 teaspoon ginseng

1 cup boiling water

Sweetener

Boil one cup of water. In a tea ball or other tea strainer, add the herbs, seeds or stems. Place the tea ball in the cup or place the herbs directly into the cup. Slowly pour the boiling water over the herbs. Cover cup tightly and let steep for 6-10 minutes. Remove tea ball or strain the tea. Add honey, sugar, or sweetener if desired. Drink when at comfortable temperature. Discard herbs.

ESSENTIAL OIL: Oil Spray for the Doshas

Essential oils have been shown to bring a person down from a euphoric high or lift them up from depression. This recipe will help with grounding, calming, and evening out a person's moods and back to their desired range. These oils contain antidepressant, stimulant, tonic, restorative and calming properties. This blend brings the all of the doshas into balance and will help you to achieve that "normal" mood level you desire.

Yield: 2 Ounces

10 drops rose oil

10 drops frankincense oil

5 drops basil oil

2 ounces' water

Using a funnel, pour all of the ingredients into a spray bottle. Label and date bottle. Oils and water separate, so you will need to shake very well before each usage. Spray your body, room or office lightly, as desired. Ensure that you do not get spray into eyes, ears, mouth, open wounds, or other sensitive areas. Store spray bottle in a dark, cool area for up to 6 months.

***ALTERNATIVE REMEDY:* Bipolar Rubdown**

Getting a massage can be such a calming and almost a spiritual experience for most people. A person with bipolar can receive numerous benefits from getting this rubdown. The oils in this rub balance out the mind, body and soul with their calming and antidepressant properties.

Yield: 2 Ounces

5 drops clary sage oil

3 drops melissa oil

3 drops rose oil

2 ounces' carrier oil

Using a bowl or a jar, combine the ingredients together using a whisk or a fork. Using your fingertips, spread the rub onto the soles of feet, back or chest area, ensuring that you do not get into eyes, ears, mouth, open wounds, genitals, mucus membranes, or other sensitive areas. You may cover area with light gauze or old clothing to prevent staining furniture. Leave mixture on until you are ready to reapply. Store remainder in a dark colored jar, in a cool, dark area for up to one year.

BLESSINGS

Bestowing blessings on another, or having blessings bestowed on you is a very powerful tool. In some religions, priests have the power to bless others. We often wish blessings on those around us, and rituals are performed all over the planet to bless people. These ceremonies, tools and rituals have been performed forever and you can use these same tips to bring blessings upon your household, or another's. You may find it hard to believe that you could have the power to actually bring blessings to another person or yourself. Most people believe that the truth is that you are simply a vessel or a tool for a Higher Power to use to channel that blessing. Simply open yourself up with prayer, meditation or any means you believe brings you closer to your Higher Power so that the blessings can flow through you.

AYURVEDA: Intention Blessing

In Ayurveda, opening up yourself to the Universe in order to help yourself or others is quite simply a matter of setting your intention. Once you have the intention set then God can use you to fulfill blessings.

- *Sit in a quiet spot, free from distractions. Make yourself as comfortable as possible. Steady your breathing as if for meditation. Set your intention by stating aloud who the blessing is for and what you wish could be accomplished by this blessing. For example, you might state aloud "My sister will have an offer for the best job that she's ever had."*
- *Think about your sister, what this job could mean for her. Feel the joy she will experience when her job offer arrives. Think about how happy she and her family will feel when she makes enough money to fulfill her family's needs. Express joy and gratitude to your higher power for using you to channel these blessings to your sister.*
- *Always end with gratitude.*

HERBS: Home Blessings Potpourri

A potpourri is a vessel containing fruits, herbs, oils or other ingredients from nature. Certain elements can bring about feelings, memories, ambiance, or in this case, blessings. Several gifts from nature can be used to impart blessings to the home. Potpourris can be dried, simmered, oil based or simply spread out on a table. Use this recipe when you wish your home to be full of all good things.

A bowl or container

2 bay leaves

Dried peel of one orange, chopped

¼ cup rosemary needles, dried

Combine all of the ingredients together in a bowl. You may add drops of your favorite aromatic essential oils, if desired. Savor the aroma from the bowl and give thanks of gratitude for all of the blessings being bestowed upon your home.

ESSENTIAL OIL: **Blessing Oils**

This oil recipe has been used throughout the ages to apply blessings to others by placing a drop of oil on a person's forehead, by placing a drop over a door or a windowsill, you could even put a drop on your car or your computer. Your intention that the oil contain blessings is paramount to the oil being used as a tool by your Higher Power to actually provide the blessing you are seeking.

Yield: 1/3 ounce

3 drops rosemary oil

3 drops bergamot oil

2 drops rose oil

2 drops sandalwood oil

1/3-ounce carrier oil

Using a bowl or a jar, combine the ingredients together using a whisk or a fork. Using your fingertips, place a drop onto forehead, if on the body ensure that you do not get into eyes, ears, mouth, open wounds, genitals, mucus membranes, or other sensitive areas. If applying to an object dip finger in oil and simply place fingertip with oil onto object to be blessed. At the same time, affirm your intention either in your mind, or out loud. Always end with a prayer of gratitude. Store remainder of oil in a dark colored jar, in a cool, dark area for up to one year.

ALTERNATIVE REMEDY: **Blessings Spray**

This spray recipe can be used throughout the home, over a child's bed, in your office, on your clothing for a job interview, or just about anywhere you wish blessings to be bestowed. The spray only lasts for a few days, so use it liberally and bring those blessings raining down. Test for use on any material with one drop before applying liberally.

Yield: 2 Ounces

2 ounces of water

1 spray bottle

1 small piece frankincense or 5 drops frankincense oil

1 small piece myrrh, or 5 drops myrrh oil

1 small gold object (ring, chain, coin)

Mix all the ingredients into the spray bottle. Shake well before each application. When spraying keep spray away from eyes and mucous membranes. Store in refrigerator at night and discard water, after straining, after 4 days.

CALMING

Ayurveda, herbs, essential oils and alternative remedies all can offer a wide variety of tips and recipes to help bring your emotions back to Earth. Being in a calm state can help you to think more clearly, offer sound advice, execute emergency plans and to just be happy. Numerous factors can lead us to feeling overwhelmed, angry, anxious and just not at peace. Try one of these blends the next time you are feeling out of control and want to bring some soothing calm to your life.

AYURVEDA: Dosha Calming Tips

When a person is over-excited, anxious, and cannot remain calm, Ayervedic practitioners believe that the vata dosha is out of balance. There are many ways to bring the doshas back into balance so that the body and mind can be calm and active.

- *Meditate – for 10-20 minutes twice daily. Find a comfortable spot, sit cross-legged, close your eyes and try to simply observe your thoughts with no reaction. Clear your mind and focus on your breathing. Breathe deep and long. It is said that praying is talking to God, meditating is listening to God. Ohm.*

- *Yoga – child's pose is the most calming of all poses. Kneel on your shins with the tops of your feet pressed to the floor, lay arms at your sides (palms up), bend forward over your thighs and lay your forehead on the floor. Breathe deeply and try to hold this pose for 5 minutes. This asana will bring calm and peace to your whole body and mind.*

- *Foods – eat warm, heavy foods to bring down the air of the vata dosha. Eat warming spices such as ginger, cumin and cinnamon. Add ghee to your diet.*

- *Drink – only warm or room temperature drinks, nothing cold. Try to keep the entire body and digestive system warm during a calming down phase.*

- *Nature – nothing calms the soul like a walk or adventure into nature. Even if it is stepping outside your door to breathe in the fresh air and look at the sky. Any amount of time spent outdoors will help you to achieve calm.*

***HERBS*: Calming Balm Bath**

These herbs have relaxing and sedative qualities that will help to relieve stress and anxiety. Immerse yourself in this lovely aroma for a bath made for the angels.

Yield: 1 application

2 tablespoons bee balm leaves

2 tablespoons lemon balm leaves

1 square cheesecloth

1-foot ribbon or twine

Make a sachet for the tub by laying out a piece of material. Place the herbs in the middle of the cloth. Bring the ends of the fabric together and tie off with a ribbon. Once the tub has filled with water, place the sachet into the water. You may remain in the tub as long as the water is comfortable. Discard the herbs after using.

ESSENTIAL OIL: **Sesame Massage Oil**

This massage is designed to use essential oils that are well known for their anti-anxiety, calming, sedative and tranquilizing properties. Even the massage itself can be a calming tool for you not to mention all the healing therapeutic properties being absorbed by your body.

Yield: 2 Ounces

5 drops mandarin oil

5 drops neroli oil

5 drops jasmine

2 ounces' sesame oil

Using a bowl or a jar, combine the ingredients together using a whisk or a fork. Using your fingertips, spread the rub onto arms, legs, feet, or other area you can reach for self-massage, ensuring that you do not get into eyes, ears, mouth, open wounds, genitals, mucus membranes, or other sensitive areas. You may cover area with light gauze or old clothing to prevent staining furniture. Leave mixture on until you are ready to reapply. Store remainder in a dark colored jar, in a cool, dark area for up to one year.

***ALTERNATIVE REMEDY:* Calming Air**

These essential oils have sedative, calming and tranquilizing properties to help you overcome that anxious, dreadful feeling and to bring you back to your peaceful and happy state of mind.

Yield: 1 application

4 drops vetiver

4 drops mandarin

Water

Each diffuser has different amounts of water and oils that can be used for that particular diffuser. Adjust the recipes according to your diffuser. Add the water, then add the oils and run your diffuser for the desired effect.

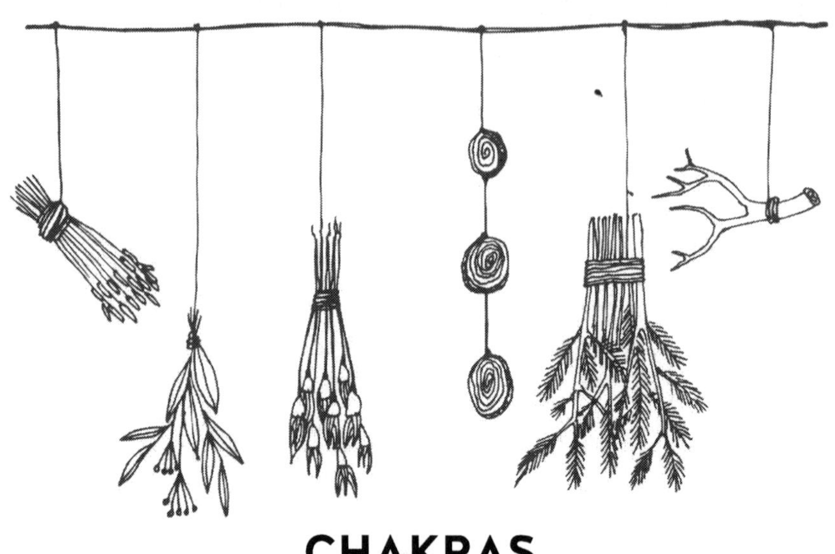

CHAKRAS

Every issue we have ever had in our lives is connected to the energy fields in our bodies called "chakras." Getting stuck in a chakra is when a particular emotion, ailment or energy is out of balance and needs to be gently realigned. Learning about and practicing healing of the chakras is at the root of many medical practices around the world. You would be surprised to learn how your ailments and mental stressors are tied to a particular chakra. This ancient form of healing (over 3000 years old) gets its beliefs from countless centuries of practice. Learn where your chakras are "stuck" and use these recipes to bring back flowing energy and chakra balance into your life.

1ST ROOT CHAKRA (Muladhara)

Stability, safety, security and shelter are all associated with the "root" chakra. Anxiety, attachment disorders, flighty emotions, bi polar disorder, these are a few of the emotional problems that we can have when our root chakra is out of balance. To get more grounded and secure in your life, follow some of these tips and recipes to get your Muladhara chakra back into balance. This chakra is located at our root, or tailbone.

***AYURVEDA:* Muladhara Ayervedic Tips**

- *Get as close to nature as possible. Walk in a garden, woods, path, or anywhere outdoors where you can get peace and solitude.*
- *Sit on the ground and meditate. Do not place any barriers between you and the Earth.*
- *Walk barefoot on the beach, in a grassy yard, or through mud puddles! Just get your feet connected to the Earth.*
- *Do not think about the past when working on this chakra. Be present and try to focus on now. In everyday situations, practice reacting and not separating yourself from unpleasant situations. Focus on what needs to be done now.*
- *Try to focus on the color red, such as red flowers or a red sunrise. Paint a wall in your home red, or accent with red pillows.*
- *Listen to some grounding music such as Krishna Das.*

***HERBS:* Muladhara Tea**

Yield: 1 cup

1 teaspoon hibiscus flowers

1 teaspoon ginger root, minced

1 cup water

Sweetener

Boil one cup of water. In a tea ball or other tea strainer, add the herbs, seeds or stems. Place the tea ball in the cup or place the herbs directly into the cup. Slowly pour the boiling water over the herbs. Cover cup tightly and let steep for 6-10 minutes. Remove tea ball or strain the tea. Add honey, sugar, or sweetener if desired. Drink when at comfortable temperature. Discard herbs.

ESSENTIAL OIL: **Muladhara diffuser**

This diffuser recipe has the properties to help you with grounding, safety and security.

Yield: 1 Application

5-10 drops of any combination of two or more of the following grounding essential oils:

Frankincense, patchouli, sandalwood, vetiver, cypress or cedarwood

Water

Each diffuser has different amounts of water and oils that can be used for that particular diffuser. Adjust the recipes according to your diffuser. Add the water, then add the oils and run your diffuser for the desired effect.

***ALTERNATIVE REMEDY:* Muladhara Affirmations**

Using your own thoughts and voice to balance your chakras is one of the oldest known methods of opening your chakras for healing. Affirmations can be used as a form of meditation, a chant, a mantra, or just something you repeat to yourself throughout the day. Here are a few examples of affirmations for your chakra balancing.

I am connected to the Earth

I am grounded

I am safe and secure

No harm will come to me

I am protected by my Higher Power

2ND SACRAL CHAKRA (Swadhisthana)

Adaptability, problem solving, sexual nature, creativity and guilt are all tied to the sacral chakra. If you suffer from guilt when undertaking the most basic pleasures in life, working on this chakra will help you better express yourself without overwhelming feelings of doubt and guilt. This chakra is located in the pelvic region.

***AYURVEDA:* Swadhisthana Ayurvedic Tips**

- *Take a solitary walk in the night under the moon.*
- *Immerse yourself in water. Healing oils and herbs added to a bath are perfect for getting in touch with this sacral chakra.*

- *Try to be aware of your emotions at all times. If you are feeling angry or sad, let someone close to you know. Work on learning to express your emotions.*
- *Try to incorporate the color orange into your life daily. Hang an orange painting in your office or get an orange candle and burn it before meditation.*
- *Learn to let your creativity shine. Do something that you think others will NOT like, and let yourself create what You want, not what you think that someone else will approve of.*
- *Learn to openly communicate your feelings and desires to others. Do not keep your emotions bottled up for fear of another person's reaction to your feelings.*

HERBS: **Sacral Tea**

Yield: 1 cup

1 teaspoon hibiscus

1 teaspoon calendula

1 cup water

sweetener

Boil one cup of water. In a tea ball or other tea strainer, add the herbs, seeds or stems. Place the tea ball in the cup or place the herbs directly into the cup. Slowly pour the boiling water over the herbs. Cover cup tightly and let steep for 6-10 minutes. Remove tea ball or strain the tea. Add honey, sugar, or sweetener if desired. Drink when at comfortable temperature. Discard herbs.

ESSENTIAL OIL: **Swadhisthana Diffuser**

Using this diffuser recipe will awaken passion and help you to be more mindful of yourself and those around you and erase any guilt you may have in your life.

Yield: 1 Application

5-10 drops of any combination of two or more of the following grounding essential oils:

Neroli, clary sage, grapefruit, cardamom, orange, jasmine or rose

water

Each diffuser has different amounts of water and oils that can be used for that particular diffuser. Adjust the recipes according to your diffuser. Add the water, then add the oils and run your diffuser for the desired effect.

ALTERNATIVE REMEDY: **Swadhisthana Affirmations**

Using your own thoughts and voice to balance your chakras is one of the oldest known methods of opening your chakras for healing. Affirmations can be used as a form of meditation, a chant, a mantra, or just something you repeat to yourself throughout the day. Here are a few examples of affirmations for your chakra balancing.

I am sure in what I am doing

I have the right to do as I wish

I am passionate

I am mindful

3RD SOLAR PLEXUS CHAKRA (Manipura)

Power, self-esteem, will, shame, confrontation, depression, fatigue and anger are related to the third chakra, which lies directly above the navel. If you feel you are blocked, out of control and have no power in these areas, then these recipes are designed to unblock your third chakra and give you the power you need to confront life head on and control your emotions.

***AYURVEDA:* Manipura Ayurvedic Tips**

- *Sit and meditate at sunrise or sunset.*
- *Surround yourself with the color yellow. Move in the sunshine, paint your office yellow, or wear a yellow shirt to meditate in.*
- *Practice yoga early in the morning, or whichever exercise regimen you prefer. This will recharge your body for the day.*
- *Work In the garden. This will get you in the sun, get you exercising, and lesson any feelings of anger you may*

have.

- *Concentrate on what you can do to change and empower yourself. Do not wait for another person to make changes for you.*
- *Make a goal for yourself and work towards this goal with baby steps. Don't be discouraged that you haven't achieved a goal, just be happy that you have a goal and that you will reach it someday.*

HERBS: **Solar Plexus Tea**

Yield: 1 cup

1 cup water

1 teaspoon lemon balm

1 teaspoon chamomile

sweetener

Boil one cup of water. In a tea ball or other tea strainer, add the herbs, seeds or stems. Place the tea ball in the cup or place the herbs directly into the cup. Slowly pour the boiling water over the herbs. Cover cup tightly and let steep for 6-10 minutes. Remove tea ball or strain the tea. Add honey, sugar, or sweetener if desired. Drink when at comfortable temperature. Discard herbs.

ESSENTIAL OIL: **Manipura Diffuser**

This diffuser recipe will release so many negative emotions and help bring calm and peace to you.

Yield: 1 Application

5-10 drops of any combination of two or more of the following grounding essential oils:

Pine, Juniper, lemon, cardamom, sandalwood, lemongrass, peppermint, rosemary, ginger

water

Each diffuser has different amounts of water and oils that can be used for that particular diffuser. Adjust the recipes according to your diffuser. Add the water, then add the oils and run your diffuser for the desired effect.

***ALTERNATIVE REMEDY:* Manipura Affirmations**

Using your own thoughts and voice to balance your chakras is one of the oldest known methods of opening your chakras for healing. Affirmations can be used as a form of meditation, a chant, a mantra, or just something you repeat to yourself throughout the day. Here are a few examples of affirmations for your chakra balancing.

My heart is joyful

I am calm, relaxed and at peace

I am open to all good things

I am energetic

4TH HEART CHAKRA (Anahata)

The heart chakra lies next to the heart. Putting up walls, blocking love, empathy and connecting to others can be issues of a person who has a blocked heart chakra. Even the ability to love yourself can be affected when your heart chakra is out of balance. Bring love, and self-worth back into your being by following the recommendations below to unblock your heart chakra.

***AYURVEDA:* Anahata Ayurvedic Tips**

- *Practice unconditional love. You may need to get a pet, a friend, or a loved one to love them no matter what they do or say. Be open and giving to this loved one.*
- *Attend grief-counseling sessions, if you have experienced a death.*
- *Meditate in a quiet place and concentrate on loving life and others. Do not think about anything related to fear or anxiety. If fear and anxiety creep into your thoughts, push them aside. Learn to be open to others and don't let fear of abandonment or separation get in your way.*
- *Do not be dependent on another person for your happiness. Learn to be happy in the moment and don't let anyone take that from you. Your happiness depends only on yourself and no one else.*
- *Surround yourself with the color green. Wear an emerald colored piece of jewelry. Get a vase and collect greenery and put in it. Sit under a tree on the grass.*

- *Love yourself.*

HERBS: **Heart Tea**

Yield: 1 cup

1 cup water

1 teaspoon rose

1 teaspoon hibiscus

sweetener

Boil one cup of water. In a tea ball or other tea strainer, add the herbs, seeds or stems. Place the tea ball in the cup or place the herbs directly into the cup. Slowly pour the boiling water over the herbs. Cover cup tightly and let steep for 6-10 minutes. Remove tea ball or strain the tea. Add honey, sugar, or sweetener if desired. Drink when at comfortable temperature. Discard herbs.

ESSENTIAL OIL: **Anahata Diffuser**

Loving yourself is the first step to opening the heart chakra. This recipe has the oils known to empower you to see yourself as the loving and giving creature that you are.

Yield: 1 Application

5-10 drops of any combination of two or more of the following grounding essential oils:

Jasmine, sandalwood, lavender, lemon balm, rose, ylang-

ylang, geranium, mandarin

water

Each diffuser has different amounts of water and oils that can be used for that particular diffuser. Adjust the recipes according to your diffuser. Add the water, then add the oils and run your diffuser for the desired effect.

***ALTERNTIVE REMEDY:* Anahata Affirmations**

Using your own thoughts and voice to balance your chakras is one of the oldest known methods of opening your chakras for healing. Affirmations can be used as a form of meditation, a chant, a mantra, or just something you repeat to yourself throughout the day. Here are a few examples of affirmations for your chakra balancing.

I love myself

I love everyone on the planet

I give my love freely

Everyone loves me

5TH THROAT CHAKRA (Vishuddha)

Sinus problems, teeth and gums, speaking, listening, communicating, self-expression, social skills and speaking your mind, these are all attributes or problems of the throat chakra. Working on your throat chakra can enable us to have a larger presence in the world. To not be afraid to speak the truth to others, and to listen better when others speak the truth to us. These recipes and tips can help us to open up our throat chakra to better communicate with the world around us.

***AYURVEDA:* Vishuddha Ayurvedic Tips**

- *At first, make small issues you have with others known to them. You may be surprised that they don't get confrontational, but desire to accept what you say to them and make the necessary changes.*
- *Learn what you are lacking in communication by writing down your fears, thoughts, desires, frustrations and hopes. What you write will be very cathartic for you.*
- *Meditate and chant the word "hum" throughout your meditation.*
- *Think before you speak. Do not ramble about meaningless things to others. Make your words count and express what you really intend for the other person to hear.*
- *Surround yourself with the color blue. Burn a blue candle. Hold a piece of a sapphire colored gem as you meditate. Buy a blue blanket for your bed.*
- *Touch is the sense associated with the throat chakra. Touch different textures as you contemplate what you wish to say to someone.*

***HERBS:* Throat Tea**

Yield: 1 cup

1 cup water

1 teaspoon peppermint

1 teaspoon spearmint

sweetener

Boil one cup of water. In a tea ball or other tea strainer, add the herbs, seeds or stems. Place the tea ball in the cup or place the herbs directly into the cup. Slowly pour the boiling water over the herbs. Cover cup tightly and let steep for 6-10 minutes. Remove tea ball or strain the tea. Add honey, sugar, or sweetener if desired. Drink when at comfortable temperature. Discard herbs.

***ESSENTIAL OIL:* Vishuddha Diffuser**

Communication and speaking your mind are the things most oppressed when this chakra is blocked. Open your throat chakra and learn to speak your truth.

Yield: 1 Application

5-10 drops of any combination of two or more of the following grounding essential oils:

Frankincense, chamomile, rose, cypress, spearmint, laven-

der, clove, sandalwood

water

Each diffuser has different amounts of water and oils that can be used for that particular diffuser. Adjust the recipes according to your diffuser. Add the water, then add the oils and run your diffuser for the desired effect.

***ALTERNATIVE REMEDY:* Vishuddha Affirmations**

Using your own thoughts and voice to balance your chakras is one of the oldest known methods of opening your chakras for healing. Affirmations can be used as a form of meditation, a chant, a mantra, or just something you repeat to yourself throughout the day. Here are a few examples of affirmations for your chakra balancing.

I will speak my truth

I will look others in the eye

I will voice my opinion

My word is gold

6TH THIRD EYE CHAKRA (Ajna)

Intelligence, wisdom and intuition are connected to our third chakra. When this chakra is blocked, and energy cannot pass through, then we do not have a good gut instinct, or give sound advice. Limits for ourselves are set when this chakra is not flowing smoothly, and society places enough limits on us, without us setting any on ourselves.

***AYURVEDA:* Ajna Ayurvedic Tips**

- *Make a vision board. On this board, place everything you want in life. Use pictures, sayings, thoughts, and express where you would like your life to be in one year from now.*
- *Pray for understanding of yourself and others. Ask for guidance and acceptance for your life and throughout your life.*
- *Surround yourself in the color indigo. Wear indigo clothing and light an indigo candle. Place an indigo colored stone on your alter or in your sacred place.*
- *Meditate to the word "ohm" for as long as you can twice daily.*
- *Forgive, forgive, forgive.*

***HERBS:* Third Eye Tea**

Yield: 1 cup

1 teaspoon lavender

1 teaspoon valerian root chopped

1 cup water

sweetener

Boil one cup of water. In a tea ball or other tea strainer, add the herbs, seeds or stems. Place the tea ball in the cup or place the herbs directly into the cup. Slowly pour the boiling water over the herbs. Cover cup tightly and let steep for 6-10 minutes. Remove tea ball or strain the tea. Add honey, sugar, or sweetener if desired. Drink when at comfortable temperature. Discard herbs.

ESSENTIAL OIL: *Ajna Diffuser*

This recipe enables us to open our minds to wisdom, intelligence, common sense, intuition and listening skills.

Yield: 1 Application

5-10 drops of any combination of two or more of the following grounding essential oils:

Clary sage, frankincense, pine, rosemary, juniper, thyme, pine, cedarwood, germander

water

Each diffuser has different amounts of water and oils that can be used for that particular diffuser. Adjust the recipes according to your diffuser. Add the water, then add the oils and run your diffuser for the desired effect.

ALTERNTIVE REMEDY: Ajna Affirmations

Using your own thoughts and voice to balance your chakras is one of the oldest known methods of opening your chakras for healing. Affirmations can be used as a form of meditation, a chant, a mantra, or just something you repeat to yourself throughout the day. Here are a few examples of affirmations for your chakra balancing.

I believe what my brain tells me

I am open to my Higher Power's message

I believe in my instincts

I trust my intuition

7TH CROWN CHAKRA (Sahasrara)

The most important of all the chakras, the crown chakra. Responsible for our spirituality and souls. Beauty, Nature, positivity, consciousness and God are all connected to our crown chakra. Working and balancing the other six chakras will naturally clear our crown chakra.

***AYURVEDA:* Sahasrara Ayurvedic Tips**

- *Surround yourself with the color violet. Accent your home with violet. Wear violet jewelry. Burn a violet candle.*
- *Practice some sort of physical exercise daily. Yoga is perfect for this exercise as it will keep you in touch with your mind and body as one.*
- *Meditate daily and chant the word "ohm". Meditation is extremely important to increase, balance and get in tune with your crown chakra.*
- *Pray to God daily and ask not only for yourself, but for others as well. Expressing gratitude for your life and soul on an ongoing basis is key to developing the Sahasrara chakra.*
- *This chakra is balanced once you balance all of your other chakras. Work daily on each and every chakra to keep them all balanced, and your crown chakra will benefit, as will your spirit, soul and self.*

***HERBS:* Crown Tea**

Yield: 1 cup

1 teaspoon Palo Santo

1 teaspoon lavender

sweetener

1 cup water

Boil one cup of water. In a tea ball or other tea strainer, add the herbs, seeds or stems. Place the tea ball in the cup or place the herbs directly into the cup. Slowly pour the boiling water over the herbs. Cover cup tightly and let steep for 6-10 minutes. Remove tea ball or strain the tea. Add honey, sugar, or sweetener if desired. Drink when at comfortable temperature. Discard herbs.

ESSENTIAL OIL: **Sahasrara Diffuser**

This recipe fills our homes with the aromatic connection to God. Use this diffuser during prayer and meditation to connect with your Higher Power.

Yield: 1 Application

5-10 drops of any combination of two or more of the following grounding essential oils:

Myrrh, rose, frankincense, lavender, petitgrain, vetiver, rosewood or angelica

water

Each diffuser has different amounts of water and oils that can be used for that particular diffuser. Adjust the recipes according to your diffuser. Add the water, then add the oils and run your diffuser for the desired effect.

***ALTERNATIVE REMEDY:* Sahasrara Affirmations**

Using your own thoughts and voice to balance your chakras is one of the oldest known methods of opening your chakras for healing. Affirmations can be used as a form of meditation, a chant, a mantra, or just something you repeat to yourself throughout the day. Here are a few examples of affirmations for your chakra balancing.

I am connected to my Higher Power

I am grateful for my place in this Universe

I am open to all knowledge

I seek wisdom and enlightenment

CONFIDENCE

Confidence in ourselves can be a lifelong process for some people. Confidence is something that you have…or you don't. Building your confidence can lead to better social interactions, self-esteem, career capabilities and an all-around happier life. Following these treatments that people have used forever to increase their own confidence may be just what you need. So, before that next speaking engagement or that confrontation you dread, just follow one or two of these recipes to increase your confidence in yourself.

AYURVEDA: Confidence Massage Treatment

This recipe will not only help you to feel great about yourself, but you will smell like a million dollars! These oils all work together to increase the serotonin levels in your brain, help your positivity and reduce any negative emotions you may have. I love this blend and it works so well for increasing my positive outlook on everything, including myself!

Yield: 2 Ounces

2 ounces brahmi or coconut oil

7 drops rose oil

5 drops sandalwood oil

5 drops chamomile oil

3 drops vitamin E oil

In a small bowl or container, mix the ingredients together using a spoon or small whisk. Dip fingertips into the container and rub onto back, neck, back of legs, soles of feet, or other areas desired. Do not apply mixture to mucus membranes, eyes, genitals, mouth, wounds or sensitive areas. Rub area desired with a circular motion until the skin absorbs the mixture. When done with massage, wipe off excess with a towel. Store the unused portion in a jar with a tight-fitting lid, in a cool, dark area for up to 3 months.

HERBS: **Confidence Tincture**

My, oh my! This little gem of a brew is just what the doctor ordered to help you to think of yourself in a more positive light. When I know I have a big meeting, or am going to be in a stressful situation, a half teaspoon of this in a cup of lemon balm tea helps me to smile, hold my head up high, and get on with business at hand while feeling great about what I am accomplishing.

Yield: 1 Pint

¾ pint vegetable glycerin or vodka

2 tablespoons borage flowers

2 tablespoons lemon balm

2 tablespoons red clover

2 tablespoons valerian root

1 tablespoon diced ginseng root

Using a pint or quart sized mason jar, fill jar 2/3 full of herbs, cover the herbs with vodka (for adults), or vegetable glycerin (for children), 1 inch from the top of the jar. Cover tightly with mason jar lid and place in a cool, dark location. Shake bottle each day for 2 weeks, and then let it set without shaking for one month (6 weeks for entire process, or longer if you wish). Strain, bottle, label and include the date you strained it. Use ½ - 1 dropper-full in tea, water or other liquid. Store up to one year if made with glycerin, or 3 years if made with vodka.

***ESSENTIAL OIL:* Confidence Boosting Balm**

These oils have properties known for their ability to help you think clearly, stay focused and on task, remain calm and be at your best. Use this balm on your wrists or neck to give yourself the confidence you need.

Yield: 1-2 Tablespoons

1 tablespoon carrier oil

1/4 teaspoon beeswax

4 drops vitamin E oil

5 drops peppermint oil

3 drops melissa oil

Add the herbs to the oil in a small pan or double boiler on the stove. Cook on extremely low heat for 1 hour, stirring occasionally. Strain the oil and herbs through cheesecloth. Discard the herbs. Add the beeswax and stir until melted. Pour into container, label and date. Once cooled, apply to pulse points. Reapply 2-3 times daily. Store in a cool, dark area for up to one year.

ALTERNATIVE REMEDY: **Natural Alternative Confidence Boosters**

There are several ways to gradually boost your confidence levels. Each day try to add a couple of these tips to your daily routine. Over time you will notice that you are walking prouder and thinking more positively about yourself. I use many of these techniques on a regular basis myself.

- *Dark chocolate. Not only does it taste good, but it promotes the good-feeling chemicals in our brains and dark chocolate is naturally healthy for our bodies and our hearts.*
- *Positive thinking. This is probably the number one way to increase your self-esteem and gain confidence. If you think it, act it and do it, you will BE it.*

- *Posture. Even if you are feeling like everyone is staring at you and judging you, walk tall and proud. You will put off an aura of confidence that will be received by others instantly.*

- *Remain calm. Use essential oils, herbs and exercise to give you a calming and powerful feeling within yourself. If you think calm, you will be calm.*

- *Diet. Do not eat heavy, spicy foods. Diet has so many factors to do with our brains. Light meals with airy foods such as broccoli, cabbage and cauliflower do great things to help us remain positive and in a good place. Honey and vitamin B play important factors in boosting our confidence and keeping negative self-doubts at bay.*

CREATIVITY

I have an idea! Why not write a book depicting various natural healing methods from all corners of the world? That was a bit of creativity I had while diffusing pink grapefruit and clary sage essential oils. Ideas, thoughts, art, and visions are often inspired by creative minds. All over the world, various techniques have been utilized to develop creativity in artists and inventors' and giving them a springboard for their next innovation. Here are a few of the ways that you can inspire your own creativity!

***AYURVEDA:* Creative Sparks**

- *Colors: the color of creativity in Ayurveda is orange. Surround your thinking space with oranges, ambers and citrines to open your mind to everything.*
- *Dream journal: write your dreams down when you wake up in the morning. Who knows? Maybe your subconscious is trying to give you that next big idea!*
- *Meditate: Sit in a quiet, comfortable spot. Close your*

eyes as you let your mind go where it wants. If you have trouble letting your mind drift, then quietly repeat over and over the word vam. This mind opening chant in Ayurveda will help you to develop creative thoughts.

- *Ida Nadi: Left nostril breathing is known for activating the creative portion of your mind. Sit comfortably with your eyes closed. Gently place two fingers of your right hand over your right nostril, blocking off the air on the right side. Now breathe deeply in and out of your left nostril ten times. You may be surprised by where your thoughts take you and how relaxed you feel afterwards.*
- *Play. When you are at your wits end trying to come up with your next idea, then just sit it all aside and play. Play with abandon and vigor. Play like you are a child without a care in the world. We were never so creative as we were when we were young.*

HERBS: Creativity Sachet

I am a sachet freak! I love these little bags of heavenly smelling magic. These herbs not only boost your brain and give your creative juices a jump start, but they smell delicious. You can tuck the bag in a drawer to scent your clothing when you are done with it.

Yield: *1 Sachet*

1 tablespoon calendula flowers

½ tablespoon rosemary needles

2 tablespoons mint leaves

3 X 6-inch piece of material

Needle and thread

Dry the herbs until no moisture present to prevent mildewing. Crunch the herbs in a bowl with your fingers until crumbly. Do not crunch so much as to make a powder of them. Next, fold the material until it forms a square with the printed sides facing each other. Sew the edges of two of the sides together, until you have a pocket formed. Turn the material right sides out. Place the herbs inside the pocket, then continue sewing the remaining side until it is completely closed. You may fashion a loop out of a scrap of material and attach to one corner of your sachet for hanging purposes. Set the sachet in a spot where you will be meditating or doing most of your thinking. I place mine on my desk by my computer. Each day give it a few squeezes with your fingers to release a new round of aromas. When not in use, you can store in a zip lock bag to retain the fragrances. I use mine for a month or two before I can no longer detect any smells.

ESSENTIAL OIL: Inspiring Oil Bath

These essential oils are known to open the mind and spark creativity and dreams. You can accomplish anything you set your mind to. Take this bath and let your mind wander, and you may be surprised where your thoughts go. Listen to yourself and believe!

Yield: 1 Application

3 drops pink grapefruit oil

1 avocado diced

Add all ingredients into a bowl. Stir and serve. Top with juice of lemon or lime. Serve with creative soup.

DEPRESSION

Depression can strike anyone, anywhere at any time. Figuring out ways to combat depression is at the forefront of modern psychiatric treatments. In the West, people are usually given a prescription to medications, and in many cases, these medications can work wonders. Clinically depressed people should be under a doctor's care as depression can oftentimes lead to suicidal thoughts and actions. Chronic depression is very serious and should not be taken lightly. In distant corners of the world, prescriptions are not an option available to most people. They must rely on plants, nature, lifestyle and home remedies to battle this vicious condition. I have gathered some of the most helpful recipes and tips for you to use on yourself or your loved ones when occasional depression leaves you feeling sad and lethargic.

AYURVEDA: Ayervedic Depression Approach

Ayerveda teaches us that when we are in a state of depression, everything is involved; our mind, spirit, body, our doshas, chakras and essentially everything we are made up of is out of balance.

Some Ayervedic tips to get back into balance following depression include:

- *Thoughts – try to think positively. Only associate with positive people when possible. When negative thoughts intrude, gently swat them aside and replace them with happy thoughts memories. This is a life-long practice, and not something that can be done on a whim. Thinking positively is hard work, but so worth it in the end.*
- *Meditation - Our consciousness is full of millions of thoughts, our environments are full of sounds, threats, needs, and the list goes on and on. Our minds are cluttered and filled with useless information every second of the day. Only through meditation can we slow the consciousness and allow the subconscious to peak through. Our subconscious knows everything about us…things that are hidden from our conscious. If we still our minds through meditation, we can let the subconscious come forward and give us the messages we so desperately need to hear. Sit in stillness for 5 minutes. Let your thoughts come and go with no reaction. Soon, after practice, the mind will still, the conscious will quiet, and our subconscious will come forward.*
- *Diet – of course a healthy diet is on the menu when struggling with depression. Some foods that will counteract depression are plenty of fresh fruits, vegetables, fruit juices and water. Do not eat processed foods when depressed as they will weigh the body down, clog up the thought processes and lead to negative thinking.*

- *Combine the following spices into a jar and sprinkle on food such as salads and vegetables to lift spirits and banish depression:*
- *Cumin, turmeric, ground ginger, rosemary and black pepper. Keep jar in a cool dark area for up to one year.*

HERBS: **Saffron Rice Casserole**

Herbal treatment for depression is thousands upon thousands of years old. Teas are the main form that herbs are used for during a depression episode, but salves, rubs and diffusers are also great ways to incorporate herbs into healing depression. The main herbs used throughout time are: St. John's wort, ginseng, lavender, chamomile, and most recently, saffron. Many foods have recently been hailed as a vehicle to treat depression. Try this vegetarian rice dish to combat those feelings of doom.

Yield: 2 servings

½ cup dried rice

1 can vegetable broth

½ cup cooked black beans

¼ teaspoon saffron

1 teaspoon ghee

½ cup peeled and cleaned vegetables

salt

Prepare the rice according to package directions but cook 5-10 minutes LESS than directions indicate. Preheat oven to 350 degrees. Place rice, black beans, broth, saffron, ghee and salt into oiled casserole dish. At this time, you can add any other herbs or vegetables you have on hand, such as sweet potatoes, broccoli, squash, cauliflower, etc. to pan. Bake for 25 minutes, or until vegetables are tender. If you have any leftovers, you may refrigerate, covered, for up to 2 days.

ESSENTIAL OIL: Uplifting Diffuser

Essential oils are gaining much popularity in the battle against depression. These little powerhouses often contain therapeutic properties that pass the blood/brain barrier and go to work immediately on your serotonin levels. There are many ways to use essential oils such as in baths, aromas, ointments and rubs. These essential oils work best for banishing depression. Mix two or three of them in your diffuser for an uplifting blend. Or try the blend listed in the recipe below. Bergamot, lavender, chamomile, ylang-ylang, clary sage, basil, vetiver, frankincense, myrrh, rose, jasmine, geranium, orange, petitgrain, neroli, patchouli, sandalwood, and valerian.

Yield: 1 application

3 drops petitgrain oil

3 drops sandalwood oil

3 drops vetiver oil

water

Each diffuser has different amounts of water and oils that can be used for that particular diffuser. Adjust the recipes according to your diffuser. Add the water, then add the oils and run your diffuser for the desired effect.

***ALTERNATIVE REMEDY*: Tips for Depression**

- *Eat healthy. Banish sugar, starches and gluten from your diet for one week. Drink plenty of water and stay hydrated. Remove caffeine and soft drinks from your diet. Enjoy fresh fruit and vegetables.*

- *Sleep. Ensure you are getting the required sleep your body needs to function optimally. Don't over-sleep, or under-sleep. If negative thoughts plague you while attempting sleep, keep returning your thoughts to something positive in the future.*

- *Goals. Set a goal for yourself. Or multiple goals. Set your intention to reach those goals. No goals or intentions are too high. List the steps needed to accomplish your goals. Envision these goals as already happening. Be grateful for being able to accomplish those goals before you complete them. Immerse yourself in the thoughts of those goals.*

- *Exercise. Set a routine for yourself to exercise each day. A healthy body is a must for a healthy mind. It doesn't matter what form of physical activity you do. Try many. Swimming, hiking, yoga, dancercise, mountain climbing. Whatever makes you move and makes you happy is the right exercise for you.*

- *Focus. Focus on feeling good. That you put your all, heart, mind, body and soul into getting better and try-*

ing everything you can to climb out of that black hole is of paramount importance. Vent to someone, spend some money, accomplish the impossible. Getting yourself back to feeling good is the most important thing in your life right now. Give it everything you have.

- *Faith. Increase your spiritual practice. It is odd how when we need our Higher Power the most we don't turn to it. Make a conscious effort to pray, meditate, chant, or whatever it is you do to increase your spiritual growth.*

DESPERATION

Desperation is an overwhelming sense of despair, hopelessness and a call to action. Oftentimes the action needed is not available to us, so the desperation leads to feelings of despair, hopelessness and helplessness. In order to dispel any feelings of desperation, we need to first look inside of ourselves and try to calm the mind to find an answer that will help us, or others, in time of need. Ancient remedies are at our fingertips to bring us clarity and peace in times of desperation.

***AYURVEDA:* Brahmi Infusion**

In Ayurvedic treatments the "vata" is considered to be out of balance for a person suffering from desperation. This gotu kola infusion recipe is one that can be used to balance the vata dosha and return one to complete calm and bring harmony to mind, body and soul. Gotu kola, or brahmi, is well known throughout India as the herb that brings balance to the brain.

Yield: 1 Cup

2 teaspoons gotu kola (brahmi)

1 teaspoon mint leaves

1 cup water

sweetener

Bring one cup water to boil. Add the herbs and remove from heat. Cover and steep for 20-30 minutes. Strain and discard herbs. Sweeten if desired. Drink by the teaspoonful within 12 hours. Refrigerate any remainder for up to 3 days.

HERBS: **Herbs for Desperation**

It has been said that "desperate people turn to desperate methods." In this case, that could not be further from the truth. Desperate people can turn to a time-honored tradition of having a cup of herbal tea to renew their hope, calm and determination to find a solution and stay focused. These herbs have been used for thousands of years as a method for renewing mental peace.

Yield: 1 cup

½ inch ginseng root, grated

1 teaspoon passion flower

sweetener of choice

1 cup water

Boil one cup of water. In a tea ball or other tea strainer, add the herbs, seeds or stems. Place the tea ball in the cup or place the herbs directly into the cup. Slowly pour the boiling water over the herbs. Cover cup tightly and let steep for 6-10 minutes. Remove tea ball or strain the tea. Add honey, sugar, or sweetener if desired. Drink when at comfortable temperature. Discard herbs.

ESSENTIAL OIL: Calming Air Diffuser

Essential oils have long been known to give you the ability to focus, remain calm, and to boost hopeful feelings. This blend is full of oils that have antidepressant properties to give you the fortitude to carry on and enable you to get back to the frame of mind to find a solution to your problems. A diffuser is a quick and easy way to access the properties inherent in essential oils.

Yield: 1 application

3 drops basil oil

3 drops lavender oil

3 drops jasmine oil

water

Each diffuser has different amounts of water and oils that can be used for that particular diffuser. Adjust the recipes according to your diffuser. Add the water, then add the oils and run your diffuser for the desired effect.

A

***LTERNATIVE REMEDY:* Healing for Desperation**

Modern Science has discovered what most cultures have known for years. Our vitamin and mineral intake play a significant part in maintaining not only physical health and balance, but emotionally as well. Foods such as walnuts, eggs, potatoes and bananas also increase the serotonin needed for emotionally stable moods.

The vitamins below are known to bring about feelings of calm, focus and balance. Incorporate the following vitamins and minerals into your diet daily to get the most beneficially healthy emotional needs to banish feelings of desperation.

Magnesium

Fish oil

Vitamin B1 (thiamine)

Vitamin B2 (riboflavin)

Vitamin B3 (niacin)

Vitamin B5 (pantothenic acid)

Vitamin B6 (pyridoxine)

Vitamin B7 (biotin)

Vitamin B9 (folic acid

Vitamin B12 (cobalamin)

Follow your physician's orders for taking vitamins daily for optimal physical and mental health and get the most recommended daily allowance for your body and mind.

DETOX

Detox is a catch phrase these days and involves ridding the body of an untold amount of toxins. From food to drugs, detoxing is a way to speed up the healing process and get our bodies back to their natural state. Detoxing can include withdrawal symptoms which can sometimes be dangerous, or even fatal. Ensure through your physician that the substance you are detoxing your body from, such as drugs, will not have any harmful consequences to you. You might be wondering why "detox" is in a book about emotional needs. If you have ever tried any detoxification process, then you know how it is a mental process as much as it is a physical process. Remedies from around the world are available to us to help rid our bodies and our minds of unnatural substances. Try a few of these easily accessible tips to get your body, thoughts, and soul back to its pristine, natural state.

AYURVEDA: **Detox Treatment**

In Ayurveda, detoxing each seasonal change is the optimal way to stay on top of your health. These Ayurvedic detox methods can be performed for anywhere from 2-7 days. The important thing in Ayurveda is to never skip any meals. Just ensure that what you do eat is easily digestible and that you detox yourself mentally as well as physically. Ensure through your doctor that you can proceed with these steps, especially if you are on medications or have been diagnosed with any conditions.

- ✔ *Diet: ensure you are eating only fresh, warm ingredients. Fresh greens, cabbage, broccoli, rice, dhal, kitchari, vegetarian, and organic, when possible. Stay away from processed foods, sugar, alcohol, fried foods, cold foods, spicy foods and foods that you know give you issues with your digestive tract.*

- ✔ *Sleep: Try to get more sleep than normal. Go to bed 15-30 minutes earlier and get up 15 minutes later. Our brain needs the extra sleep time to give our bodies a little special healing care. Slowing down and relaxing is the process that will help us through this detox phase.*

- ✔ *Hydrate: Drink an extra couple of glasses of water these few days to help the body flush out the system.*

- ✔ *Exercise: Don't do any running or cardio during this time. Gentle yoga or walking in nature are two examples of the easy exercise you need to keep your limbs supple and gives you enough movement to squeeze toxins out of your joints and muscles.*

- ✔ *Oil Shower: Before your shower, rub your body down with sesame oil. Use long, firm strokes over your entire body. Then commence with your shower, washing with soap only those parts that need extra cleanliness such as feet, genitals, ears, etc. Leave the oil on the rest of your body. When done, gently pat dry being careful to not remove the sesame oil that is left on your skin.*

- ✔ *Read self-help or spiritual materials before bed each night. This helps the brain with its healing process throughout the night, gives you positive reinforcement, and helps you to learn about your journey through your life and the path you are to take.*
- ✔ *Surround yourself with positivity, good, beautiful, quiet places, and simple delights. Don't be around gossip, evil, noisy places, or anything with any negative connotations.*

HERBS: **Detox Tea**

This tea has the herbs that will speed up the detox process. Try to drink at least 3 warm cups of herbal tea daily during this process. Dandelion and clover are full of therapeutic properties to help expel toxins and provide an abundance of purifying and cleansing properties to our bodies.

Yield: 1 Cup

1 teaspoon dandelion flowers

1 teaspoon red clover flowers

1 cup water

½ teaspoon honey

Boil one cup of water. Add the herbs, flowers, seeds or stems.

Slowly pour the boiling water over the herbs. Cover the cup of herbs and steep for 6-10 minutes. Strain the tea and discard the herbs. Add honey, cream, or sweetener if desired. Drink when at comfortable temperature.

ESSENTIAL OIL: Detox Foot Bath

This citrusy foot bath gives great results. I have had very expensive footbaths before that left the water looking cloudy but didn't produce any significant results. With this particular detoxifying foot bath, I felt lighter, cleaner, and positively happier after soaking for 15 minutes. Try this during your days of detox and watch yourself not only experience the detoxifying effects, but you will be giving your home an aroma makeover.

Yield: 1 application

1 large container (big enough for your feet)

2 gallons of hot water

½ cup Epsom salts

1 tablespoon milk

10 drops citrus oil

10 drops wild orange oil

10 drops lemongrass oil

Pour the hot water into the container. Dissolve the Epsom salts into the hot water. Cool the water down enough that it is comfortable for your feet. Add the milk to the water (this helps to keep the essential oils from adhering to, and burning, your skin), add the essential oils. Immerse your feet into the comfortable water and relax as long as your feet are comfortable with the temperature. As soon as the water is no longer warm, remove your feet from the vessel and pat dry. Be careful that you don't slip, as feet may be slightly oily. Discard remainder.

***ALTERNATIVE REMEDY:* Detox the alternative way**

Detoxing consists of ridding your body (and your mind) of any toxins, negativity build-up, poisons, unhealthy foods, addictive substances and evil. There are many ways to create an environment of detoxification for yourself. These detox home remedy tips have been used throughout time and in hundreds of cultures.

- *Coconut Oil Pulling: Add the oil to a large spoon. Place the spoonful of oil into the mouth. Very gently, swish oil between all teeth, over tongue and in all areas of the mouth for 10 – 15 minutes. After you are done, spit all of the oil out of your mouth. The oil is now full of toxins. Do not swallow oil. Repeat twice daily as needed.*
- *Hydrate: Drink water as often as you can. Flushing the toxins out of your body is more easily done if you are well hydrated.*
- *Herbal teas: drinking warm herbal teas gives your body energy, vitamins, minerals, and can help to eliminate toxin build-up.*
- *Long term diet: a balanced diet of fresh fruits, vegetables, water, and healthy food can keep you naturally detoxed for life. Stay away from processed foods.*

- *Juice fasting for 24 hours, with "no sugar added" juices, is a quick way to detox, but the benefits may not be as good, or with as long-lasting results as a slower, healthier way to detox.*

- *Meditate, pray, read spiritual books, say affirmations, write down your gratitude list, walk in silence, and other self-help practices can help you to begin on a journey of "mental detoxification."*

DEVOTION

Devotion is an act of truly giving yourself, mind, body and soul, to a belief, faith, project, or person. The act of increasing devotion in ourselves and in others takes a lifetime of practice. For example, I meditate each day to increase my devotion to God. Using these techniques and recipes below only magnifies this process and helps to open us up to devotion and increase our beliefs in a higher power, ourselves, or another.

***AYURVEDA:* Morning Routine for Devotion**

Incorporating a morning routine in your life is not only of paramount importance to your overall health, it can do wonders for increasing your devotion in your spiritual journey. This routine is the highlight of my day and *the most important part of my life.*

- *Find an area in your home devoted solely to your spiritual practices. You can fill with things you love such as candles, diffuser, music, mala beads, self-help books, tapestries, salt lamps, pillows, whatever you want to make your morning routine all about you and your spirituality.*

- *Create ambiance. Light your candles, turn on your Zen music, burn incense, or run your diffuser. Create a devotional area that gets you in the mood to have a great day.*
- *First meditate for at least 5 minutes. Sit on a comfortable pillow and close your eyes. As you breathe in, think the word "peace." As you exhale, think the word "calm." After you practice meditating for a while, you can try different meditation techniques to see which ones you like the best. Push aside any negative thoughts.*
- *Read some sort of spiritual material, or self-help material. This step is so very important. Even if you can only read for 3 minutes. Learning how to advance in our spiritual journey from others is an on-going, life-time journey. Never quit.*
- *Pray. Say your prayers however feels comfortable to you. I use mala beads to ensure that I am saying over 100 prayers of gratitude each and every day. I thank God for each member of my family, my material possessions, for my positive thoughts, for the things I don't yet have, and for my spiritual journey. Gratitude is the key.*
- *Affirmations. Don't forget to say some pretty amazing things about yourself. Use positive language. Instead of saying "I am losing weight," say "I am thin and healthy." Say affirmations about the things you want to accomplish on your day. Today I said, "I will finish ten recipes today." And I will.*

- *Do some morning stretches. Yoga, jumping jacks, karate, whatever gets you moving and your heart racing. Try to move for 5 minutes. It makes all the difference. I have a 7-minute routine that I complete each morning. Then when I can't do my regular yoga practice, I feel great knowing I have done at least the minimum of what I need.*

- *Write a few things in your gratitude journal. You won't believe how happy and thankful this will make you. This step right here has turned around some of the most difficult relationships in my life. Instead of concentrating on the negative aspects of my relationships, I thought and was grateful for the positive aspects. Wow! Talk about stress relieving.*

- *Each night when I go to bed, I hold a small crystal in my hand. I have a box of different types of crystals by my bed. I will blindly grab one and hold it tightly in my palm while I say my prayers. Then I go over my day in my head and try to find the best part of my day and say a prayer of gratitude for that moment.*

- *Completing even a few of these steps each day will have you on a path of devotion, love, worship, and peace like you have never experienced. You will find that on days you are unable to perform your morning routine, you are longing for your space and prayers. But remember, you can pray and be thankful anytime, anywhere.*

HERBS: Devotional Herbal Massage Oil

When devoting yourself to a person, or wanting a person to devote themselves to you, what better way than a massage. These herbs have been used throughout history to increase devotion in ourselves or to others. Making this massage oil takes a while, so make enough to last.

Yield: 1 Cup

1 cup almond oil or jojoba oil

¼ cup thyme

¼ cup calendula flowers

10 drops angelica oil

2 tablespoons lavender flowers

2 tablespoons basil leaves

7 drops vitamin E oil

Combine the carrier oil and the herbs into an oven-safe dish. Heat in 200-degree oven for 4 hours. Remove from oven and cool. Strain through cheesecloth. Discard the herbs and retain the oil. Add the vitamin E oil, and the angelica essential oil. Bottle and label. To use: put 1 teaspoon of the oil into your hands, and lightly massage yourself or the person in which you are trying to increase their devotion. Ensure that they are laying on towels or other area that you don't mind the oil getting on, because it will stain. To store, place bottle in a cool, dark area for up to six months.

ESSENTIAL OIL: Devotional Perfume

This perfume can be made in a roll-on bottle, or just a small glass container with a lid. These essential oils have been used for centuries to increase devotion in ourselves and in others. This is a fun, easy way to make your own perfumes, and can be used with a multitude of essential oils. The ones we are using here are the best ones for devotion.

Yield: 1 ounce

1 teaspoon grapeseed oil

1 teaspoon vodka

8 drops rose oil

7 drops melissa oil

5 drops orange oil

5 drops sandalwood oil

Add the ingredients into a small glass bowl. With a whisk, stir the ingredients together. Using a small funnel, fill a bottle with the perfume. Set in a cool, dark area for 2 weeks, remembering to shake the bottle every day or two. After two weeks, label, and use as you need to increase desired devotional effect.

ALTERNATIVE REMEDY: Help for Devotion

Old home remedies for increasing devotion is as easy as saying a prayer. Pray unceasingly. Ensure that each and every prayer begins with the words "thank you." Praying for devotion to a higher calling, a person, or your own journey begins and ends in your mind. Praying, no matter your beliefs, is the most profound thing you can do for yourself and your devotional experiences.

DOSHAS

We all know what type A personalities and type B personalities are and have probably at one time or another referred to ourselves or someone we know as such. The doshas are personality types that not only tell how you typically work, walk and talk, but can give us insights into the types of diseases you may eventually have and how to stave off or even eliminate the inevitable.

The three main dosha types, (vata, kapha and pitta) are used throughout the world as a beginning point of medical practice. There are seven actual combinations of dosha types, but the goal is to keep the doshas in balance, hence reducing the chance of the diseases associated with your dosha. For example, if you are a pitta type (prone to quick judgments, laughter, anger and argumentative) then you could possibly end up with stroke or high blood pressure related diseases. Vata types, (quick, fearful, flighty, thin and cold) usually have arthritis, anxiety and mental issues. Kapha types (physically inactive, smart, non-judgmental, obese) can have issues with heart, joints and congestion.

Learning which dosha is most prominent in you can help you to learn to balance those doshas, thereby reducing the chances of winding up with those diseases. The recipes below are common in Ayurvedic and other medicinal practices in many cultures, and are used to lower the prominent dosha, and raise the other two doshas, bringing them into balance. Balancing your doshas is a lifelong practice, as they can change from day to day. Your diet is the number one way that you can incorporate into your daily routine to balance your dosha. You will find that when you begin working on balancing your doshas, that all areas of your life improve dramatically. Read the descriptions below for each of the three doshas and see which one you or a family member most resembles.

KAPHA

Always tired, unmotivated to move, procrastinators, obesity and chronic sinus issues are prevalent in the kapha type person. Kaphas are also non-judgmental, intelligent, can see all sides of every issue and are creative. Kaphas are usually over weight, with oily face and hair, reddish skin tones and prefer to be inactive. Kaphas tend to be the one everyone goes to for advice, for they are wise, helpful, and calm. Reducing your kapha will seriously decline the chances of you getting those sedentary lifestyle illnesses such as high blood pressure, stroke, morbid obesity, bad knees and heart attacks. These diet tips are used all over the world to help reduce kapha and raise vata and pitta doshas for balancing.

***AYURVEDA:* Kapha Reducing Diet**

- *Eat: apples, prunes, strawberries, lemon, cherries, cranberries, raisins, asparagus, beets, broccoli, Brussels sprouts, cabbage, cauliflower, celery, corn, eggplant, greens, mushrooms, okra, peas, squash, cooked tomatoes, oats, rice, black beans, lima beans, navy beans, pinto beans, cottage cheese, ghee, goats milk, yogurt, chicken, eggs, shrimp, turkey, mustard, sprouts.*
- *Avoid eating: avocado, bananas, oranges, pineapple, grapefruit, plum, potatoes, zucchini, raw tomatoes, bread, white rice, wheat, soy, dairy, beef, tuna, chocolate, mayonnaise, pickles, soy sauce, coconuts, peanuts, pistachios and walnuts, alcohol, soda, cold drinks.*

***HERBS:* Kapha Herbal Tea**

This tea has the therapeutic properties needed by kaphas to increase their energy and get them moving. These herbs increase vata and pitta doshas, thereby balancing the doshas for a healthier life.

Yield: 1 Cup

½ teaspoon lemongrass

½ teaspoon ginseng

½ teaspoon peppermint

1 cup water

honey

Boil one cup of water. Add the herbs, flowers, seeds or stems.

Slowly pour the boiling water over the herbs. Cover the cup of herbs and steep for 6-10 minutes. Strain the tea and discard the herbs. Add honey, cream, or sweetener if desired. Drink when at comfortable temperature.

ESSENTIAL OIL: **Kapha Oil Rub**

These essential oils have the therapeutic properties needed to reduce kapha and increase vata and pitta. This rub can be used daily to reduce kapha.

Yield: ½ ounce

8 drops Orange oil

8 drops Lemongrass oil

8 drops Rose oil

½ ounce Coconut oil

4 drops Vitamin E oil

Using a bowl or a jar, combine the ingredients together using a whisk or a fork. Using your fingertips, spread the rub onto various areas of your body, ensuring that you do not get into eyes, ears, mouth, open wounds, genitals, mucus membranes, or other sensitive areas. You may cover area with light gauze or old clothing to prevent staining furniture. Leave mixture on until you are ready to reapply. Store remainder in a dark colored jar, in a cool, dark area for up to one year.

ALTERNATIVE REMEDY: ***Kapha Mover***

The best way to reduce kapha is to move. Kaphas tend to sit a lot and to do everything they can to avoid getting up. But in order to eliminate those chances of getting those kapha diseases, movement is extremely critical for a kapha's lifetime of wellbeing. Yoga poses are easy and can provide kapha's with enough energy to get going for the rest of the day. Try some of these simple yoga poses and get movement into that body. Take just 5 minutes to do a few of these asanas to assist you in getting that blood pumping.

- *Cat/cow – Get on your hands and knees in tabletop. Lower your head, chin to chest while exhaling deeply. Arch your back like a mad cat. Upon inhaling, slowly raise your head while swaying your back for cow. Alternate your inhaling and exhaling with arching and swaying your back. Repeat entire sequence 3-5 times. Repeat daily as needed.*
- *Child's pose – (Balasana) – On your hands and knees, spread your knees a little more than hip distance apart. The tops of your feet rest on floor. Lower your head down and let your belly rest between your thighs. Walk your fingers out until comfortably on the floor in front of you. Breathe. Keep this position for 1-3 minutes. Repeat daily as needed.*
- *Down dog***-** *(adho mukha svanasana) Begin in tabletop position on your hands and knees. Tuck your toes under and slowly rise your hips into the air. Your palms and fingers are spread on the floor with your weight evenly distributed throughout them. Straighten, but do not lock your knees. Stretch your heels to the floor as close as you*

can get them. Thighs are tightened and turned inward. Shoulder blades are widened and pushed towards the hips. Hold position.

- *Forward bend- This is a wonderful reliever for back spasms. Stand straight and tall, feet hip distance apart. Lean forward until your fingertips touch the floor or get as close as you can. Ball your fists and place them inside of the crook of your elbows of opposite arms while still in forward bend position. Stay for 5 deep breaths. Elongate the head and neck and sway slightly from side to side.*
- *Legs up the wall pose – In this simple and easy pose, you will find comfort, relaxation in tense muscles, positive thoughts and energy. Lay on your back next to a wall, with your rear facing the wall. Lift your legs and place them up the wall. Your body should be making the letter "L", with your legs up, and your body down. Relax and just let the positivity and energy flow through you. Your arms can be either at your sides, or on your torso. Remain in this position 3-5 minutes.*

VATA

Vatas tend to walk fast, talk fast and are typically thin with dry skin and hair. Vatas, historically, end up with very painful joint, muscle and nerve diseases. Reducing vata will also reduce the chances of getting a mood disorder, arthritis and skin diseases, to name a few. Vatas are flighty, anxious, fearful and nervous. For a vata person, getting yourself grounded every day is of utmost importance. These calming, grounding tips and recipes help to reduce vata and raise the kapha and pitta, thereby balancing out the doshas for optimal health.

AYURVEDA: Vata Reducing Diet

- *Eat: Apples, avocado, bananas, berries, melons, oranges, peaches, pineapple, raisins, cooked vegetables, carrots, green beans, lettuce, okra, onions, peas, sweet potatoes, oats, quinoa, rice, wheat, mung dahl, soy, tofu, butter, cheese, sour cream, beef, fish, salmon, tuna, ketchup, mayonnaise, mustard, soy sauce, coconut, cashews, peanuts, walnuts, pecans, soups, stews and ghee.*
- *Avoid eating: watermelon, pears, figs, artichokes, Brussels sprouts, broccoli, cabbage, cauliflower, celery, corn, eggplant, mushrooms, peppers, onions (raw), potatoes, squash, tomatoes, bread, crackers, pasta, black beans, black eyed peas, navy beans, pinto beans, pork, turkey, chocolate, popcorn, flax, caffeine, alcohol, sodas, and sugar.*

HERBS: Vata Herbal Tea

This tea recipe has the grounding and calming therapeutic properties that vatas need to reduce vata and increase pitta and kapha.

Yield: 1 Cup

½ teaspoon ginger, grated

½ teaspoon hibiscus flowers

1 pinch fennel seeds

1 cup water

honey

Boil one cup of water. Add the herbs, flowers, seeds or stems. Slowly pour the boiling water over the herbs. Cover the cup of herbs and steep for 6-10 minutes. Strain the tea and discard the herbs. Add honey, cream, or sweetener if desired. Drink when at comfortable temperature.

ESSENTIAL OIL: ***Vata Oil Rub***

These essential oils have the therapeutic properties needed to reduce vata and increase kapha and pitta. This rub can be used daily to reduce vata.

Yield: ½ ounce

8 drops Neroli oil

8 drops Mandarin oil

8 drops Vetiver oil

½ ounce Sesame oil

4 drops vitamin E oil

Using a bowl or a jar, combine the ingredients together using a whisk or a fork. Using your fingertips, spread the rub onto various areas of your body, ensuring that you do not get into eyes, ears, mouth, open wounds, genitals, mucus membranes, or other sensitive areas. You may cover area with light gauze or old clothing to prevent staining furniture. Leave mixture on until you are ready to reapply. Store remainder in a dark colored jar, in a cool, dark area for up to one year.

***ALTERNATIVE REMEDY*: Vata Reducing Remedy**

With someone who is fearful, nervous, hyperactive, it is best to find an old way that has worked for thousands of years to reduce these anxiety provoking feelings. Alternate nostril breathing is the perfect technique for calming and grounding vata.

Ida Nadi: Left nostril breathing is known for activating the creative portion of your mind, while at the same time providing you with comfort and grounding. Sit comfortably with your eyes closed. Gently place two fingers of your right hand over your right nostril, blocking off the air on the right side. Now breathe deeply in and out of your left nostril ten times. You may be surprised by where your thoughts take you and how relaxed you feel afterwards.

PITTA

The great orators, public speakers and politicians of the world are usually pitta in nature. Quick to anger, laughter and love, pittas are fiery and outspoken. Pittas are usually of medium build, complain of heat, and are charismatic and have a lot of friends. Pittas are leaders and doers. But too much pitta can lead to strokes, back and neck problems, stress, high blood pressure and social and personal relationship issues. Learning to think before you speak, breathe before yelling and trying not to judge others is a prerequisite for lowering pitta in a person. These hints and tips can assist you in lowering that explosive pitta and raising the vata and kapha doshas.

AYURVEDA: Pitta Diet

- *Eat: apples, avocados, berries, coconut, dates, grapes, melons, oranges, pears, pineapples, plums, raisins, asparagus, broccoli, Brussels sprouts, cabbage, carrots, cauliflower, cucumber, celery, green beans, leafy greens, tomatoes, cereal, crackers, oats, pasta, flour, black beans, lima beans, navy beans, peas, pinto beans, soy, tofu, dairy, ghee, chicken, eggs, fish, turkey, almonds, coconut, flax, popcorn, white wine, almond milk, cool drinks, herbal tea, peppermint, turbinado sugar.*
- *Avoid eating: Apricots, bananas, grapefruit, grapes, mangoes, peaches, plums, beets, corn, eggplant, garlic, olives, onions, peppers, zucchini, pear, radishes, spinach, tomatoes, brown rice, soy sauce, hard cheese, sour cream, plain yogurt, beef, lamb, pork, salmon, tuna, chocolate, mustard, mayonnaise, salt, vinegar, black walnuts, peanuts, pecans, walnuts, chia, sesame, corn oil, caffeine, coffee, lemonade, pineapple juice, rosemary, thyme, white sugar and molasses.*

HERBS: PITTA Herbal Tea

This cooling tea has the ability to calm that pitta fire and increase the vata and kapha doshas that the pitta is lacking.

Yield: 1 Cup

½ teaspoon juniper berry

½ teaspoon rose hip

½ teaspoon sage

1 cup water

honey

Boil one cup of water. Add the herbs, flowers, seeds or stems. Slowly pour the boiling water over the herbs. Cover the cup of herbs and steep for 6-10 minutes. Strain the tea and discard the herbs. Add honey, cream, or sweetener if desired. Drink when at comfortable temperature.

ESSENTIAL OIL: *Pitta Oil Rub*

These essential oils have the therapeutic properties needed to reduce pitta and increase vata and kapha. This rub can be used daily to reduce pitta.

Yield: ½ ounce

8 drops Spearmint oil

8 drops Petitgrain oil

8 drops Tea tree oil

½ ounce almond oil

4 drops vitamin E oil

Using a bowl or a jar, combine the ingredients together using a whisk or a fork. Using your fingertips, spread the rub onto various areas of your body, ensuring that you do not get into eyes, ears, mouth, open wounds, genitals, mucus membranes, or other sensitive areas. You may cover area with light gauze or old clothing to prevent staining furniture. Leave mixture on until you are ready to reapply. Store remainder in a dark colored jar, in a cool, dark area for up to one year.

***ALTERNATIVE REMEDY*: Thousand-Year-Old Pitta Reducer**

Meditation is one of the oldest forms of therapy for pittas. Try this technique for just 5 minutes to reduce anger, stress and those fiery thoughts and feelings that pittas experience.

- *Meditation should be completed in a quiet, peaceful area. Low music may be played. Try to find an area free of negativity and distractions.*
- *Sit on a pillow, folded towel, or a rug. Cross your legs comfortably. Sit erect, but not stiffly.*
- *Closing your eyes, think of peaceful things that make you happy. Controlling the mind is difficult and you may find your thoughts returning again and again to negativity. Just tell those negative thoughts to go away and replace with happy thoughts. Observe your thoughts, don't react to them. Just watch them as if you are watching a movie, then send each thought on its way.*

- *Breathe. Each time your thoughts return to you, direct your thoughts to your breathing patterns. Try to completely empty the lungs of air with deep, slow, inhales and exhales. Continuously return your thoughts to your breathing.*

- *For 5 minutes, sit in silence, or softly chant a mantra such as the words "thank you", and give your mind the positivity it needs to get you through another hectic day. You will find each day becoming easier, and your thoughts beginning to reflect the positivity you focus on each time you meditate. Problem solving, spirituality, grounding, communication, love, social interaction and peace all become deeply affected by meditating.*

EMPATHY

The ability to connect with another person by emotionally feeling their pain or joy is empathy. When many of us work in the care-giving field, we find our empathy waning, due to burn out. It is difficult to be empathetic when you see someone making the same mistakes time and again that repeatedly brings them back to the same adverse situation that they have been in many times before. But care-givers must have empathy, or they cannot perform their job to the best of their abilities. Putting others first is the ultimate goal of being a healthy care-giver, but putting others first often comes at a price for the care-giver, both physically and mentally. These recipes were designed to help bring back those emotions of empathy and help us to better understand those we serve, whether we agree with their decisions, or not, while keeping us at our best and healthiest. Try a few of these to make yourself a more understanding, better and empathetic caregiver and friend.

***AYURVEDA:* Empathy Tips**

- *Vinyasa yoga, to connect the body to mindful breathing,*

can bring you to connecting with your emotions, mind and body. Grounding yourself and listening to your own body and thoughts can assist you with being stronger and more capable of helping others. This practice can develop your ability to protect yourself, while at the same time helping others.

- *Bhastrika (energizing Breathing Technique)*
- *Sit in a comfortable position with erect spine, relaxed neck, head and jaw. Take a few deep inhales and exhales. Begin forcefully breathing out from your diaphragm in rapid, one second intervals. After 15-20 seconds stop and take a deep inhale and exhale. Begin round 2 of rapid breathing. Complete 3 rounds to energize the body and mind.*
- *Abhyanga*
- *Use an oil such as sesame or coconut, any oil that you like and that helps you to feel grounded, calm, and able to empathize with others. You can add a few drops of grounding essential oils, such as cypress, ylang-ylang or patchouli, to add to your experience.*
- *Warm the oil by placing it into a small glass container of hot water for 5 minutes.*
- *Pour the warmed oil into a bowl with any added ingredients.*
- *Gently massage entire body (avoiding eyes, mucus membranes, genitals, open wounds or other sensitive areas), starting with the scalp, down to the soles of your feet.*

- *While massaging yourself, repeat words of affirmation, calming and self-love. It is of paramount importance that you be good to yourself.*
- *Ensure that you are standing on a towel, or sitting, to avoid slipping with the oil on your feet.*
- *When done, towel off the excess oil, or shower.*
- *Take note of how you feel. Enjoy the pleasant emotions that you are experiencing.*

***HERBS:* Empathy Herbal Tea**

This tea has been used forever to help us to open ourselves to others and feel closer to their spirit. This tea also protects us by allowing us to stay grounded and not to become totally absorbed in another's emotional negativity.

Yield: 1 Cup

½ teaspoon rosehips

½ teaspoon calendula flowers

½ teaspoon jasmine

1 Cup water

sweetener

Boil one cup of water. Add the herbs, flowers, seeds or stems. Slowly pour the boiling water over the herbs. Cover the cup of herbs and steep for 6-10 minutes. Strain the tea and discard the herbs. Add honey, cream, or sweetener if desired. Drink when at comfortable temperature.

ESSENTIAL OIL: Empathetic Massage

Giving yourself this massage in the morning before you begin your care-giving duties will give you energy, grounding and the ability to protect yourself from the emotions of others that can weigh heavily on your soul.

Yield: ½ ounce

5 drops rose oil

5 drops jasmine oil

½ ounce carrier oil

Using a small glass bowl, mix all of the ingredients together using a small whisk. Using your fingertips apply the oils to the back, neck, temples, legs, soles of feet, or where desired. Ensure that you do not get any of the mixture into the eyes, ears, mouth, mucus membranes, genitals, open wounds, or sensitive areas. Store remainder in a dark colored jar, label and date, and place in a cool, dark area for up to 6 months.

ALTERNATIVE REMEDY: Gemstones for Empathy

These gemstones have been used since the beginning of time to help bring emotions under control and to help regulate the separation of our mental state from the emotions of others. You can carry them, wear as jewelry, or sleep with one of these beauties under your pillow.

- *Rose Quartz*
- *Malachite*
- *Emerald*

EMPOWERING

Empowering yourself is giving yourself the ability to conquer any goal or idea that you set forth for yourself. You can empower yourself in a million different ways, but you have to work at it every day. Learning to empower ourselves is giving ourselves the freedom to think, act and speak in a way that lets others around us know that we are in charge of ourselves and have faith in our own abilities. Various cultures around the world use different techniques and recipes to bring empowerment to themselves or others. Try using one of these a couple of times a week and see if you don't bring new facets of yourself to your life on your own.

AYURVEDA: **Sankalpa (Setting intentions)**

Sankalpa is an Ayurvedic word that means to set your intentions, believe that it will come true, work towards your goal, and bring your intention to fruition by using sankalpa. This is a simple outline for empowering yourself to reach the intention you have for your life path. Don't reach low…reach for the stars. It's yours for the asking. Believe in yourself.

- *Think long and hard what your actual intention is. To help others? To have a new home? To work at your dream job? Recognize what your deepest desire in life is.*
- *Write what your intention for your future is on paper and read it several times a day.*
- *Give prayers of gratitude and feel the empowering emotions as if you have already received your intention.*
- *Map out the steps you need to take to make that intention come to life.*
- *Work every single day on reciting, reading, praying about and taking steps to reach your goal.*
- *And most importantly, give thanks, give thanks, give thanks.*

HERBS: Empowering Tincture

These herbs work well to balance your spirit and give you the strength and empowerment you crave. Take a few teaspoons of this throughout your day to increase your confidence, ground you, and give you the energy you need. This empowering tincture is a staple in times of stress and helps reduce anxiety and promote a calm, level-headed determination.

Yield: 1 quart

1-quart vodka, or vegetable glycerin

½ cup lavender flowers

½ cup lemon rind

½ cup clary sage leaves

Place herbs in a pint or quart jar until it's 2/3 full, and cover the herbs with a high proof vodka, or vegetable glycerin (for children), 1 – 1 ½ inches from the top of the jar. Cover tightly and place in a cool, dark location. Shake vigorously every day for 2 weeks, then let it set without shaking for one month. Strain, bottle, label and put the date you decanted it (strained herb). Use ½ - 1 dropper-full in tea, water or other liquid. (Tincture made with alcohol will last several years if kept in a cool dark place). Take during times of stress, to empower yourself by giving you the inner strength to take the steps needed in your life.

***ESSENTIAL OIL:* Empowering Morning Oil Lotion**

Essential oils have been used for thousands of years to give a sense of empowerment to people. These top six essential oils have all been reported to instill confidence, energy and a willingness to do what it takes for you to reach your goals. Choose three of the essential oils to use in the lotion recipe below; *Bergamot, geranium, ylang-ylang, frankincense, peppermint or orange.*

Yield: 1 pint

15 drops of a combination of 2 or 3 of the above oils

4 drops vitamin E oil

1-pint unscented lotion

Any of your favorite unscented lotion will work well. Measure out a pint of the lotion and using a whisk, add the ingredients to the lotion, mixing well. Apply to areas needed, 2-3 times daily, but especially in the morning to start your day off with confidence and the ability to forge ahead. Pour into glass container, label and date, and store for up to 6 months.

***ALTERNATIVE REMEDY:* Nature's Alternative Gift**

Exploring the vast wonder of nature can greatly empower us to do what is needed. Just sitting outside in the morning, before your hectic day, can completely change the frame of mind you were in when you woke up. Try a couple of these nature inspired tips to bring empowerment into your daily living.

- *Walking in nature can relieve you of stress and give you a more focused mind. Take a short stroll and try to concentrate on the beauty around you.*
- *Meditate outside. Find a nice quiet spot, spread a blanket, and absorb the energy of the space around you.*
- *Work in the garden. Digging in the soil and connecting with the Earth is a very empowering task. Even if you are just pulling weeds. Get your hands dirty, and your mind clean.*
- *Pick wild flowers for a vase. Quietly strolling along and visualizing the arrangement you wish to make can help to reduce stress, help you to line up tasks needed to be accomplished, and give you much needed peace of mind.*

ENCOURAGEMENT

This section deals mainly with giving yourself encouragement. Being self-encouraging can help you to gain the confidence and the strength needed to face an obstacle or deed. Oftentimes we can self-soothe and give ourselves the support we need, when we can't get it from anyone else. In the end, you only have yourself to rely on. These practices have been used for centuries to bring bravery, fearlessness and encouragement to people from many cultures. Practice self-encouragement as part of your daily ritual to help you to face the world head-on!

***AYURVEDA*: Encouragement Routine**

- *Find an area in your home devoted solely to your spiritual practices. You can fill with things you love such as candles, diffuser, music, mala beads, self-help books, pillows, lamps, spiritual relics, whatever you want to make your morning routine all about you and your spirituality.*
- *Create ambiance. Light your candles, turn on your Zen*

music, get out that salt lamp, burn incense, or run your diffuser. Create a devotional area that gets you in the mood to have a great day and to promote self-confidence.

- *First meditate for at least 5 minutes. Sit on a comfortable pillow and close your eyes. As you breathe in, think the word "peace." As you exhale, think the word "calm." After you practice meditating for a while, you can try different meditation techniques to see which ones you like the best.*

- *Read some sort of spiritual material, or self-help material. This step is so very important. Even if you can only read for 3 minutes. Learning how to advance in our spiritual journey from others is an on-going, life-time journey. Never quit.*

- *Pray. Say your prayers however feels comfortable to you. I use mala beads to ensure that I am saying over 100 prayers of gratitude each and every day. I thank God for each member of my family, my material possessions, for my positive thoughts, for my confidence, for the things I don't yet have, and for my spiritual journey. Gratitude is the key to receiving everything the Universe and God has to offer.*

- *Affirmations. Don't forget to say some pretty amazing things about yourself. Use positive and self-encouraging language. Instead of saying "I am losing weight," say "I am thin and healthy." Say affirmations about the things you want to accomplish on your day. Today I said, "I will research ten recipes today." And I will.*

- *Write a few things in your gratitude journal. You won't believe how happy and thankful this will make you. This step right here has turned around some of the most difficult relationships in my life. Instead of concentrating on the negative aspects of my relationships, I thought and was grateful for the positive aspects. Wow! Talk about stress relieving. This can be a life-changing exercise, especially for care-givers.*

- *Do something for someone else. Anything. Even smiling and saying "Hi" to someone can completely turn their day around. Give.*

- *Do some morning stretches. Yoga, jumping jacks, karate, whatever gets you moving and your heart racing. Try to move for 5 minutes. It makes all the difference. I have a 7-minute routine that I complete each morning. Then when I can't do my regular yoga practice, I feel great knowing I have done at least the minimum of what I need.*

- *Completing even a few of these steps each day will have you on a path of devotion, love, worship, confidence, joy and peace like you have never experienced. You will gain encouragement from these actions every day. You will find that on days you are unable to perform your morning routine, you are longing for your space and prayers. But remember, you can pray and be thankful anytime, anywhere.*

HERBS: Encouraging Herbal Eye Pads

Take some time for yourself. These relaxing eye pads will soothe you, reduce anxiety, and bring confidence and stamina to your thinking. Relax and sit back, meditate on your wonderful self and repeat words of affirmation while experiencing a whole new way to bring up your confidence in yourself.

Yield: 2-4 applications

1 teaspoon sage leaves

1 teaspoon thyme leaves

sprinkle of rosemary needles

¼ cup water

Heat the herbs and the water in the microwave for 3 minutes, or simmer on stovetop. Remove from microwave, strain, discard herbs and cool the liquid. Once the liquid has cooled, soak 2 cotton rounds in the mixture. Wring out slightly and place over closed eyes. Rest for up to 15 minutes, or as long as is comfortable. Discard after using. Store any remainder in the refrigerator, covered, for up to 3 days.

ESSENTIAL OIL: Encouraging Bath Salts

This recipe contains oils that have been used to bring empowerment, confidence and capability to the user. Try this bath the next time you want to give yourself that added boost. There are a variety of salts on the market today that have not been so readily available to us in the past. Use whichever one you prefer: Epsom salts, Himalayan salt, sea salt, the possibilities are endless.

Yield: 1 Cup

1 cup salts

¼ cup baking soda

10 drops bergamot oil

10 drops petitgrain oil

10 drops orange oil

2 tablespoons carrier oil

In a mason jar, or a glass bowl, add the salts and the essential oils. Whisk well. Cover with lid and leave in a cool, dark area for up to 24 hours. Whisk well once more. Run comfortably warm, not hot, bathwater. After the water is done filling the tub, add ½ cup bath salts, and a tablespoon of milk (optional). Store the remainder in a tightly covered jar, in a cool, dark area for up to 3 months.

***ALTERNATIVE REMEDY:* Encouraging Gemstones**

Using gemstones, which contain alternative energy, to bring up your confidence level and to promote self-encouragement has been practiced for thousands of years. These stones are known to activate your energy, your self-esteem and your self-love.

Turquoise

Citrine

Bloodstone

While holding at least one of these stones, say the following affirmations to yourself:

I am enough

I am confident

I am Happy

I am grateful

Repeat these mantras, or say some of your own, by whispering them while concentrating on your stone, and then repeat them again out loud. You will be surprised at how much better you feel afterwards. Then keep that gemstone close to you all day or sleep with it near your head all night.

ENDURANCE

Having the drive and the ability to endure has been a much sought-after accomplishment for eons. Caregivers and parents, in particular, can use some endurance remedies, as their job never ends, never gets a break, and is beyond mentally and physically exhausting. Using these recipes and blends from around the world can help you to have the endurance you need for those tough-to-tackle days and projects.

AYURVEDA: Alternative Color Therapy for Endurance

Color therapy is one of the fastest growing forms of therapy in America and has been utilized for centuries in Ayurveda. Using color to help us calm down, sleep, perform tasks and to be happy has been practiced by all of us for eons. Doesn't a bright bouquet of flowers instantly make you smile? The blue sky makes us feel serene, and the green grass grounds us. Incorporating the colors that match the effect you want is easy and fun. Try these colors the next time you need a boost of strength, confidence and endurance.

Yellow

Orange

For a boost of endurance use yellow and orange, which signify vitality, endurance, strength, optimism and laughter. Wear yellow and orange clothes, make a banana/orange fruit salad. Paint your room a soft yellow with bright orange accents.

***HERBS:* Enduring Herbal Tea**

Dandelion and ginseng are the herbs for confidence, strength and enduring qualities. Make this tea as a morning boost, or an evening relaxer. It's both powerful in therapeutic properties and tastes delicious.

Yield: 1 Cup

1 teaspoon dandelion

½ teaspoon grated ginseng

1 Cup water

sweetener

Boil one cup of water. Add the herbs, flowers, seeds or stems. Slowly pour the boiling water over the herbs. Cover the cup of herbs and steep for 6-10 minutes. Strain the tea and discard the herbs. Add honey, cream, or sweetener if desired. Drink when at comfortable temperature.

ESSENTIAL OIL: Athletes Oil Rub

This rub is made specifically for athletes who have sore muscles but have an endurance trial ahead of them. These essential oils are loaded with the therapeutic properties needed reduce pain, heal and bring comfort to the sorest of muscles so that you can endure what is ahead.

Yield: 1 ounce

1-ounce carrier oil

9 drops peppermint oil

9 drops lavender oil

7 drops lemon oil

5 drops clove oil

5 drops vitamin E oil

Using a bowl or a jar, combine the ingredients together using a whisk or a fork. Using your fingertips, spread the rub onto the affected area, ensuring that you do not get into eyes, ears, mouth, open wounds, genitals, mucus membranes, or other sensitive areas. Rub into the muscles and joints with soft massaging strokes. You may cover area with light gauze or old clothing to prevent staining furniture. Leave mixture on until you are ready to reapply. Store remainder in a dark colored jar, in a cool, dark area for up to one year.

***ALTERNATIVE REMEDY:* Super Enduring Herbal Salad**

This salad has the vegetables and fruit to boost your supply of magnesium, B vitamins and vitamin C. Make plenty, because as good as it is for your endurance, it tastes just as yummy.

Yield: 2 servings

2 cups mixed salad greens

¼ onion, diced

¼ cup carrots, shredded

1 orange peeled, de-seeded and diced

2 tablespoons raisins

2 tablespoons olive or coconut oil

1 teaspoon wine vinegar

1 clove garlic minced

½ teaspoon dried herbs

1/8 teaspoon ground saffron needles

In a small bowl, mix the saffron, herbs, garlic, vinegar and oil with a whisk. Set in refrigerator while you make the rest of the salad. Add the rest of the ingredients into a large bowl, stir lightly. Add the chilled dressing to the salad mixture. Serve with cheese and crackers, or as a side to a meal.

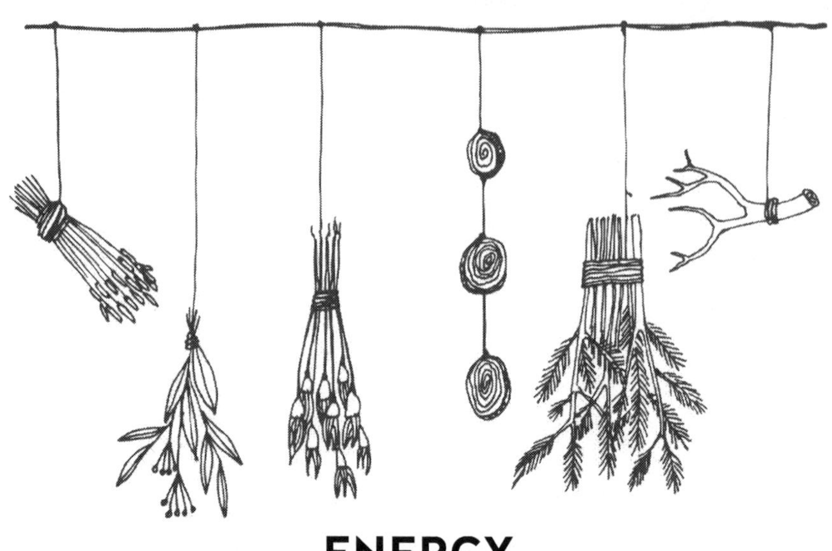

ENERGY

Lacking energy can be annoying, draining and in some cases, life-threatening. Having the energy to get through a normal day can elude us due to lack of sleep, illness or depression, to name a few reasons. If you don't have the energy to do what you need to do in life on a daily basis, you should consult with your physician to ensure something more than just fatigue isn't wracking havoc on your body. Energy is more of a state of mind than a physical ailment in most cases. These recipes and tips can help you to provide yourself with energy to spare! Just try them all to give yourself not only the energy to get through the day, but a little energy to spare for yourself.

AYURVEDA: Alternative Energy Crystals

There are so many crystals and gemstones that are brimming with energy inducing powers. Just think, until 50 years ago, crystals ran radios! The gemstones for energy include black quarts, smoky quarts, amethyst and hematite.

Place each of your crystals in your hand and close your eyes for a few seconds. Which crystal "feels" right to you in this moment, in your current state of emotions. Choose that crystal as your "energy" crystal. You can carry that crystal with you, wear it as jewelry, or any number of ways you wish to keep your crystal close enough to you to absorb your negative emotions and to promote positive emotions. One of the best ways to incorporate the healing power of your crystal is to lie on a flat, comfortable surface. Place the crystal in the middle of your chest. Lay your hands loosely at your sides, and let your feet fall where they may. As you lie still for 5-15 minutes, think about that crystal and the energy it is spreading throughout your body. Imagine its healing effects coursing through your blood veins, your organs, your heart and finally through your brain. Once your emotions are calm and under control, sit up, take a few breaths and walk away feeling energized and renewed.

HERBS: Energy Tonic

This energy tonic is a strong tea that takes 8 hours to make. This particular recipe uses herbs that are energy inducing and fatigue clearing. Make this before you go to bed when you know you have a big day the next day and you need to be on top of your game. This tonic will provide you with the mental and physical energy to do what needs to be done.

Yield: 1 Quart

1 ginseng root chopped

½ cup gingko biloba

½ cup gotu kola

Fruit (optional)

1-quart water

sweetener

Crush, and/or chop the herbs, seeds or stems and add to a mason jar. Pour boiling water over the herbs and cap the jar tightly. Shake well and let sit undisturbed, at room temperature, for 8 hours. It's good to make this in the evening and let sit all night. Strain, and add sweetener of choice to the tonic. Fruit may be added to tonic for taste. Discard herbs. Drink tonic at intervals throughout the day for desired effect. Store in refrigerator in a jar with a tight-fitting lid for up to 24 hours.

ESSENTIAL OIL: **Bottle of Energy**

These essential oils contain fatigue fighting properties and will assist you in staying alert. Mental energy fatigue is sometimes more overpowering than a lack of physical energy. These essential oils contain enough energy producing therapeutic properties to help you to focus, think clearly and precisely, and to take command of any situation. Carry this roller bottle in your purse, or put it in your desk drawer, so it will be handy whenever you start feeling foggy, tired and confused.

Yield: 1 ounce

1-ounce carrier oil

3 drops vitamin E oil

4 drops peppermint oil

3 drops lemon oil

4 drops frankincense oil

2 drops basil oil

Combine the ingredients into a small bowl. Using a tiny funnel, pour the mixture into roller bottles. Label and date. Roll on to areas needed as desired, 2-3 times daily. Do not roll onto open wounds, mouth, eyes, genitals, sensitive areas or mucus membranes. Store, upright, in a cool, dark area for up to 6 months.

***ALTERNATIVE REMEDY:* Mental Energy Salad**

This salad is full of the mind-clearing, focusing, energetic properties needed to give you that afternoon pick-me-up that will help you through the rest of the day. The brain-boosting benefits of these foods provide enough energy to get you motivated and meeting those deadlines. Not to mention it's tasty too!

Yield: 1 serving

2 cups greens chopped

1 hard-boiled egg diced

1/8 cup quinoa prepared

1/8 cup blueberries

1 teaspoon flax seeds

1 tablespoon celery diced

1 avocado sliced

1 tablespoon coconut oil

½ teaspoon lemon juice

1 clove garlic minced

Whisk together the coconut oil, garlic, and lemon juice in a small bowl. Set the dressing aside. In a salad bowl, combine the rest of the ingredients. Mix lightly. Add nuts if desired, and top with dressing.

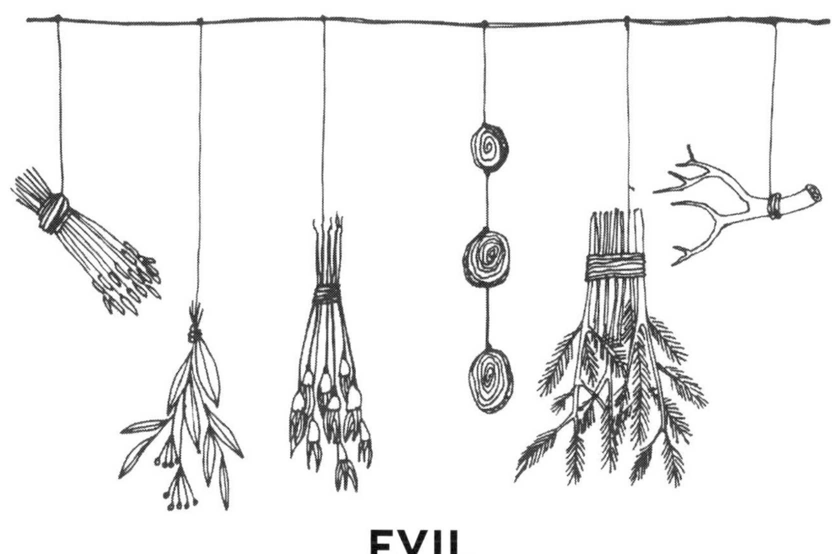

EVIL

There is an ages old debate about whether or not evil is born into the world or if people create it. I personally don't care, if it's out there, I don't want any of it. Keeping evil at bay has been practiced in thousands of different ways throughout time. When we genuflect, say gesundheit after a sneeze, or knock on wood, we are practicing, in essence, deflecting evil. Here are a few of the remedies used by various cultures to eradicate evil and protect ourselves from that which we cannot see.

AYURVEDA: Tips for Protection Against Evil

There are many Ayurvedic tips for reducing evil and negativity in your life. Try to incorporate a few, or all of these tips to become immersed in light, positivity and love.

Cleansing Soul – An old practice involves the full moon. Dress yourself in the color green (for grounding), or white (for purity), and walk barefoot under a full moon, while chanting the protection mantra "I am surrounded by white light which no evil can penetrate."

Yarrow – plant yarrow around your home. Yarrow is said to be the herb of protection against all evil and negativity.

Sweat – To reduce the amount of negative and evil illness inducing toxins in the body, sweat them out. Whether through steam bath, hard work, or sunshine, it's important to let the sweat flow.

Bath – add ½ cup sea salt to the bathwater. Soak for up to 15 minutes or as long as comfortable. It is said that the sea salt absorbs all negativity.

Smudge – An ages old practice is the art of smudging. White sage is especially powerful against evil. Light the end of the sage stick and blow out the fire. Walk from room to room in the space you wish to rid the evil. Say affirmations of positivity as you wave the smoke in all the corners.

HERBS: Protection Ointment

Herbs contain powerful properties known for ridding oneself of evil and providing protection. This ointment will last a long time and has a pleasing aroma. Wear especially when surrounding yourself in an environment where there is a lot of negativity or hard feelings.

Yield: 1 Cup

1-ounce lavender chopped

1-ounce cedarwood, chopped

1 cup carrier oil

5 drops vitamin E oil

1-ounce beeswax grated

Combine the oils and the herbs and cook on very, very low heat in oven (250) for 1-3 hours. Strain, discard herbs, add one ounce of beeswax and the vitamin E oil, melt and stir. Pour mixture into a jar with a lid. Apply to temples, throat, soles of feet, or wrists when cool. Store in a jar with a tight-fitting lid in a cool, dark area for up to onc year.

***ESSENTIAL OIL:* Home Oil Protection**

This diffuser uses essential oils that are reported to rid the home or office of evil, negativity, grudges, hatred and anger. Run this diffuser when you want to bring peace and calm to an area.

Yield: 1 application

3 drops angelica oil

3 drops juniper oil

3 drops myrrh oil

water

Each diffuser has different amounts of water and oils that can be used for that particular diffuser. Adjust the recipes according to your diffuser. Add the water, then add the oils and run your diffuser for the desired effect.

***ALTERNATIVE REMEDY*: Crystal/Gem Protection**

There are many crystals and gems that you can use to protect yourself from all types of evil. Try using these treasures from the Earth to give yourself protection all day long.

- *One of the best ways to clear negativity and evil from your home is to run a salt lamp. Salt lamps are reported to reduce negative ions and increase positivity and calm.*
- *These gems can be carried, worn, held, or placed under your pillow or at your bedside table for protection: Amethyst, amber, smoky quartz, black obsidian, black onyx or turquoise*

EXHAUSTION

Exhaustion can overtake the stoutest among us. Overwork, mental fatigue, tragedies and triumphs can all lead to a bout of exhaustion. Of course, the best remedy to deal with exhaustion is sleep, but sometimes that is just not possible. These remedies will help you to regain your faculties and forge ahead for a while longer. People have been known to be hospitalized with exhaustion when it is chronic and includes both physical and mental exhaustion. If you have chronic exhaustion, check with your physician to get a proper diagnosis and uncover any underlying problems or issues.

AYURVEDA: Abhyanga

This massage will wake up your senses, making you feel more alive and energetic. This massage can be given to yourself, and is especially good for the morning, after your shower.

Yield: 1 application

¼ cup oil of either oil: sesame, avocado, jojoba, apricot, grape seed, or oil of choice.

- *Warm the oil by placing it into a small glass container and placing it in a bowl of hot water for 5 minutes.*
- *Pour the warmed oil into a bowl with any additional essential oil ingredients.*
- *Gently massage entire body (avoiding eyes, mucus membranes, genitals, open wounds or other sensitive areas), starting with the scalp, down to the soles of your feet.*
- *While massaging yourself, repeat words of affirmation, calming and self-love. It is of paramount importance that you be good to yourself.*
- *Ensure that you are standing on a towel, or sitting, to avoid slipping with the oil on your feet.*
- *When done, towel off the excess oil, or shower.*
- *Take note of how you feel. Enjoy the pleasant emotions that you are experiencing.*

HERBS: Awakening Herbal Eye Pads

Peppermint has long been a great energizing herb. Using leftover peppermint tea or making a fresh batch to use for your eye pads will bring you refreshment and energy.

Yield: 2-4 applications

2 teaspoons peppermint

¼ cup water

2 cotton pads

Heat the herbs and the water in the microwave for 3 minutes. Remove from microwave, strain, discard herbs and cool the liquid. Once the liquid has cooled, soak 2 cotton rounds in the mixture. Wring out slightly and place over closed eyes. Rest for up to 15 minutes, or as long as is comfortable. Discard after using. Store any remainder in the refrigerator, covered, for up to 3 days.

***ESSENTIAL OIL:* Energizing Diffuser**

Use these oils to give yourself a treat. The aroma is amazing, and the effects are quick to give your brain that boost to get you through the rest of the day when mid-afternoon exhaustion sets in.

Yield: 1 application

3 drops bergamot

3 drops wild orange

3 drops peppermint

water

Each diffuser has different amounts of water and oils that can be used for that particular diffuser. Adjust the recipes according to your diffuser. Add the water, then add the oils and run your diffuser for the desired effect.

***ALTERNATIVE REMEDY:* Yoga for Exhaustion**

Yoga combats fatigue better than anything I have ever tried. These poses are reported to ramp up your brain power while lending physical prowess to your tired and aching body.

Begin by setting comfortably and stating your intention for this practice, which would be to banish your fatigue and increase your energy levels.

Complete three sun-salutations:

- *Mountain*
- *Forward fold*
- *Half-way lift*
- *Forward fold*
- *Plank*
- *Low plank*
- *Up dog*
- *Down dog*
- *Complete tree poses on each leg*

FAITH

Faith…doubt…faith…doubt. They creep in and out of our lives, our minds, our hearts and never remain consistent. How do we increase our faith in ourselves? In our Higher Power? In the Universe? In humanity? We try. We commit. We keep trying every time our faith waivers. People have turned to outside influences all throughout history to find a way to increase their faith. I have included a few of those remedies here to help you to increase your faith, in yourself and in your higher power, and hold on to your beliefs.

AYURVEDA: Faith Boosters

Holding on to your faith in yourself and in your beliefs, is a daily ritual that you can include each morning as you get ready to face the day. Incorporate a few of these time-tested tips to get you believing in yourself and your ability to forge ahead.

- *Affirmations: One of the best ways to increase your faith in your abilities and strengths is to state them out loud to yourself. Believe in what you say. You can even make a list of affirmations and carry it with you to repeat as you need throughout the day. What you say to yourself reflects what others think of you.*

- *Gratitude: Be grateful for your strengths. Say prayers of thanks to the Universe for everything you desire in yourself. This part of your ritual will not only increase your faith in yourself, but in your higher power. Giving thanks is the highest form of prayer. Gratitude opens us up to receive everything the Universe has to offer.*
- *Communication: Commit to talking positively and remove all negativity from your communication with others. You will strengthen your faith and abilities, your spirit and your life when you speak only good. The tongue is the deliverer of our innermost being. Let yours be as bright as the sun.*
- *Commit: Give yourself permission to take time for yourself each morning to perform these rituals of faith. Having a faith-based ritual every morning is the single most important skill-set you will ever develop in your life.*

HERBS: Faith Fragrance

This beautiful aroma fills the home with luscious smells while imparting positive emotions, just right for filling one with faith. These herbs have been utilized for centuries as a way to connect people with their spiritual selves. Give your home, and everyone in it, a dose of uplifting positivity and faith by making a batch of this herbal concoction.

Yield: 1 application

1 tablespoon lavender flowers

1 tablespoon holy basil leaves

1 tablespoon lemon balm leaves

1 tablespoon rose petals

3 cups water

Mix herbs together in a small, heavy-duty sauce pan on the stove. Cook herbal mixture, on very low, until water is 1 inch from bottom of pan, then add more water. Continue to add water throughout the day as the water will evaporate. The home will fill with the aroma from the herbs. Do not let water get so low that the herbs will burn. When done, discard herbs.

***ESSENTIAL OIL:* Faith Anointing Oil**

Anointing oneself in essential oils is a practice that has been upheld since before recorded history. Increasing ones' faith through this practice is as old as humankind. Not only will this ritual restore faith in yourself and in your Higher Power, but possibly in your fellow human beings.

Yield: 1 Ounce

1-ounce carrier oil (sesame or jojoba is perfect for faith)

9 drops angelica oil

9 drops frankincense oil

3 drops sandalwood oil

3 drops vitamin E oil

3 drops vetiver oil

3 drops ylang-ylang oil

Using a small glass bowl, mix all of the ingredients together using a small whisk. Using your fingertips apply the oils to the back, neck, temples, legs, soles of feet, or where desired. Ensure that you do not get any of the mixture into the eyes, ears, mouth, mucus membranes, genitals, open wounds, or sensitive areas. Store remainder in a dark colored jar, label and date, and place in a cool, dark area for up to 6 months.

***ALTERNATIVE REMEDY*: Methods to Increase Faith**

These tips may seem like common sense, but it never hurts to repeat what is so beneficial for us to have a healthy faith in ourselves and our Higher Power.

- *Vitamins: B vitamins are vital to our overall mental health. Ensure that you are getting enough B vitamins through your diet, or through supplements.*
- *Yoga: Practicing any form of yoga can help to instill an abundance of faith in yourself. It is said that "Practicing yoga three times a week will change your body; Practicing yoga five times a week will change your life."*
- *Pray: Start your gratitude prayer ritual today. Just close your eyes, right now, and say "thank you" three times*

with each slow exhale. See what I mean? Smiling, aren't you?

- *Nature: Walking in nature is a sure-fire way to restore your faith in everything. Just think about nothing but the beauty of mother Earth and the joy that can be found in the simplest blade of grass or leaf from a tree.*

FATIGUE

A host of factors can lead one to feel extreme fatigue. And you know how it usually goes…the more fatigued you are, the harder it is to fall asleep. These recipes will help you to either gain energy to continue on as you should or help you to sleep and put that fatigue to an end once and for all. If you have chronic fatigue plaguing you, then it is best to be thoroughly checked out by your physician to discern if there are any underlying issues.

AYURVEDA: **Fatigue Tips**

The vata dosha is out of balance when you are fraught with mental fatigue. Physical fatigue is caused by an imbalance in the kapha dosha. When you are emotionally drained, the pitta dosha is out of balance. Balancing the doshas to bring yourself up to your optimal physical, emotional and mental best are easy by following these dosha balancing tips.

- *Diet: by following the diet to balance doshas, you will bring kapha, pitta and vata into harmony and feel at your optimal best.*

- *Cut out caffeine, alcohol, and diet drinks. Drink plenty of water and herbal teas.*
- *Cut out all processed foods. Eat nature's bounty.*
- *Eat fruit, veggies, ghee, nuts, herbs, and plenty of food from God's garden.*
- *Sleep. It cannot be stressed enough how much a good night's sleep can impact you positively throughout the following days.*
- *Exercise. Do what you like to do, walk, swim, run, yoga. Whatever it is, try to sneak it in when you can.*
- *Positive thoughts. Try to eliminate any thoughts that you don't want to be your future. Think about things that you DO want in your future.*

HERBS: **Decoction Herbal Boost**

When fighting fatigue, both mentally and physically, these herbs have been touted by the experts to restore feelings of vitality and wellness. This decoction can be made the night before and drink it before you start off on your day.

Yield: 1 Cup

1 teaspoon ginger diced

1 teaspoon ginkgo biloba, ground or powdered

1 teaspoon gotu kola, ground or powdered

1 cup water

sweetener

Bring the water to boiling in a pan on the stove. Add the herbs, and immediately turn the heat to simmer. Simmer for 30 minutes for leaves and flowers, simmer for one hour for woodier herbs, seeds and bark. Remove from heat and strain through cheesecloth. Discard herbs and add sweetener (optional) to the drink. Drink slowly by sips over the course of a few hours. Store remainder in a jar with a lid in the refrigerator for up to 24 hours.

ESSENTIAL OIL: ***Energy Inhale***

This quick, easy recipe can take you from afternoon fatigue, to let's get these tasks done now. You can keep a vial of peppermint oil in your purse, or office desk so that you have this with you at any moment of need.

Yield: 1 application

2 drops peppermint oil

Slowly drop the essential oil drops onto the palm of your hand, a tissue, or an essential oil inhaler. Using your thumb and forefinger, cover one nostril while inhaling deeply the aromas with your open nostril. Repeat process on other side as needed.

ALTERNATIVE REMEDY: **Superfood Smoothie**

This powerful smoothie contains the superfoods reported to provide energy, mental sharpness, and physical strength when taken. Combine these great tasting treats into a fatigue-fighting drink in the morning and feel the energy coursing through your body the entire day.

Yield: 2 servings

1 orange

½ banana

4 walnut halves

1/8 cup yogurt

¼ cup spinach

½ teaspoon chopped ginseng

½ cup juice of choice (unsweetened)

Combine all the ingredients into a blender, or smoothie machine. Add ice if you like your drink more of a frozen consistency. Blend until the blades no longer have a chopping sound. Pour into 2 glasses and enjoy. Refrigerate remainder. It's best if drank within 12 hours.

FEAR

Fear at the right time is a blessing as it helps our minds and bodies react in a way that may save our lives. But fear for unknown or imagined reasons is detrimental to us and a sign of anxiety, paranoia or a host of more serious issues. Therapy can help to assuage a lot of chronic fear, and medical tests could find underlying issues that sometimes lead to chronic fear and paranoia.

The same chemicals that course through our bodies in moments of fear to help us react, will turn on us and cause disease if we continue to live with chronic fear. These recipes have helped many people for ages to overcome crippling fear. Take hold of your lives and thoughts by trying these and give yourself that safe, protected, comforting feeling that you need.

AYURVEDIA: Breath Technique

Breathing properly for different emotions is paramount in Ayurvedic medicine. Try this simple tip to calm your fears and instill a sense of peace throughout your mind and body. Fear and anxiety often spill over into many areas of our lives. Different breathing techniques are easy and free. You always have your breath with you. Use it to control your emotions.

- *Diaphragmatic – Find a comfortable position and lay in corpse pose, on your back. Arms down at sides, palms up. Eyes closed, and feet relaxed. Place a 5-10-pound comfortable, soft weight (such as a sand bag, or a large bag of rice) onto the diaphragm, right below the rib cage. Continue lying in corpse pose and breathe as normal as possible. The weight will strengthen the diaphragm and force the patient to take long, slow, deep breaths. This exercise can be performed for 5-15 minutes a day until diaphragm is strengthened. It can also be used in times of significant stress, anxiety or fear, as it has many calming properties.*
- *Ujjayi – sit in a comfortable position. Hold your hand up like it is a mirror. Exhale as if you are trying to fog the mirror. Now close your mouth and constrict your throat muscles in the same way, exhaling low and loudly. Inhale longer than normal, now slowly exhale making the sound of an ocean. Repeat ocean breath for 2 minutes. Ujjayi breathing is very relaxing and stress reducing.*

HERBS: **Fear Dispelling Tea**

Sitting over a cup of calming tea must be one of the most relaxing acts a person can do. These herbs are specifically made by the Creator to give you a taste of heaven on Earth. Drink a cup of this herbal delight the next time your anxiety and fear take hold of your mind. The therapeutic benefits of these herbs include sedative and tranquilizing properties.

Yield: 1 Cup

1 teaspoon St. John's wort

1 teaspoon lemon balm

1 cup water

sweetener

Boil one cup of water. Add the herbs, flowers, seeds or stems. Slowly pour the boiling water over the herbs. Cover the cup of herbs and steep for 6-10 minutes. Strain the tea and discard the herbs. Add honey, cream, or sweetener if desired. Drink when at comfortable temperature.

***ESSENTIAL OIL:* Calming Touch Oils**

I like to blend these oils with sedative and calming properties when I am feeling anxious or fearful about a specific situation. It only takes a small amount to bring about great results.

Yield: ½ ounce

½ ounce carrier oil

5 drops clary sage

4 drops neroli

4 drops vetiver

3 drops jasmine

4 drops vitamin E oil

Using a small glass bowl, mix all of the ingredients together using a small whisk. Using your fingertips apply a small dot of oil to the neck, temples, soles of feet, or third eye (forehead). Ensure that you do not get any of the mixture into the eyes, ears, mouth, mucus membranes, genitals, open wounds, or sensitive areas. Store remainder in a dark colored jar, label and date, and place in a cool, dark area for up to 6 months.

***ALTERNATIVE REMEDY:* Gemstones to Banish Fear**

These gemstones have been used for thousands of years to dispel fear, anxiety and stress. Some of them are familiar to you, while others may be foreign and sound strange. It's a good idea to learn about the different gemstones and how they can work with your various emotions. They can be quite powerful.

Choose one of the following gemstones as your "fear dispeller" stone. Sit it in the sunlight for one hour, or overnight under the moonlight to magnify its energy. After having completed this, you can carry the gemstone with you. Wear it in a pouch or as a piece of jewelry. Sit it on your office desk, or your bedside table. Holding the stone in your hand while praying, meditating, or saying your mantras is a perfect way to absorb its calming energies.

Amethyst, citrine, sapphire, tourmaline, ruby, turquoise, diamonds, jade, blue lace agate, fluorite, emerald, opal, calcite, selenite, meteorite, pearls, onyx.

FORGETFULNESS

Memory loss is a horrible, devastating fact of life as we age. We have issues remembering recent events, but can recount, in detail, something that happened 40 years ago. The mind is a funny thing. These recipes and tips are designed to help people with age-related memory loss, and I do believe that they work very well, as I use them at times when I need memory skills, such as teaching yoga classes, or giving a speech. Give these a try and watch your memory improve as mine does when I need it most.

AYURVEDIA: Memory Drink

Ashwagandha and brahmi are two of the most well-respected memory enhancers in Ayurvedic medicine. These two herbs are considered a tonic for the brain, (if you have rheumatoid arthritis, be aware that ashwagandha is a "nightshade"). Drink this mixture at night before you go to sleep, and it will work on restoring your brain all night long.

Yield: 1 serving

½ teaspoon brahmi powder

½ teaspoon ashwagandha powder

1 cup milk

Combine the ingredients in a heavy saucepan on stovetop. Simmer for 5-10 minutes. Remove from stove and cool until warm enough to drink. Sip slowly before bedtime. Discard any remainder.

***HERBS:* Lemon Forget-Me-Not Tea**

Lemon verbena and rosemary have long been held as memory enhancing herbs. Studies have proven that these herbs can help to reduce forgetfulness due to age, stress, or concentration issues. This tea also tastes as good as it is helpful.

Yield: 1 Cup

1 teaspoon lemon verbena

1/3 teaspoon rosemary needles

sweetener

Boil one cup of water. Add the herbs, flowers, seeds or stems. Slowly pour the boiling water over the herbs. Cover the cup of herbs and steep for 6-10 minutes. Strain the tea and discard the herbs. Add honey, cream, or sweetener if desired. Drink when at comfortable temperature.

ESSENTIAL OIL: Temple Roller

These essential oils have long been reported to enhance memory caused by age-onset forgetfulness. It's easy to make, and the oils have memory boosting therapeutic properties that will help you to be on top of your game.

Yield: 1/3 ounce

1/3-ounce carrier oil

2 drops citrus oil

2 drops clary sage oil

2 drops melissa oil

2 drops lemon grass oil

Combine the ingredients into a small bowl. Using a tiny funnel, pour the mixture into a 1/3-ounce roller bottle. Label and date. Roll on temples or neck, 2-3 times daily. Do not roll onto open wounds, mouth, eyes, genitals, sensitive areas or mucus membranes. Store, upright, in a cool, dark area for up to 6 months.

ALTERNATIVE REMEDY: Methods for Forgetfulness

There are thousands and thousands of tips and hints for increasing your memory skills and banishing forgetfulness. I have chosen the ones that either I have used, or that have been proven through various studies to work. I try to incorporate a few of these into my daily routine and diet to stave off forgetfulness in myself as well as getting family members with memory issues to try. The results seem good.

- *Diet: Do eat ghee, coconut, seafood, carrots, milk, pistachios, blueberries, spices, eggs, leafy greens, and almonds as much as possible.*
- *Do: Use salt lamps (to reduce negative ions), work on puzzles, learn a foreign language, exercise, add spices to food, do yoga, try to meditate, and get out in nature as much as possible.*
- *Diet: Do not eat sugar, wheat, processed food, alcohol, and chemical derivatives when possible.*
- *Don't: Drink alcohol, use tobacco, sleep too little, let depression or negative thoughts linger, have toxic cleaning solutions in your home, or neglect to learn something new every day.*

GLOOM

Gloom is an all-encompassing feeling of sadness, despair and negativity. When someone is feeling "gloomy" everyone around them is affected. Bring some positivity, happiness and spiritual awakening to the home by using these recipes that have been used for centuries. Gloom has no place in our lives, and we should do whatever is in our power to cast it out.

AYURVEDA: **Panchakarma**

In Ayurveda, a person who is suffering from gloom or depression has a build-up of toxins, or Ama, in the body. An ancient method of reducing and removing toxins is called panchakarma, which is a purification process. This used to be quite a horrific process of detoxification involving blood-letting, enemas and vomiting. But throughout the years Ayurveda has changed the steps for Panchakarma, although the old ways are still practiced in some areas. Panchakarma is time consuming, emotional and extremely healing. Ensure through your physician that panchakarma techniques are safe for you, especially if you are on any medications or have any illnesses. Panchakarma is usually practiced for 3-5 days. Ensure that you are away from technology, in a quiet, peaceful area, with no distractions or stress. This is my own interpretation of present day panchakarma. The following steps will help you to detox, and rid your body of the Ama, or toxin build-up that is responsible for those gloomy, depressing emotions.

- *Wake up early with the sunrise. Go outside if weather permits, if not, have a dedicated quiet room. Sit and meditate, followed by a gentle, stretching yoga practice.*
- *Clean your teeth, have an oil pull, clean your ears. You may also perform tongue scraping and nasya at this time, if you wish. Cleansing and purifying the body involves the outside as well as the inside.*
- *Drink a cup of herbal tea. The most common detoxifying herbs to use in this process are listed in "step #9". You can use other herbs suitable for your dosha if you want.*
- *Sesame oil body massage. Oil yourself from your scalp to your toes. Do not get in eyes, ears or mucus membranes. You can add herbs or essential oils to the massage oil if you wish. Leave on for 15 minutes to 1 hour. Wash off in a warm bath.*
- *Kitcheree or dal for lunch.*
- *Spend the afternoon alternately in nature or in meditation. Some light reading of self-help or spiritual materials is permitted. Being alone with your thoughts for such a long time is mind-expanding, emotional and draining.*

- *At this point, you can take an enema if you wish, (overseen by doctor or Ayurvedic practitioner), or you can have another head to toe oil treatment with sesame oil.*
- *Eat kitcheree for supper, or you may have light, steamed vegetables with rice.*
- *Drink a relaxing, calming cup of detox herbal tea and add some relaxing herbs such as St. John's wort, lemon balm, valerian root or chamomile.*
- *Meditate, pray, read, journal, say your affirmations, use visualization techniques for your future (gloom-free), do a few gentle yoga stretches, or sit under the moon light. Use your evening hours to relax, unwind, and prepare for the night.*
- *Eat 1-2 tablespoons ghee. This will work its way through the system all night, leaving you with a gentle elimination upon wakening.*
- *Coat the feet with sesame oil. Sleep with thick socks on to keep the oil from getting on your furniture, and to help you to not slip when you walk.*
- *Read a favorite and profoundly inspirational chapter from a book, then sleep with a deep, satisfying, relaxing sleep.*

***HERBS:* Gloom-Free Tea**

The therapeutic properties in this tea make it the perfect tea for lifting the spirits, banishing any negative emotions, and it tastes delightful. These herbs contain sedative and tranquilizing properties, so it's best to drink it at night, or when spending a few hours relaxing. This is a great tea to drink when performing Pancha karma or any other negativity dispelling rituals.

Yield: 1 Cup

1 teaspoon lemon balm

½ teaspoon chamomile

½ teaspoon St. John's wort

1 cup water

sweetener

Boil one cup of water. Add the herbs, flowers, seeds or stems. Slowly pour the boiling water over the herbs. Cover the cup of herbs and steep for 6-10 minutes. Strain the tea and discard the herbs. Add honey, cream, or sweetener if desired. Drink when at comfortable temperature and reduce any negative emotions for a peaceful night's sleep.

ESSENTIAL OIL: **Gloom Dispelling Bath Salts**

What better way to lift your spirits, dispel negativity, and focus on the good things about yourself other than a salt bath? Light a candle, turn on the soft music, and soak in these essential oils to bring you some peace and smiles. There are a variety of salts on the market today that have not been so readily available to us in the past. Use whichever one you prefer: Epsom salts, Himalayan salt, sea salt, the possibilities are endless.

Yield: 1 Cup

1 cup salts

¼ cup baking soda

10 drops Palo Santo oil

10 drops neroli oil

5 drops rose oil

2 tablespoons carrier oil

In a mason jar, or a glass bowl, add the salts and the essential oils. Whisk well. Cover with lid and leave in a cool, dark area for up to 24 hours. Whisk well once more. Run comfortably warm, not hot, bathwater. After the water is done filling the tub, add ¼ cup bath salts, and a tablespoon of milk (optional). Soak until the water is no longer a comfortable temperature. Store the remainder in a tightly covered jar, in a cool, dark area for up to 3 months.

***ALTERNATIVE REMEDY:* Joyful Diet**

One alternative therapy method for dispelling gloom is to eat a diet rich in vitamins and minerals. Fresh veggies and fruits cannot be beat in the vitamin provision department. Try incorporating this salad into your diet a couple times a week to keep yourself happy and joyful.

Yield: 2 servings

1 ½ Cups fresh salad greens

1 avocado diced

1 Tablespoon grapes halved

1 Tablespoon scallions diced

1 Tablespoon walnuts chopped

½ cucumber, sliced

1 radish sliced thinly

(dressing)

½ lemon

½ orange

1 saffron needle powdered

In a small bowl, squeeze the lemon and orange and pour juice in to bowl. Whisk in the saffron powder. Refrigerate while preparing the salad.

In a large bowl, mix the vegetables and fruit. Pour dressing over the top and serve with crackers. Refrigerate any remainder for up to 12 hours.

GRATITUDE

In 2010, I learned that having gratitude for every little thing in my life was the most powerful tool I had for physical, mental and spiritual growth. I have clung to the belief that saying, "thank you" for everything in my life, whether I have received it or not, is the most powerful defense against depression, sadness and despair. I am grateful every day and pray the prayers of thanks unceasingly. These recipes have helped me in multiple ways to focus on my gratitude and express my love of my Higher Power and family. Try one of these recipes every day, before meditation, or before a bath time ritual and feel your love, gratitude and peace grow by leaps and bounds.

AYURVEDA: Sankalpa (Setting intentions)

Sankalpa is an Ayurvedic word that means to set your intentions, believe that it will come true, work towards your goal, and bring your intention to fruition. Expressing gratitude is the most important part of a Sankalpa ritual.

- *Think long and hard about what your actual intention is. To help others? To have a new home? To work at your dream job? Recognize what your deepest desire in life is. No goal is too huge or too impossible to reach. The Universe is yours.*

- *Write what your intention for your future is on paper. Be specific. Read it several times a day, with belief, emotion and conviction. I include my intentions for the future on my vision board each year.*

- *Give prayers of gratitude as if you have already received your intention. Just say "thank you." These are the most powerful words in the universe.*

- *Map out the steps you need to take to make that intention come to life. Take small steps toward reaching that goal. Be grateful for each step.*

- *Work every single day on reciting, reading, praying about and taking baby steps to reach your goal. Think positively about reaching your goal. Experience in your mind what that is going to feel like. Experience the emotions that will come with reaching your goal.*

- *And most importantly, say thank you, thank you, thank you.*

***HERBS:* Gratitude Infusion**

Red clover and cinnamon make the most beautifully colored infusion. This drink will help you to stay focused on your gratitude all day long. Remaining in a state of positivity, peace and calm are paramount in expressing gratitude and gratefulness to your higher power. This drink has stomach calming properties as well, so drinking this and saying your prayers of gratitude before a big event in your life will bring about great results.

Yield: 2 cups

2 cups water

¼ cup red clover flowers

½ cinnamon stick

sweetener

Bring 2 cups of water to a boil. Place the flowers and cinnamon stick into a large mason jar. Pour the boiling water over the herbs into the jar. Leave 8-10 hours, covered. Strain, discard herbs. Add sweetener, if desired. Drink 1-2 cups daily, as desired. Store remainder in the refrigerator, in a jar with a tight-fitting lid, for up to 2 days.

ESSENTIAL OIL: **Gratitude Spray**

These essential oils are well renowned for their ability to help you express your gratitude. Much like the incense used in ceremonies and rituals all over the world, these oils are used to express devotion, gratitude, and a willingness to accept what is coming your way. I like to use this spray when I know that my expression of gratitude to the universe is changing my life in monumental ways.

Yield: 2 ounces

10 drops bergamot oil

8 drops grapefruit oil

6 drops ylang-ylang oil

4 drops rose oil

2 ounces of water

spray bottle

Using a funnel, pour all of the ingredients into a spray bottle. Label and date bottle. Oils and water separate, so you will need to shake very well before each usage. Spray the area lightly as desired. Ensure that you do not get spray into eyes, ears, mouth, open wounds, or other sensitive areas. Store spray bottle in a dark, cool area for up to 6 months.

ALTERNATIVE REMEDY: *Gratitude Mantra*

Saying a gratitude mantra is like a prayer of thankfulness that you repeat many times. I like to say mantras when I am meditating, or if I am very upset or anxious. The calming, soothing chant will lead you into a state of absolute peace. One of my favorite mantras is below, but feel free to write your own mantra. You must say it at least three times. You can say mantras in your mind, in a whisper, or with a shout…but you must feel every word as you say it and mine always start with "thank you."

"Thank you for my soul. Thank you for my spiritual journey and for opening my eyes every day. Thank you for this path

where I may be of service to others. Thank you, thank you, thank you."

GRIEF

Grieving is a natural process and has many stages. A person must grieve for certain events in their lives in order to come out of the other side with some semblance of normalcy. If we do not grieve when it is needed, our bodies can turn that grief into illness and disease. Support from others is a fundamental part of the grieving process and is needed to help us stay in contact with reality and society. Each person grieves differently and that is ok. Some people scream and cry, others talk about their grief with friends and family, some people grieve inwardly and privately. There is no correct way to grieve or to go thru the stages of grief in a step-by-step manner. Each person must figure out the processes in which to connect with and pass through the grieving process. These recipes gathered from various cultures help us to move through those grieving stages as easily as possible and in our own way.

AYURVEDA: Grieving Pancha Karma

Pancha karma is traditionally used to complete a detox process. I actually used Pancha karma as a way to help rid my body of negativity and depression during my grieving process. Pancha karma is an emotional, physical and spiritual way to reconnect to your best self. It is practiced for a multitude of issues all over the world. You can adapt Pancha karma to be compatible to your lifestyle. Pancha karma used to be very invasive to the body with enemas and vomiting. This tamed down version still has the same great effects, but without damage to the digestive system. Try 3-5 days of Pancha karma and work through your grief during this time. The results are amazing.

- *Wake up early with the sunrise. Go outside if weather permits, if not, have a dedicated quiet room. Sit and meditate, followed by a gentle, stretching yoga practice.*
- *Clean your teeth, have an oil pull, clean your ears. You may also perform tongue scraping and nasya at this time, if you wish. Cleansing and purifying the body involves the outside as well as the inside.*
- *Drink a cup of herbal tea. The most common grieving herbs are rose, marjoram, ginseng, motherwort, holy basil and St. john's wort. You can use other herbs suitable for your dosha if you choose.*
- *Sesame oil body massage. Oil yourself from your scalp to your toes. Do not get in eyes, ears or mucus membranes. You can add essential oils to the sesame oil if you wish. Leave on for 15 minutes to 1 hour. Wash off in a warm bath.*
- *Kitcheree or dal for lunch. (Or any type of light soup)*

- *Spend the afternoon alternately in nature or in meditation. Some light reading of self-help/grieving materials is permitted. Being alone with your thoughts for such a long time is mind-expanding, emotional and draining.*
- *At this point, you can take an enema (overseen by doctor or Ayurvedic practitioner), or you can have another head to toe oil treatment with sesame oil.*
- *Eat kitcheree for supper, or you may have light, steamed vegetables with rice.*
- *Drink a relaxing, calming cup of herbal tea and add some relaxing herbs such as St. John's wort, lemon balm, valerian root or chamomile.*
- *Meditate, pray, read, journal, say your affirmations, use visualization techniques for your future (grief free), do a few gentle yoga stretches, or sit under the moon light. Use this time to turn your thoughts toward happier times with your lost loved one. Think about the joy and love you shared. Use your evening hours to relax, unwind, and prepare for the night.*
- *Eat 1-2 tablespoons ghee. This will work its way through the system all night, leaving you with a gentle elimination upon wakening.*
- *Coat the feet with sesame oil. Sleep with thick socks on to keep the oil from getting on your furniture, or to help you to not slip when you walk.*
- *Read a favorite and deeply meaningful inspirational chapter from a book, then sleep with a deep, satisfying,*

relaxing sleep.

Repeat for 3-5 days.

***HERBS*: Grief Tea**

Having a nice cup of herbal tea at any time can be a spiritual experience in itself, but during the grieving process, it takes on new meaning. Learning to let go and relax into our feelings is sometimes hard to do. Allowing yourself to feel the way your mind and heart want to feel can be overwhelming and intimidating. During your "herbal grief tea time", just allow yourself to relax, and watch your thoughts as they pass through your head. Allow yourself to feel whatever feelings arise. These herbs can help you to relax and meditate on the things you push to the back of your mind all day.

Yield: 1 Cup

1 cup water

1 teaspoon St. John's wort

1 teaspoon rose petals

sweetener

Boil one cup of water. Add the herbs, flowers, seeds or stems. Slowly pour the boiling water over the herbs. Cover the cup of herbs and steep for 6-10 minutes. Strain the tea and discard the herbs. Add honey, cream, or sweetener if desired. Drink when at comfortable temperature.

***ESSENTIAL OIL*: Grieving Self-Massage**

Giving yourself a massage with essential oils meant to calm and lift your spirits is an extraordinary experience at any time during your life. Completing this process during the stages of grief can be beneficial to both mind and body. Sesame oil is a great grounding oil that can keep you from living inside of your head and reconnect you to those loved ones around you.

Yield: ½ cup

½ cup sesame oil

5 drops ylang-ylang oil

5 drops frankincense oil

5 drops sandalwood oil

4 drops vitamin E oil

Using a small glass bowl, mix all of the ingredients together using a small whisk. Using your fingertips apply the oils to the back, neck, temples, legs, soles of feet, or where desired. Ensure that you do not get any of the mixture into the eyes, ears, mouth, mucus membranes, genitals, open wounds, or sensitive areas. Store remainder in a dark colored jar, label and date, and place in a cool, dark area for up to 6 months.

***ALTERNATIVE REMEDY:* Grief Sachet**

I like to use sachets in my car, my office desk, my linen drawers, and just about anywhere that I may be sitting for a while. These herbs are relaxing, uplifting and contain properties to help you feel your best. Sachets used to be very common but have been replaced by stronger chemical fragrances.

Yield: 1 sachet

1 six-inch piece material

1 teaspoon rose petals

1 teaspoon basil leaves

1 teaspoon marjoram

Dry the herbs until no moisture present to prevent mildewing. Crunch the herbs in a bowl with your fingers until crumbly. Do not crunch so much as to make a powder of them. Next, fold the material until it forms a square with the printed sides facing each other. Sew the edges of two of the sides together, until you have a pocket formed. Turn the material right sides out. Place the herbs inside the pocket, then continue sewing until it is closed. You may fashion a loop out of a scrap of material and attach to one corner of your sachet for hanging purposes. Set the sachet in a spot where you will be meditating or doing most of your thinking. Each day give it a few squeezes with your fingers to release a new round of aromas. When not in use, you can store in a zip lock bag to retain the fragrances. I use mine for a month or two before I can no longer detect any smells.

GROUNDING

I am in constant need of grounding. My personality is un-proportionally vata, so I must eat, exercise, socialize, and think grounding activities in order to be a more grounded person. When you can't focus, have too many plans and ideas, don't think about consequences, have flighty thoughts and actions, and run through friendships and relationships, you need more grounding. All over the world, grounding oneself is at the forefront of a lot of medical practices. Being more connected to the Earth, slowing down, and focusing on important tasks is easy for some people, but almost impossible for others. I use many of these grounding techniques every day to bring myself down to reality and out of my normal manic state.

AYURVEDA: Get Outside

In Ayurveda, the most grounding practice you can immerse yourself in, is nature. No matter your mood, disposition, thoughts, or actions, being outside in nature can quickly make you feel more at peace with yourself and others. Below are a few grounding activities you can partake in outside.

- *Take a walk or a hike in a new area. Just familiarize yourself with the flora and fauna.*
- *Sit on the grass, without a blanket, and just observe your surroundings. Use all of your senses.*
- *Work in a garden, whether it be weeding, planting or harvesting. Working with the dirt is just about more grounding than anything you can do.*
- *Meditate outdoors, whether sitting on your patio, at a lakeside, or in an orchard. Just being under the sky and on the Earth has very grounding properties. Meditation is always a grounding activity no matter where you decide to practice.*
- *Complete a yoga sequence outside. Take your mat and make the outdoors your own personal studio.*
- *Invite a friend over to sit outside and drink some herbal tea. Herbal teas and sitting with a friend are both grounding practices that you can combine with your outdoor needs.*

***HERBS:* Grounding Bowl**

I love to use herbal bowls throughout my home and fill with various pinecones, pieces of wood, sea shells, and crystals. I often throw in some herbs to send a pleasing fragrance throughout my home. Every now and then I will just walk by the bowl and give the herbs a crush, then the air is filled with delightful aromas. Using these grounding herbs can help me to stay centered and focused. Make your own herbal bowls and give some as presents to friends.

Yield: 4 cups

¼ cup dried lavender stems and flowers

¼ cup dried rosemary twigs and needles

¼ cup sage leaves

¼ cup nettle leaves

¼ cup dried lemon or orange rinds

2 cups various wood chips, pine cones, twigs or other natural treasures.

Combine all of the ingredients into a bowl and slightly crush the leaves and herbs at least once every few days. You can halve or double the ingredients, depending on the size of your bowl. You can be very creative with this and use different herbs for different moods. At the end of a month, discard into compost pile.

ESSENTIAL OIL: Grounding Roll-On

This recipe contains so many grounding essential oils. Just carry it and when you need to feel more peaceful, relaxed and not so impulsive, just roll it on.

Yield: ½ ounce

½ ounce sesame oil

3 drops vetiver oil

3 drops ylang-ylang oil

3 drops juniper oil

1 ½ ounce roller bottle

2 drops vitamin E oil

Combine the ingredients into a small bowl. Using a tiny funnel, pour the mixture into roller bottles. Label and date. Roll on to areas needed as desired, 2-3 times daily. Do not roll onto open wounds, mouth, eyes, genitals, sensitive areas or mucus membranes. Store, upright, in a cool, dark area for up to 6 months.

***ALTERNATIVE REMEDY*: Crystal Grounding**

Crystals have been known for centuries to contain healing properties. Using the right crystal for the right need takes time, patience and practice. For grounding purposes, the crystals listed below will meet your needs.

Use one or two of the following crystals:

Black tourmaline quarts

Selenite

Hematite

Lie on a yoga mat, your bed, or carpet. Someplace comfortable, relaxing, and free from distractions. Place the gem stone of your choosing in the center of your forehead, about an inch above your eyebrows. Relax your entire body and brush aside any negative or fearful thoughts. Try to concentrate on your forehead, and the energy you are directing from other areas of your body to your forehead. You will begin to feel happier and have much less anxiety. You will feel yourself getting heavier, and more grounded the longer you lay there. Continue as long as you wish, anywhere from 2-20 minutes. Repeat as needed.

HAPPINESS

Why is happiness so elusive and fleeting? Is it because life gets in the way? Negativity of others? There are many reasons for us to lose our sense of happiness. Developing a practice for your spiritual base and living in a state of gratitude can vastly improve and increase your periods of happiness. These recipes contain ingredients that can boost the chemicals in certain areas of your brain to enhance feelings of peace, calm and contentedness; which are emotions that are needed for us to be happy. The tips, blends and actions below can help you on your journey to obtain that "happy" that you desire.

AYURVEDA: Happy Tummy

In Ayurveda it is believed the stomach and digestive system is the source of all ailments, unhappiness and mood swings. Keeping your digestive system in check is paramount to happiness in Ayurvedic teachings. One sure way to keep the stomach in line is by following the Ayurvedic diet for each particular dosha type. Your dosha, either vata, pitta or kapha, determines your personality, your health and your overall self. Below is a list of the foods that are good for balancing each particular dosha type and works to keep digestive systems working at the most optimal.

> *Kapha: cranberries, apples, barley, rye, corn, ginger, broccoli, cabbage, white meat, low fat milk, kale, potato, beans, honey, almonds, seafood, pumpkin, Mexican food, spicy food, pear, goats' milk, Indian food,*

> *Pitta: coconuts, pomegranate, cold cereal, melon, limes, chicken, turkey, milk, vegetables, lettuce, okra, Brussel sprouts, squash, zucchini, carrot, mushrooms, lettuce, okra, cauliflower, cabbage, bananas, avocados, butter, ghee, prunes, raisins*

> *Vata: rice, wheat, butter, fat, seafood, salty, honey, cream, warm soups, bread, herbal tea, asparagus, onions, chicken, sweet potatoes, cucumber, carrot, cherries, grapes, citrus, avocados, cooked/warm food.*

***HERBS:* Happy Herbal Veggies**

Eating for our moods is something we all do without realizing it. Usually we eat unhealthy foods, trying to make ourselves feel better. And they may make us feel better *while we are eating them, but when we are through, we just feel worse. Eating healthier as a way to feel better in the long run is finally getting mainstream attention. These herbs have properties in them to help dispel any negative feelings and boost our good moods. Paired with healthy veggies, and eaten at least once a week, can only benefit us in the end. (Double the herbs, if using fresh).*

Yield: 2 servings

1 teaspoon ghee (or other healthy oil)

1 carrot roughly chopped

1 sweet potato peeled and diced

1 onion chopped

½ bell pepper, diced

3 mushrooms chopped

1 clove garlic minced

¼ teaspoon thyme

1 teaspoon parsley

¼ teaspoon marjoram

1-foot square of tin foil

Grease one side of the foil with ghee. Pour the chopped/grated vegetables onto the foil. You may add more ghee or healthy oil over the vegetables. Top with the herbs. Fold foil over the vegetables and seal, making an air-tight pouch. Bake in oven for 30 minutes at 350 degrees or cook on grill until tender. May top with sour cream or cheese. Store any leftovers in an airtight container for up to two days.

***ESSENTIAL OIL:* Happy Bath Salts**

These essential oils release aromas that increase happiness and are infused with the therapeutic properties that affect the endorphin releasing areas of our brains. Bath salts in themselves bring a sense of calm and peace, but combined with these powerhouses, will bring delight to your day. There are a variety of salts on the market today that have not been so readily available to us in the past. Use whichever one you prefer: Epsom salts, Himalayan salt, sea salt, the possibilities are endless.

Yield: 3 cups

1 cup salts

¼ cup baking soda

12 drops orange oil

12 drops jasmine oil

12 drops rose oil

2 tablespoons carrier oil

In a mason jar, or a glass bowl, add the salts and the essential oils. Whisk well. Cover with lid and leave in a cool, dark area for up to 24 hours. Whisk well once more. Run comfortably warm, not hot, bathwater. After the water is done filling the tub, add ¼ cup bath salts, and a tablespoon of milk (optional). Store the remainder in a tightly covered jar, in a cool, dark area for up to 3 months.

ALTERNATIVE REMEDY: ***Happiness Tips***

These alternative tips from around the world have epitomized the true path to happiness. The reason is that it works. Employing some of these habits into your daily life will certainly lead you to a place that is healthier, happier and much more meaningful than to live life as if it were pure drudgery.

- *Gratitude is and always will be the number one path to happiness. Close your eyes right now and simply state the words "thank you" quietly to yourself a few times. You will instantly feel calmer, happier and more peaceful. Express your gratitude for everything in your life, including your life, multiple times daily. You will begin to see a change in not only the way you feel, but in the way in which you view the world around you.*

- *Develop healthy habits, such as an exercise routine. Even if it is just ten minutes of yoga, or a brisk walk or simple stretches each day. Getting the heart pumping can release feel good endorphins which can increase happiness. You can work your way up to as long as you feel happy working out.*

- *Meditate. If praying is talking to God, meditation is listening to God. Give yourself a chance to hear what your higher power might be wanting to tell you. Simply sit quietly on a pillow in a distraction-free area and close your eyes. Watch your thoughts, without judgement or reaction. Start 5 minutes a day and try to increase to 20 minutes daily. It has been said that meditation is the single most important thing that a person can do for themselves.*

- *Diet. Try to eat fresh, local, and healthy. It may make you feel good to indulge in bad, fast food for a few minutes, but eating healthy will make you feel good for a lifetime.*

HARMONY

I am continually searching for harmony between myself and my family and friends. But I also want harmony with my mind, body and soul. These various techniques have been used worldwide for thousands of years to help people live in harmony with themselves, nature, society, and in all areas of life.

AYURVEDA: Tip for Harmony

Go outside. No matter the weather, the time of year, or the time of day. As long as you are in a safe environment, enjoy what the Earth has for you. Use all of your senses to feel, touch, smell and see the beauty that surrounds you. Walk, sit, pray, garden, clean, meditate; do whatever activities you feel drawn to, simply surround yourself with nature to let true happiness and harmony enter your soul. When you feel at one with nature, you can't help but to feel love for your fellow human beings. Harmony with nature also brings harmony to your mind and spirit. Go outside.

HERBS: Harmony Tea

What could be more harmonious than to sit down for a cup of tea to talk about your issues with a friend? When that tea also contains therapeutic properties that promote harmony, then you will have a productive and enlightening conversation.

Yield: 1 cup

1 teaspoon lavender flowers

1 teaspoon chamomile flowers

1 cup water

Sweetener

Boil one cup of water. Add the herbs, flowers, seeds or stems. Slowly pour the boiling water over the herbs. Cover the cup of herbs and steep for 6-10 minutes. Strain the tea and discard the herbs. Add honey, cream, or sweetener if desired. Drink when at comfortable temperature.

ESSENTIAL OIL: Come Together Air

These essential oils are reported to bring peace, harmony and calm. The tranquil properties of these oils make them the perfect diffuser for the office, or your home.

Yield: 1 application

3 drops lemon

3 drops palmarosa

2 drops angelica

Water

Each diffuser has different amounts of water and oils that can be used for that particular diffuser. Adjust the recipes according to your diffuser. Add the water, then add the oils and run your diffuser for the desired effect.

***ALTERNATIVE REMEDY:* Harmonious Color Healing Method**

Colors often can bring various emotions to our brains, ambiance to a room, and even increase visual perceptions. Color therapy is used throughout the world to bring emotions under control, to promote energy, instill harmony or provide therapeutic treatments to thousands of people and businesses every day. Try using color therapy to bring harmony to your life.

The color green is the color of nature, growth, harmony and peace. To bring color therapy into your chaotic, divided times of life, try using green colors in various ways to mend any dissolutions to relationships you may have. Carry green stones or wear jewelry made from jade or adventurine. Paint the family room one of the hundreds of shades of green on the market today. Or simply meditate while looking at the green foliage of a tree or plant.

HOPE

When hope is gone, you have nothing. Situations can spiral beyond our control and leave us feeling weak and vulnerable. But having hope to get us through those most difficult of times can sometimes be the only thing we have to cling to. Hope can empower you, sustain you, and instill the desire to carry on. These tips and recipes have been handed down for generations to inspire, instill belief of a positive outcome and bring hope to the hopeless.

AYURVEDA; Saffron/Ginger Inspirational Rice

In Ayurveda, what we eat can set our moods, control our health, and bring about certain emotional needs. Instilling hope for the future starts with a positive attitude. Saffron and ginger both can leave us feeling more positive and hopeful with their calming and healing therapeutic properties. Try this rice dish and share a soothing meal with those you think need a little uplifting.

Yield: 4 servings

1 cup rice of choice

2 tablespoons ghee

¼ teaspoon salt

Water

Vegetable broth (optional)

1-2 saffron needles

½ inch piece of ginger, grated

½ cup veggies of choice

Cook the rice, salt and ½ of the ghee according to rice package directions. In a small saucepan, heat the rest of the ghee on low. Add chopped veggies such as broccoli, cauliflower, sweet potatoes, onion, peppers or any type of vegetables you prefer. Ensure the veggies are chopped or diced small. Heat the veggies for a couple of minutes until tender. You can add vegetable broth if the veggies are a long cooking variety. Add the sautéed veggies to the rice. Add the saffron and stir and heat one additional minute. Remove from heat and serve. Store any leftovers in the refrigerator for up to 3 days.

***HERBS:* Empowerment Herbal Tonic**

This tonic does just what the name implies. It brings empowerment and hope when life seems hopeless. These herbs are known world-wide for their ability to help people overcome negative attitudes and have the will to move forward in a calm and rational manner.

Yield: 1 Quart

½ cup St. John's Wort

½ cup Chamomile

1-quart water

Crush, and/or chop the herbs and flowers and add to a mason jar. Pour boiling water over the herbs and cap the jar tightly. Shake well and let sit undisturbed, at room temperature, for 8 hours. Strain, and add sweetener of choice to the tonic. Discard herbs. Drink tonic at intervals 3 or 4 times a day, a teaspoon at a time, for desired effect. Store in refrigerator in a jar with a tight-fitting lid for up to 3 days.

***ESSENTIAL OIL:* Hope Is in The Air**

Using essential oils to set a certain ambiance, bring about a precise frame of mind, and establish hope has been used for thousands of years all over the world. Using your diffuser, you can help to elevate and bring encouragement to your friends and family when situations seem beyond hope. These essential oils have been used forever to empower and uplift.

Yield: 1 application

3 drops vetiver

3 drops ylang-ylang

3 drops frankincense

Water

Each diffuser has different amounts of water and oils that can be used for that particular diffuser. Adjust the recipes according to your diffuser. Add the water, then add the oils and run your diffuser for the desired effect.

ALTERNATIVE REMEDY: ***Hope in the Soul***

Hopefulness and faith are closely correlated. Having a spiritual base, keeping grounded, and living with conviction for a better future are the source of hope. It is my firm creed that a daily routine, of your own choosing, that helps you work on your faith and spirituality can bring so much hope, support and belief into your life. Try a couple of these simple, time-limited, steps each morning when you wake up. You will soon find your spiritual practice that leads to increasing your hope to be the best part of your day.

- *Find an area in your home devoted solely to your spiritual practices. You can fill with things you love such as candles, diffuser, music, mala beads, self-help books, pillows, whatever you want to make your morning routine all about you and your spirituality.*
- *Create ambiance. Light your candles, turn on your Zen music, lay out your crystals, burn incense, or run your diffuser. Create a devotional area that gets you in the mood to have a great day.*
- *First meditate for at least 5 minutes. Sit on a comfortable pillow and close your eyes. As you breathe in, think the word "peace." As you exhale, think the word "calm." After you practice meditating for a while, you can try dif-*

ferent meditation techniques to see which ones you like the best.

- *Read some sort of spiritual material, or self-help material. This step is so very important. Even if you can only read for 3 minutes. Learning how to advance in our spiritual journey from others is an on-going, life-time journey. Never quit.*

- *Pray. Say your prayers in whatever fashion feels comfortable to you. I use mala beads to ensure that I am saying over 100 prayers of gratitude each and every day. I thank God for each member of my family, my material possessions, for my positive thoughts, for my hope for the future, for the things I don't yet have, and for my spiritual journey. Gratitude is the key.*

- *Affirmations. Don't forget to say some pretty amazing things about yourself. Use positive language. Instead of saying "I am losing weight," say "I am thin and healthy." Say affirmations about the things you want to accomplish on your day. Today I said, "I will finish editing this book today." And I will.*

- *Write a few things in your gratitude journal. You won't believe how happy and thankful this will make you. This step right here has turned around some of the most difficult relationships in my life. Instead of concentrating on the negative aspects of my relationships, I thought and was grateful for the positive aspects. Wow! Talk about stress relieving. If my world is feeling dire and hopeless, I can get my hope back in the forefront with journaling my gratitudes and realizing how many positive things I do have in my life.*

- *Do some morning stretches. Yoga, jumping jacks, walking, karate, whatever gets you moving and your heart racing. Try to move for 5 minutes. It makes all the difference. I have a 7-minute routine that I complete each morning. Then when I can't do my regular yoga practice, I feel great knowing I have done at least the minimum of what I need.*
- *Completing even a few of these steps each day will have you on a path of devotion, love, worship, hopefulness and peace like you have never experienced. You will find that on days you are unable to perform your morning routine, you are longing for your space and prayers. But remember, you can pray and be thankful anytime, anywhere.*

INTELLIGENCE

It has been said that intelligence is the wisdom to know enough about something that you know you don't know enough about it. Intelligence is having a series of thought processes that can convey understanding about a matter. Whether that matter is another person, a diagram, a subject or anything under (or above) the sun. Reading, socializing, traveling and working all increase our intelligence. These recipes, essential oils, herbs and Ayurvedic remedies have all been viewed as intelligence boosters. Increasing wisdom should be a never-ending, life-long quest, so incorporating these into your life on a daily basis may be just the "wisest" thing to do.

AYURVEDA: Yoga for the Mind

In Ayurveda, having a healthy, supple body leads to a healthy, supple mind. Yoga is the number one way to exercise your mind and your body at the same time. Ayervedics believe that you can increase your intelligence by working through mental hardships brought about by hardships to the body. If you can work your way through holding a difficult pose for a great length of time, then you can develop the ability to control your mind and your thoughts. Try these yoga poses and hold them for longer than you think you can. Each day increase your hold by a minute or even half of a minute. This will cause your mind to stay in the present and not let your thoughts drift.

- *Plow Pose – Lying on your back, lift your feet, legs and hips into the air. Support your hips by splaying your fingertips across your rear, with your elbows supporting your weight, on the floor. If you wish to take it further, slowly lower your flexed feet down onto the floor behind your head. Hold pose for 1-3 minutes. Repeat daily.*
- *Knees to Chest pose -Pawanamuktasana – Laying on your back, hug your knees into your chest. Relax your shoulders, jaw and neck. Lie quietly, concentrating on your breath for 3-5 minutes. Repeat daily.*

HERBS: **Wisdom Thoughts**

There is a reason this trinity of herbs is known far and wide as a thought-provoking blend. Become a wise old sage by imbibing on sage in your tea. This tea is very delicious and especially good for an evening of pleasant talk followed by a good night's sleep.

Yield: 1 cup

½ teaspoon sage leaves

½ teaspoon lemon balm leaves

½ teaspoon holy basil

1 cup water

Sweetener (optional)

Boil one cup of water. Add the herbs, flowers, seeds or stems. Slowly pour the boiling water over the herbs. Cover the cup of herbs and steep for 6-10 minutes. Strain the tea and discard the herbs. Add honey, cream, or sweetener if desired. Drink when at comfortable temperature.

ESSENTIAL OIL: **Air of Intelligence**

These memory and wisdom inducing oils will ensure you are on top of your game as you go about your day. Work better, multi-task, and keep your home running smoothly with these oils permeating the air.

Yield: 1 application

2 drops rosemary oil

2 drops clary sage oil

2 drops frankincense oil

2 drops orange oil

water

Each diffuser has different amounts of water and oils that can be used for that particular diffuser. Adjust the recipes according to your diffuser. Add the water, then add the oils and run your diffuser for the desired effect.

ALTERNATIVE REMEDY: *Brain Gains*

These tips and hints from all over the world are already known by most of us, but we need to practice them for the theory to work. Keeping your brain active is the same as keeping your muscles active. Use it or lose it.

- *Work puzzles daily*
- *Stay hydrated*
- *Get plenty of sleep*
- *Exercise daily*
- *Take your vitamins*
- *Learn a new language*
- *Work at something new every day*
- *Stay away from processed foods*

INTENTION

Setting an intention is something we do to empower ourselves or to try to help someone else. We are in effect telling the Universe how we want things to be. You can't get what you want if you don't know what it is that you want. When setting your intentions, be specific. Feel the feelings you will have when your goal is achieved. Give thanks for that which you desire. All of these things help to set an intention in stone so that it will soon be yours.

AYURVEDA: Intention Setting

In Ayurveda, setting your intention is something you cannot put aside for another time. Your intentions are the basis for everything you need and desire. You can't expect to live the life of your dreams if the Universe doesn't even know what it is you are desiring. Here are the basic and simple steps in Ayurveda for setting your intention.

- *Ground yourself by sitting on the floor, or outside in nature. Diffuse some grounding oils such as vetiver or ce-*

darwood.

- *Concentrate on your breathing. Take slow, deep, steady breaths in through your mouth and out your nose. If your thoughts wander, bring them back by concentrating on the breath.*
- *State your intention out loud, then in a whisper, then as a thought. Be specific in what your intention is.*
- *As you meditate on your breath and your intention, feel the joy you will have when you receive what you are asking for. Really feel the love and gratitude that will encompass your whole being on that day.*

***HERBS:* Intention Infusion**

This recipe promotes dreams, induces calm, grounds, and gives you the ability to set your intentions even in a distraction filled atmosphere. Drink it over a period of a day before you complete your intention work.

Yield: 1 Cup

1 teaspoon rose petals

½ teaspoon ashwagandha powder

½ cinnamon stick

1 cup water

honey (optional)

Bring one cup water to boil. Add the roses and remove from

heat. Stir in the ashwagandha with the cinnamon stick, and let the stick sit in the tea as it steeps. Cover and steep for 20-30 minutes. Strain and discard herbs. Sweeten if desired. Drink by the teaspoonful within 12 hours. Refrigerate any remainder for up to 3 days.

ESSENTIAL OIL: Intention Self-Massage Oil

These essential oils have the ability to give us the focus and clarity needed to perform our intention rituals. Before you meditate or pray about your intention, apply this oil to your arms, legs or chest as you concentrate on the intentions you want to come to fruition.

Yield: 1 Ounce

5 drops clary sage oil

5 drops frankincense oil

4 drops angelica oil

1-ounce sesame oil

In a small bowl, mix the carrier oil and the essential oils together. Dip fingertips into the container and rub oil onto neck, chest or areas desired in a gentle circular motion. Do not apply mixture to mucus membranes, eyes, genitals, mouth, wounds or sensitive areas. Rub area with a circular motion until the skin absorbs the mixture. When done with massage, wipe off excess with a towel. Store the unused portion in a jar with a tight-fitting lid, in a cool, dark area for up to 3 months.

ALTERNATIVE REMEDY: **Crystal Clear Intention Setting**

Using crystals and gem stones to set intentions is an old time-honored tradition in many countries. Crystals themselves have energy and are thought to be a conduit between people and their Higher Power.

> *Choose several crystals and gemstones. Place them on a table or on the floor where you can easily gaze at them. Hold each crystal in your hand and set two or three aside that give you a special feeling, warmth or vibration. Once you have chosen your intention crystals, hold them in your hand. While gazing at them, state your intentions out loud. After you have done that, hold the crystals to your heart and whisper your intentions. Once that is completed hold the crystals to your forehead and think about your intentions. Try to repeat this process daily until your intentions become facts.*

INTUITION

Intuitively speaking, intuition may just save your life. Slowing your car down at just the right moment, breaking up with a person who later abuses others, or a myriad of circumstances in your life can be viewed as either coincidence, or it could be that your intuition is exceedingly strong. I try to listen to that feeling in my gut, or my subconscious, because sometimes my inner mind knows more about what's going on than my conscious mind does. Developing your intuition can be achieved through practice, herbs, thought processes, essential oils, and numerous ways and means. Read through these tips and recipes and see if any of them "intuitively" speak to you.

***AYURVEDA:* Crystals for Intuition**

Lie on a yoga mat, your bed, or carpet during sunset or sunrise; someplace comfortable, relaxing, and free from distractions. Place the crystal of your choosing in the center of your forehead, about an inch above your eyebrows. This is your third eye, the area of intuition. Relax your entire body and brush aside any negative or fearful thoughts. Try to concentrate on your forehead, and the energy you are directing from other areas of your body to your forehead. You will begin to feel lighter, happier, and have much less anxiety. Continue as long as you wish, anywhere from 2-20 minutes. Listen to what your mind is telling you. This intuitive inducing ritual has been observed since people discovered crystals. Repeat as needed.

***HERBS:* Intuition Sachet**

These herbs have been used in remedies and rituals for increasing intuition since time began. Each of these herbs has a specific job to do in the area of increasing your ability to discern feelings. Put this sachet where you will smell it often. You can also make this into a simmering potpourri by just putting the herbs into a small saucepan on the stove and simmering very low and slow with water.

12 inch square linen or cheesecloth

1 tablespoon laurel leaves

1 tablespoon patchouli

1 tablespoon sandalwood chips

1-foot ribbon

Dry the herbs until no moisture present to prevent mildewing. Crunch the herbs in a bowl with your fingers until crumbly. Do not crunch so much as to make a powder of them. Next, fold the material until it forms a square with the printed sides facing each other. Sew the edges of two of the sides together, until you have a pocket formed. Turn the material right sides out. Place the herbs inside the pocket, then continue sewing until it is closed. You may fashion a loop out of a scrap of material and attach to one corner of your sachet for hanging purposes. Set the sachet in a spot where you will be meditating or doing most of your thinking. I place mine on my desk by my computer. Each day give it a few squeezes with your fingers to release a new round of aromas. When not in use, you can store in a zip lock bag to retain the fragrances. I use mine for a month or two before I can no longer detect any smells.

ESSENTIAL OIL: **Intuition Oil Rub**

These essential oils have been chosen for eons due to their intuitive powers. Rub this on before you have to make a big decision or are going on a trip when you need your intuitivism the most.

Yield: 1 ounce

5 drops sandalwood oil

5 drops frankincense oil

5 drops myrrh oil

Using a bowl or a jar, combine the ingredients together using a whisk or a fork. Using your fingertips, spread the rub onto the affected area, ensuring that you do not get into eyes, ears, mouth, open wounds, genitals, mucus membranes, or other sensitive areas. You may cover area with light gauze or old clothing to prevent staining furniture. Leave mixture on until you are ready to reapply. Store remainder in a dark colored jar, in a cool, dark area for up to one year.

***ALTERNATIVE REMEDY*: Intuition Strengthener**

Try completing these rituals to increase your intuition. Listening to your subconscious can be learned with practice and using a few aids such as the tips below.

- *Automatic Writing: sit in a comfortable place with no distractions. Using a pen and pad, just allow yourself to simply write. No matter that it doesn't make any sense. Try not to think about what you are going to write. Just write. When you go back and read it, you may find some answers you have been seeking.*
- *To increase intuition, surround yourself with the color blue.*

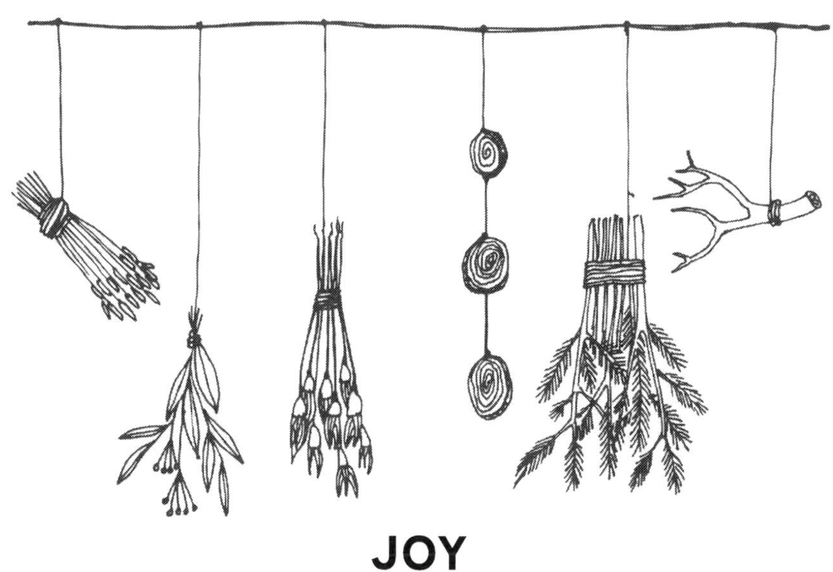

JOY

The unbridled inner feeling we get from everyday simple things can be ascribed to joy. I can get joy from a great meal, a sunset, my dog, or a conversation with someone I learn from. Joy can be attributed to chemicals in our brain, our heart, or our way of thinking. For centuries people have turned to alternative methods to increase the receptiveness in their hearts for receiving joy. Using some of these recipes can help you to achieve that elusive feeling that you crave.

AYURVEDA: Spice Blend

This recipe is used with spices that have therapeutic properties that have been known to increase feelings of joy and happiness. Use this blend of spices on all your favorite salads, soups, fish and veggie recipes.

Yield: 1 cup

1 tablespoon cumin

1 tablespoon turmeric

1 tablespoon coriander seeds

1 tablespoon dried ginger

1 tablespoon cardamom

¼ teaspoon saffron needles

1 teaspoon black pepper

Whisk the spices together in a bowl. Pour into a glass container with a lid. Use a teaspoonful in your meals. Label and date the container. Use within 6 months.

HERBS: **Joy Blend**

Herbs have long been sought for their joy producing properties. One that is in the midst of much debate today is cannabis. But if you are not a fan of the "happy herb" then try a tea with one or more of these herbs for an uplifting drink.

Yield: 1 Cup

1-2 teaspoons of one or two of the following herbs: dandelion, chamomile, holy basil, angelica or ginseng.

1 cup water

Sweetener (optional)

Boil one cup of water. Add the herbs, flowers, seeds or stems. Slowly pour the boiling water over the herbs. Cover the cup of herbs and steep for 6-10 minutes. Strain the tea and discard the herbs. Add honey, cream, or sweetener if desired. Drink when at comfortable temperature.

ESSENTIAL OIL: Joyful Attire

This laundry detergent is mild enough for HR washers, but powerful enough to get out those stains while at the same time imparting joyful components to the wearer. I have made my own laundry detergent for many years and find it great for my sensitive skin.

Yield: 2 gallons

¼ block Fels Naptha, grated

½ cup washing suds or powders

25-30 cups water

16 drops essential oils (a combination or one of the following: bergamot, geranium, grapefruit, jasmine, neroli, orange, spearmint, rose, sandalwood or tangerine)

Pour one cup water and the grated Fels Naptha into a small pan and heat on very low, stirring constantly, until Fels Naptha is melted. Do not boil. In a very large bowl add the melted Fels Naptha, the washing suds and 10 cups of water. Stir vigorously with a whisk until well blended. Pour one half of the mixture into 2 one-gallon size jugs. Put the caps on the jugs and shake well. Let sit undisturbed for 12-24 hours. Add 10 cups of water to each jug. Shake well. Add the essential oils to the jugs. Shake well before each usage. Use ¼ cup for each load of laundry.

***ALTERNATIVE REMEDY:* Best Joy Ever**

Learning to give is the greatest joy of all. Teaching your family members to give is just as joyful. Give a meal to a friend. Give a smile to someone who is feeling down. Give a portion of your earnings to a charity. Giving is the ultimate joy as it brings joy to all of the parties involved. Giving doesn't have to cost anything. Give your services to someone. Use your talent for crafting in a way to bring happiness to others. Just give.

LOVE

Love is that eternal desire to be cherished by another human being. Sometimes love is elusive, fake, ugly, bitter or fleeting. To ensure that the love you treasure and want is true, use these recipes that have been used for thousands of years. These blends can envelop the heart, mind and soul and bring you peace, contentment and trust in that someone special. Using this blend in the home can harmonize and envelop the souls within in a blanket of loving feelings, hopes and dreams.

AYURVEDA: Love Practices

In Ayurveda, thinking positively, having intentions of love and affirmations of love are what you need to put out to the Universe in order to bring love your way and to spread your love to others.

- *Law of Attraction: What you put out is what you get back. Think loving thoughts towards others. Try not to let your jealousy of love that others have invade your thinking process. Think about the type of lover you would like to attract and think thoughts constantly about how that person is attracted to you.*

- *Vision Board: To help inspire your positive thinking about love, craft a vision board that has everything on it you would like to have in a lover. Cut pictures out of magazines that have words that you wish your partner (and yourself) to have as attributes. Cut pictures out of your dream wedding, your future family, your day to day life-goals. Look at this board every day and believe that what it contains is already yours.*

- *Affirmations: Repeat words to yourself daily that reiterate what you want for your future. Whisper the words, then say them out loud. Say "my true love is thinking of me right now," "My lover has my best interest at heart," "My true love will soon find me and love me with their whole heart."*

- *Journal: Write 10 things every day that you want your future to hold. Write things like: I have found the love of my life; I am beyond happy and joyful with my _____; I have someone who loves me as much as I love them. And be thankful for those things you write. Feel the gratitude.*

HERBS: Love Linen Powder

If you are sleeping with someone whom you wish to stay in love with you, this linen powder is perfect. This has been used forever by people who are falling out of love and wish to rekindle that spark and romance.

Yield: 1 cup

1 cup cornstarch

1 tablespoon finely ground lavender flowers

1 Tablespoon finely ground rose petals

6 drops vitamin E oil

Combine all ingredients into a large bowl. Stir well with a whisk until all clumps disappear. Let sit in open air for 12-24 hours. Poke several holes in mason jar lids using a nail and a hammer. Spoon the powder mixture into the mason jars and cover with lid. Use this lid as a shaker and shake the ingredients into pillowcases, and under sheets on bed. The herbs will be mild, but have a soothing, loving effect on the person sleeping on them all night. I like to get a piece of plastic wrap, remove the mason jar lid, and place the plastic wrap over the top of the jar, and replace the ring. This will keep the powder from accidently spilling out when not in use. Store in a cool, dark area for up to one year.

ESSENTIAL OIL: Red Package of Love

The following essential oils are reputed to bring about love between two people. These oils have been used for centuries to grasp love and to even bring love to areas where there was previously a forbidden or lost love. Use one or more of these oils to bring the results you desire.

Yield: 1 Application

10 drops of one or more: Rose, Cardamom, cinnamon, coriander, frankincense, ginger, jasmine, lavender, lime, myrtle, peppermint and rose

1 6-inch square red fabric

6 inches red ribbon

Get a square of fabric and sprinkle the essential oils onto the red fabric. Fold and tie with a ribbon. Place the square of material next to your heart when you know you will be in the same vicinity as the person you desire. Think positive and loving thoughts toward this person and try to get close to them and talk if given the chance. Sleep this same night with the square of fabric under your pillow.

***ALTERNATIVE REMEDY:* Love Recipe**

I heard about this recipe when I was a small child. It may be a common thing to do, but I felt the need to include it here.

Yield: 1 Application

½ inch x ½ inch paper

3 inches Red thread

Red pen

1 tablespoon honey

½ ounce bottle

With the red pen, write the full names of both parties you wish to have love forever. Roll the paper and tie it as a scroll with the red thread. Place into the bottle and fill the bottle with honey. Secure the lid tightly. Keep it in a safe and secure place for the rest of your life. When we were young, we would buy the little bottles beneath trees.

LUCK

Good luck or bad luck, we have all had both in our lives. Some people seem to be surrounded by bad luck. They don't do anything to purposefully bring bad circumstances into their lives, it just appears…day after day after day. If you are one of those people, then you should try a few of these recipes and up your luck for a change. Let me know what good fortune came your way after you try this out!

AYURVEDA: Alternative Luck Method

Many superstitions and practices have been passed down generation after generation regarding luck, either good or bad. Sometimes they work, and sometimes they don't. It's really up to you to try various techniques for bringing luck to yourself. I have found that for myself, I bring about my best luck by practicing gratitude and positive thinking.

> *Do everything you can, every time you think about it, to think positively. Even if you just say the words "thank you" over and*

over. Putting what you want to happen out into the Universe is a guarantee that you will get it back. Being grateful for it, before you get it, is top priority in the game of luck. Think about the outcome you want, picture it, believe it, and be grateful for it. Practicing positive thinking will tip the scales in your favor.

HERBS: Herbal Luck

In ancient times, before the gladiators fought, or the chariot races began, wreaths of rosemary crowned those potential victors. Rosemary has been used for thousands of years to bring luck in cultures the world over. Try your hand at a little luck with a rosemary sachet. You can carry it in your purse, put it in your office drawer, or put it anywhere you would like.

Yield: 1 Application

2 tablespoons rosemary needles

1 square linen

1-foot ribbon

Dry the herbs until no moisture present to prevent mildewing. Crunch the herbs in a bowl with your fingers until crumbly. Do not crunch so much as to make a powder of them. Next, fold the material until it forms a square with the printed sides facing each other. Sew the edges of two of the sides together, until you have a pocket formed. Turn the material right sides out. Place the herbs inside the pocket, then continue sewing until it is closed. You may fashion a loop out of a scrap of material and attach to one corner of your sachet for hanging purposes.

Each day give it a few squeezes with your fingers to release a new round of aromas. When not in use, you can store in a zip lock bag to retain the fragrances. I use mine for a month or two before I can no longer detect any smells.

ESSENTIAL OIL: Lucky Oil Diffuser

Many essential oils have been used forever to bring about good luck (or bad luck to enemies). These oils have been used throughout time to give or bring luck to us or others. Try using some of these oils for yourself the next time you need things to go your way.

Yield: 1 Application

5-10 drops essential oils (frankincense, ginger, lime, patchouli, sandalwood, or spikenard)

Water

Each diffuser has different amounts of water and oils that can be used for that particular diffuser. Adjust the recipes according to your diffuser. Add the water, then add the oils and run your diffuser for the desired effect.

ALTERNATIVE REMEDY: Good Luck Symbols

Around the world, elephants have long been believed to bring good luck. You can use wooden, ceramic, resin, or any kind of elephant. The important points when purchasing your elephant for luck is that the trunk is raised. It is also thought that one of the legs raised also brings good luck to a home. Try incorporating one of the following in your home as a symbol and attraction for good luck.

- *Elephant*
- *Horseshoes*
- *red front door*
- *lucky 4 leaf clover*
- *posted prayers in the home*
- *symbols of faith*

MEDITATION

Whether you call it meditation, prayer, or soul searching, meditation belongs in every person's life, every day. During meditation you can give prayers of gratitude, receive elusive answers, learn to remove negative thinking from your life, reduce stress, learn about yourself, begin to have control over your thoughts, the possibilities are endless. Meditation has changed my life in so many ways, I can't even name them all. Try these meditation enhancing exercises and find one which one works best for you. And follow through with it. So many studies have been conducted that prove meditation reduces stress, anxiety, pain, and it has an overall healthy impact on our brain function. It has been said that the most important thing a person can do for their health, their life, their happiness, is to meditate.

AYURVEDA: Doshas for Meditation

Each dosha requires a different action for their own individual meditation practice. Incorporating meditation can significantly balance the doshas, which is what we strive for our whole lives.

Find which dosha is your primary, and include the practice listed as part of your meditation ritual.

- Vata: *Repeating a mantra over and over is very grounding for a vata, can extend meditation, and quiets and soothes a vatas jumbled thoughts. I like to use mala beads for this purpose. There are 108 beads on a mala, and I like to meditate and move my fingers over each bead while repeating "thank you" prayers. This practice has given me more comfort, power and grounding than any single thing I have ever done in my life.*
- Pitta: *to slow those rushes to anger, arguing and quick mood changes, meditation is the key. Pittas can balance their doshas and incorporate more vata and kapha in to their lives by practicing alternate nostril breathing.*

Sit in a comfortable chair, or on a spot on a rug or carpeted floor.

Sit up straight, shoulders back, thereby expanding your lungs. Cross your legs, resting your palms, face up, on your knees.

Begin by breathing long, slow, even, deep breaths. Repeat for 10 breaths. Relax.

Begin to push yourself when breathing out, by going 2-4 seconds longer on the exhales.

Begin holding your breath for 4 counts between inhales and exhales.

You are now inhaling for 4 counts, holding your breath for 4 counts and exhaling for 6-8 counts. Complete this process for

10 breaths.

Cover one of your nostrils by pinching it lightly with your thumb. Inhale and exhale deeply for 10 counts through one nostril, then repeat with the other nostril.

Finish by letting yourself fall into a regular breathing pattern. You should feel very relaxed and your lungs will feel light and airy.

Kapha: To meditate for a kapha can be challenging as kaphas tend to just sit a lot and often just let their minds wander. To have a great session that will get the circulation and the brain moving in order to add a little vata and pitta to your life, a kapha should practice walking meditation. Choose an area with a lot of nature or activity. Walk and try to think about the things you see, the rocks, the traffic, the people, the trees. Keep your arms moving and try to fall into a pattern of breathing and stepping. This should culminate in the kapha feeling a little lighter and less weighed down.

HERBS: Sage Meditation Room

Sage and thyme have both been used for centuries to bring a peaceful, positive and healthy charge to a room or area. Burning sage and/or thyme is a great way to get your mind ready to embark on a transformative session of meditation.

Yield: 1 application

3 thyme stems

1 sage stick

Wrap the thyme stems around the sage stick. Light the end with fire, blowing it out after it starts to flame. Carefully hold over a plate so that the embers won't fall on the carpet or floor. Carefully fan the smoke away from your body with your hand or a feather, while walking around your meditation area. Think positive and healthy thoughts and wishes as you pray and meditate. Ensure that you don't lay the sage stick down anywhere except in a glass or metal dish.

ESSENTIAL OIL: Meditation Bath

People have used long, slow, luxurious baths as a form of meditation ever since time began. You can increase your meditative experience by adding these essential oils known for their grounding and soothing properties.

Yield: 1 Application

10 drops frankincense oil

5 drops clary sage oil

5 drops cedarwood oil

1 tablespoon milk

Add the oils to the water as it is running. After filling the tub with water, you may add milk to keep the oils from sticking to your skin. Milk helps the oils combine with the water. Ensure that the water is not too hot, as the oils will be rendered ineffective. Relax and enjoy your bath as long as you are comfortable.

ALTERNATIVE REMEDY: Meditation Practice

Below are the guidelines for a simple, straightforward meditation session. Begin with only a few minutes each day, and as you become more comfortable, increase your time by a minute or two until you can sit for at least 20 minutes each day.

Meditation should be completed in a quiet, peaceful area. Low music may be played. Try to find an area free of negativity and distractions.

Sit on a pillow, folded towel, or a rug. Cross your legs comfortably. Sit erect, but not stiffly.

Closing your eyes, think of peaceful things that make you happy and content. Controlling the mind is difficult and you may find your thoughts returning again and again to negativity. Simply tell those negative thoughts to go away and replace with happy thoughts.

Observe your thoughts, don't react to them. Just watch them as if you are watching a movie, then send each thought on its way.

Breathe. Each time your thoughts return to you, direct your thoughts to your breathing patterns. Try to completely empty the lungs of air with deep, slow, inhales and exhales. Continuously return your thoughts to your breathing.

For 5-30 minutes, sit in silence, or softly chanting a mantra, and give your mind the positivity it needs to get you through another hectic day. You will find each day becoming easier, and your thoughts beginning to reflect the positivity you focus on each time you meditate. Problem solving, spirituality, grounding, communication, love, social interaction and peace all become deeply affected by meditating.

MELANCHOLY

Sometimes we get the wistful, longing for something...we just can't put our finger on it. Melancholy is the definition of a lonely, numb, all-consuming emotion that can last for days, and for some people, even years. Learning to live in the present and bring joy and happiness back to your life can be greatly enhanced by using remedies from the past. These recipes from various cultures can help you, or someone you love, to rejoin present day society with enthusiasm and hope.

AYURVEDA: Melancholy Pancha Karma

This used to be quite a horrific process of detoxification involving blood-letting and vomiting. But throughout the years Ayurveda practioners have changed the steps for Panchakarma, although the old ways are still practiced in some areas. Panchakarma is time consuming, involved, emotional and extremely healing. Ensure through your physician that panchakarma techniques are safe for you, especially if you are on any medications or have any illnesses. Panchakarma is usually practiced for 3-5 days. Ensure that you are away from technology, in a quiet, peaceful area, with no distractions or stress. This is my own interpretation of present day panchakarma. The following steps will help you to detox and rid your body of the negative feelings and emotions that are taking over your life.

- *Wake up early with the sunrise. Go outside if weather permits, if not, have a dedicated quiet room. Sit and meditate, followed by a gentle, stretching yoga practice.*
- *Clean your teeth, have an oil pull, clean your ears. You may also perform tongue scraping and nasya at this time, if you wish. Cleansing and purifying the body involves the outside as well as the inside.*
- *Drink a cup of herbal tea. The most common detoxifying herbs to use in this process are cardamom, cinnamon, dandelion, red clover, ginger. You can use other herbs suitable for your dosha if you desire.*
- *Sesame oil body massage. Oil yourself from your scalp to your toes. Do not get in eyes, ears or mucus membranes. You can add essential oils to the sesame oil if you wish. Leave on for 15 minutes to 1 hour. Wash off in a warm bath.*
- *Kitcheree for lunch.*
- *Spend the afternoon alternately in nature or in meditation. Some light reading of self-help materials is permitted. Being alone with your thoughts for such a long time is mind-expanding, emotional and draining.*

- *At this point, you can take an enema (overseen by doctor or Ayurvedic practitioner), or you can have another head to toe oil treatment with sesame oil.*
- *Eat kitcheree for supper, or you may have light, steamed vegetables with rice.*
- *Drink a relaxing, calming cup of detox herbal tea and add some relaxing herbs such as St. John's wort, lemon balm, valerian root or chamomile.*
- *Meditate, pray, read, journal, say your affirmations, use visualization techniques for your future (addiction free), do a few gentle yoga stretches, or sit under the moon light. Use your evening hours to relax, unwind, and prepare for the night.*
- *Eat 1-2 tablespoons ghee. This will work its way through the system all night, leaving you with a gentle elimination upon wakening.*
- *Coat the feet with sesame oil. Sleep with thick socks on to keep the oil from getting on your furniture, or to help you to not slip when you walk.*
- *Read a favorite and deeply meaningful inspirational chapter from a book, then sleep with a deep, satisfying, relaxing sleep.*

Repeat daily for 3-5 days.

HERBS: **Melancholy Herbal Tea**

These herbs have been used for centuries to lighten the mental load that we all carry occasionally. When melancholy becomes overwhelming and seems to invade every aspect of your life, drink a cup of this to soothe the spirit and brighten your outlook. These herbs have calming, peace inducing and joy invoking properties.

Yield: 1 Cup

1 teaspoon peppermint leaves

1 cup water

½ inch grated ginger

Honey

Boil one cup of water. Add the herbs, flowers, seeds or stems. Slowly pour the boiling water over the herbs. Cover the cup of herbs and steep for 6-10 minutes. Strain the tea and discard the herbs. Add honey, cream, or sweetener if desired. Drink when at comfortable temperature.

ESSENTIAL OIL: Melancholy Air

Spreading these aromas throughout your home is a surefire way to lift your spirits and get you out of that funk you're in. The therapeutic properties inherent in this blend include uplifting and inspiring components.

Yield: 1 Application

3 drops jasmine oil

3 drops melissa oil

2 drops tangerine oil

water

Each diffuser has different amounts of water and oils that can be used for that particular diffuser. Adjust the recipes according to your diffuser. Add the water, then add the oils and run your diffuser for the desired effect.

***ALTERNATIVE REMEDY*: Tips for Melancholy**

These tips are used in every culture in the world to get a person feeling back to their normal selves. These remedies can invoke certain energy and healing properties to the mind and the spirit.

- *Diet: try to avoid inflammatory producing foods such as red meat, sugar, alcohol, wheat and processed foods.*
- *Exercise: when feeling melancholy, sadness and a general unhappiness, it's important to get exercise in your life. Whether it be a walk, in nature, yoga, or a bike ride, just getting up and moving releases feel-good chemicals in our brains.*
- *Sunshine: The sun gives us life. Spend some time outdoors to absorb some vitamin D. If you can't be outdoors, try to open the blinds, light some candles if it's night time, or just brighten up a room the best way you can.*
- *Journal: A gratitude journal can lead to feelings of peace and joy. Try writing down five things you are grateful for, whether you have received them yet or not.*

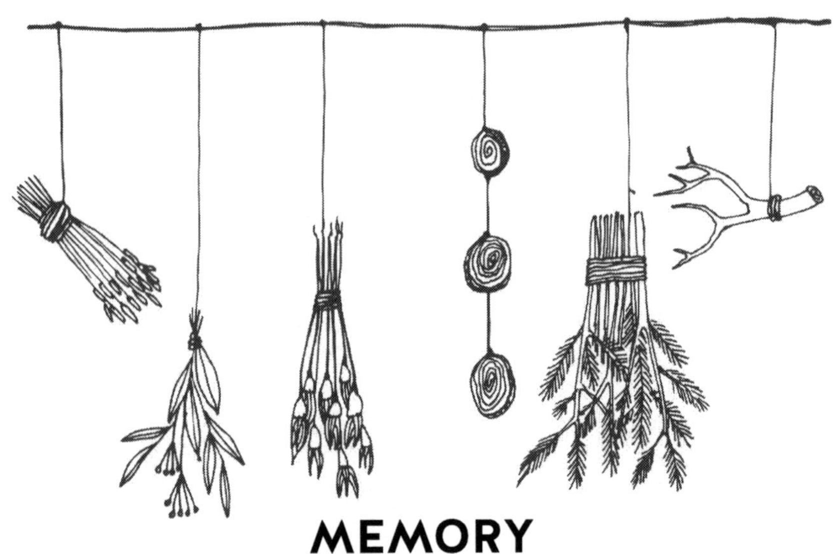

MEMORY

For everyday tasks, and for remembering all the good times we've had in our lives, it's important to keep our memories sharp. These recipes have been handed down from generation to generation and can help to improve our memories through various methods. Improve your short-term and your long-term memory with these time-tested concoctions.

AYURVEDA: Memory Spices

In Ayurveda your memory is considered to be very important to having a vital life force. These herbs and spices have long been utilized for improving memory, and as a preemptive strike against memory loss.

Yield: 2 Ounces

½ ounce Turmeric powder

½ ounce brahmi powder

½ ounce ashwagandha powder

½ ounce shankhapushpi powder

In a bowl, combine all of the spices with a whisk. Once well stirred, pour the mixture into a jar with a tight-fitting lid. Label and date the jar. Use within six months. Sprinkle the spices into casseroles, stews, salads, veggies and on your meat.

***HERBS:* Memory Tea**

These herbs have been used for thousands of years to increase our memory skills. Make yourself a cup of this tea, sit back, and let the good times roll.

Yield: 1 Cup

¼ teaspoon rosemary needles

1 teaspoon peppermint leaves

¼ teaspoon sage leaves

1 cup water

Sweetener (optional)

Boil one cup of water. Add the herbs, flowers, seeds or stems. Slowly pour the boiling water over the herbs. Cover the cup of herbs and steep for 6-10 minutes. Strain the tea and discard the herbs. Add honey, cream, or sweetener if desired. Drink when at comfortable temperature.

ESSENTIAL OIL: **Memory Lotion**

These essential oils have long been reported to improve memory. It is well known that an aroma can take you back to a certain period in your lifetime. Using these essential oils everyday can sharpen your short-term memory as well.

Yield: 2 Ounces

2 ounces unscented lotion

5 drops lemongrass oil

4 drops patchouli oil

4 drops peppermint oil

4 drops white fir oil

5 drops vitamin E oil

Any of your favorite unscented lotion will work well. Measure out the lotion and using a whisk, add the ingredients to the lotion, mixing well. Apply to areas needed, 2-3 times daily, and shake well each time. Do not get into eyes, ears or sensitive membranes. Pour into glass container, label and date, and store for up to 6 months.

ALTERNATIVE REMEDY: **Diet for Memory**

You are what you eat, so if you eat junk, your memory will be junk as well. Try this fresh and healthy diet to stay sharp and focused on daily tasks.

Fish Oil: fish oil has long been proven to contain memory

boosting and sharpening components. You can take this in a capsule form which is easily available.

Meat: try to eat as little red meat as possible, which can lead to brain fog. A vegetarian, vegan, pescatarian or a lean/white meat diet can help to increase memory.

Vegetables: Eat light, fresh, organic vegetables, and preferably ones that are in season. Eating seasonal fruits and vegetables can reduce inflammation in the body, thereby keeping our brains sharp and running a peak performance.

Avoid: alcohol, sugar, red meat, packaged/processed foods.

NEGATIVITY

Negativity is that all-encompassing energy that can turn the happiest of people, places, events and situations into utter disaster and despair. The energy of negativity can come from so many places and things that it is hard to know them all or recognize them for what they are. Sometimes even the people we love the most can fill us with so much negativity and it can take a lifetime to figure it out. Pay attention to how people, places and things make you feel. When you leave them do you feel better or worse? Are your thoughts upon encountering them positive or negative? Here are some recipes to help you dispel negativity and remove it from your life.

AYURVEDA: **Negativity Dispelling Tips**

In Ayurveda it is believed that negative energy can become toxic in your body and can cause harmful illnesses, both physically and mentally. Doing a negativity banishing practice weekly can improve your chances of staying healthy. These tips can be incorporated as a part of your daily or weekly practice.

- *Visualization – Clear your mind of any negativity by bringing your thoughts and your mental images to a place of peace and happiness. Imagine you are sitting on the shore of a pristine beach or hugging a puppy. You can think of many positive experiences from your life and with your eyes closed, recreate those peaceful and joyful moments.*
- *Prayer – Often when we are around negative people, their bad way of talking or acting can bring us down and leave us feeling depressed, anxious or sad. This is a time to reflect on the better aspects of your life. Give thanks and express gratitude to your Higher Power for all of the wonderful things you have and all of the wonderful people you know. Nothing dispels negativity like happiness and gratitude!*
- *Nature – Taking a walk, through nature, after interacting with a person or a place that makes you feel uncomfortable will banish those bad thoughts. Get to know each tree, leaf and flower. Revel in the goodness of nature. Smile.*

HERBS: **Negativity Dispelling Bowl**

Herbs have been used throughout time to bring feelings of peace, dispel negativity and evil and to instill a generalized feeling of well-being in a home. Try this ancient recipe to spread joy in your home and rid your surroundings of any negative connotations.

Yield: 3 Cups

¼ cup dried lavender stems and flowers

1 cinnamon stick, broken up

¼ cup sage leaves

1/8 cup dried thyme stems and leaves

4 bay leaves

¼ cup dried lemon or orange rinds

2 cups various wood chips, pine cones, twigs or other outdoor findings.

Combine all of the ingredients into a bowl and slightly crush the leaves and herbs at least once every few days. If you are expecting company that is usually negative, place the bowl in the room you will be visiting in. You can halve or double the ingredients, depending on the size of your bowl. You can be very creative with this and use different herbs for different moods. At the end of a month, discard into compost pile.

***ESSENTIAL OIL:* Negativity Oil Spritz**

This spritzer can be used anytime, anywhere. These essential oils have positive properties and have been used for centuries to dispel evil and negativity. If you know you are going to be around someone who is negative towards you, negative about others, or just generally makes you feel down, then spritz the area and yourself as a shield against negativity.

Yield: 1 Ounce

1-ounce water

3 drops vitamin E oil

3 drops lavender oil

3 drops citrus oil

3 drops sage oil

3 drops eucalyptus oil

Spritzes are a lighter, airier form of spray. They lend themselves well to hair and body spraying. Use to spray a room, your car, yourself, or anywhere you may come in contact with negativity. Combine all of the ingredients into a spray bottle. Label and date bottle. Shake well before using as the oils and water will separate. Spray where needed, as often as needed. Do not spray into eyes, mouth or genitals. Store bottle into a dark, cool area for up to 6 months.

***ALTERNATIVE REMEDY*: Ridding Negativity**

This old technique is still practiced quite a bit for removing any residual negative energy from the home. Try this and if you don't get results, repeat the next day and continue until you achieve the results you desire.

Yield: 1 Application

2 tablespoons sea salt

2 tablespoons white vinegar

½ cup water

Pour the water into a clear glass or vase. Add the vinegar and the sea salt. Do not stir. Sit the glass in a corner of the room of your home that you feel has the most negative energy. Leave undisturbed for 24 hours. At the end of 24 hours, check the salt. If the salt is at the bottom of the glass, then you have successfully removed all of the negative energy from the home. If the salt is at the top or up the sides of the glass, then your home still has negative energy, and you must repeat the process daily until the salt settles to the bottom of the glass.

NIGHTMARES

I have had some horrendous nightmares in my life. I am not one of those people who knows that they are dreaming and can summon the will to wake up. I suffer through nightmares like they are real. Incorporating these recipes into my life has helped me to sleep soundly, without horrific and soul wrenching nightmares. Children are prone to nightmares and can disrupt an entire family with their shrieks in the middle of the night. Some people who suffer nightmare disorders such as night terrors or PTSD can benefit from medications from your physician. Practice what many cultures around the world do and begin using some of these tips and blends at night time and give everyone in the household some peaceful and calming sleep.

***AYURVEDA*: Nightmare Release**

In Ayurveda, picturing how you would like your dreams to end through a visualization process can help with giving you the power to control your dreams. Ensuring your diet is best for your dosha will only add to your peaceful dream experience. Try this activity before bedtime to reduce the chances of anything bad happening in your dreams.

Find a comfortable spot on the floor. You can sit on a pillow or folded blankets. Cross your legs into your meditative position. Close your eyes and picture yourself in the last nightmare you had. Choose the outcome for your dream that you wish had taken place. Visualize ending your dream with love. Repeat this sequence until you are comfortable with your nightmare being replaced by this outcome. Once you get in bed, go over the dream again in your mind. When you have the nightmare again, you can let your subconscious replace the horror with the love.

HERBS: **Nightmare Bowl**

These herbs induce a great, dreamless sleep and will have you feeling great when you wake up. Herbal bowls are wonderful to use with children because it is something tangible that they can see and feel.

Yield: 4 Cups

¼ cup dried lavender stems and flowers

¼ cup dried valerian flowers

¼ cup sage leaves

¼ cup dried lime flowers

¼ cup dried lemon or orange rinds

2 cups various wood chips, pine cones, twigs or other outdoor findings

Combine all of the ingredients into a bowl and slightly crush the leaves and herbs at least once every few days. You can halve or double the ingredients, depending on the size of your bowl. You can double up on the herbs you do have to replace any you may not have on hand. Sit this bowl next to the bed and give a slight squeeze at bedtime for a peaceful and uninterrupted night's sleep. Covering the bowl during the day with plastic wrap can help prolong the life of the herbs. At the end of a month, discard into compost pile.

ESSENTIAL OIL: **Good Dreams Air**

These essential oils are said to bring good and vivid dreams to the inhaler. Run this diffuser all night (if your diffuser is safe to run unattended.) These oils also help with falling asleep and staying asleep.

Yield: 1 Application

4 drops chamomile oil

4 drops lavender oil

2 drops sandalwood oil

Water

Each diffuser has different amounts of water and oils that can be used for that particular diffuser. Adjust the recipes according to your diffuser. Add the water, then add the oils and run your diffuser for the desired effect.

***ALTERNATIVE REMEDY:* Yoga Nightmare Remedy**

Many cultures use yoga to overcome nightmares. These relaxing poses can help you to have a more positive outlook toward the night, sleep better, and you will also wake up feeling refreshed.

- *Cat/Cow – Get on your hands and knees in tabletop. Lower your head, chin to chest while exhaling deeply. Arch your back like a mad cat. Upon inhaling, slowly raise your head while swaying your back for cow. Alternate your inhaling and exhaling with arching and swaying your back. Repeat entire sequence 3-5 times each night.*
- *Child's Pose – (Balasana) – On your hands and knees, spread your knees a little more than hip distance apart. Lower your head down and let your belly rest between your thighs. Walk your fingers out until comfortably on the floor in front of you. Breathe. Keep this position for 1-3 minutes. Repeat nightly as needed.*
- *Corpse pose (Savasana)- Lay on your back with your arms down at your sides, palms up. Let your feet naturally sway to one side or the other. Be perfectly still and let your back muscles, shoulder muscles and neck muscles relax completely. Concentrate on your breathing or just observe your thoughts. Relaxing in Savasana is said to be the most important of all yoga poses. Stay in this position at least 4-10 minutes before bedtime.*

OCD

(Obsessive Compulsive Disorder)

Several family members of mine live with OCD. They compulsively clean, check and re-check everything, some have tics, some can't concentrate due to counting everything. The ways in which OCD affects people is endless. These compulsions are often a direct link to chemicals in our brains, are hereditary or stem from events in our past. To come to terms with OCD, there are various therapies that can be very healing and helpful. All over the world people have used natural healing and have often had success with the recipes below. Try them and see if they make a difference in the way that your OCD controls you.

AYURVEDA: OCD Tea

In Ayurveda, ashwagandha is the go-to relief for OCD symptoms. Ashwagandha has been shown recently to relieve symptoms of neurodegenerative diseases, boost the immune system, and work on glands to reduce anxiety. All which can help to alleviate OCD behaviors.

Yield: 2 Cups

½ inch Ashwagandha root, grated

2 cups water

1 teaspoon honey

Grind root. Add the root to two cups of boiling water. Simmer for 20 minutes. Turn off burner and let sit in hot water for 10 more minutes, after removing from stove. Strain, cool, add sweetener and drink throughout the day for desired effect. Drink within 24 hours. Store any remainder in a jar with a tight-fitting lid in the refrigerator for up to 24 hours.

***HERBS:* Borage Herbal Tea**

Sometimes depression, rather than anxiety, can lead to episodes of overly active OCD behaviors. Borage leaves have long been used to combat depression and bring a sense of well-being to people all over the world. Try this tea, relax, and let those symptoms disappear. Chamomile or lemon balm tea can have the same antidepressant effect.

Yield: 1 Cup

2 teaspoons borage leaves

1 cup water

Sweetener

Boil one cup of water. Add the herbs, flowers, seeds or stems.

Slowly pour the boiling water over the herbs. Cover the cup of herbs and steep for 6-10 minutes. Strain the tea and discard the herbs. Add honey, cream, or sweetener if desired. Drink when at comfortable temperature.

ESSENTIAL OIL: **OCD Spray**

These essential oils work to bring calm to a person having anxiety which leads to OCD behaviors, thoughts and actions. Spray this blend in your home, office, car or anywhere you feel like stress or anxiety is out of control.

Yield: 2 Ounces

6 drops vetiver oil

5 drops clary sage oil

4 drops ylang-ylang oil

4 drops cypress oil

2 ounces water

Using a funnel, pour all of the ingredients into a spray bottle. Label and date bottle. Oils and water separate, so you will need to shake very well before each usage. Spray the area lightly as desired. Ensure that you do not get spray into eyes, ears, mouth, open wounds, or other sensitive areas. Store spray bottle in a dark, cool area for up to 6 months.

ALTERNATIVE REMEDY: **OCD Therapy**

There is nothing on Earth that can soothe us as well as music. Music therapy has become a big part of helping people to overcome OCD. When I am feeling anxious, I ask Alexa to play "meditation music" and this is always instantly calming to me. Make yourself a few playlists for certain times in your life when you feel like you need to reduce anxiety or depression. Play the songs that you listened to at a happier time in your life.

Try to fully immerse yourself into the music while it is playing. It doesn't matter if it's classical, rock, R&B, country...just play whatever music makes you feel the best. Remove yourself from all distractions, including social media. Close your eyes and get into the sounds, or even get up and dance. Hopefully this therapy will have great results for you.

PAIN

Essential oils, herbs, Ayurveda and alternative remedies from various cultures, have been used since the beginning of time to help people deal with their pain. Pain can often be an indicator of something more serious, and of course a physician should diagnose the cause of chronic pain. For minor pain, these tips, hints and recipes can assist in alleviating the pain in various parts of the body.

AYURVEDA: Abhyanga

Abhyanga is a self-massage and the various herbs and spices added are specific to your need. These particular spices and herbs help to alleviate pain. You can find these herbs and spices in combination/powder forms to make this oil easier to assemble.

Yield: 1 Ounce

1-ounce sesame or grapeseed oil

1 teaspoon powdered turmeric

1 teaspoon dried/ground ginger or powder

Warm the oil by placing it into a small glass container and sitting in a bowl of hot water for 5 minutes. Pour the warmed oil into a bowl with added ingredients. Gently massage entire body (avoiding eyes, mucus membranes, genitals, open wounds or other sensitive areas), starting with the scalp, down to the soles of your feet.

While massaging yourself, repeat words of affirmation, calming and self-love. It is of paramount importance that you be good to yourself. Ensure that you are standing on a towel, or sitting, to avoid slipping with the oil on your feet. When done, towel off the excess oil, or shower. Take note of how you feel. Enjoy the pleasant emotions that you are experiencing.

***HERBS*: Spice Shaker**

These herbs and spices have various therapeutic properties to help relieve pain. Using a shaker of this blend on your soups and salads daily could help you to get past the chronic pain that consumes your thoughts.

Yield: ¼ Cup

2 Tablespoons Turmeric powder

2 Tablespoons ginger powder

1 Tablespoon garlic powder

1 teaspoon Himalayan salt

1 Tablespoon valerian powder

1 Tablespoon skullcap powder

Combine all of the ingredients together in a bowl, with a whisk. Pour into a shaker bottle, or a bottle with holes punched in the lid. Use this spice blend daily on any food that you like spices on. You can even add some capsaicin (red pepper flakes), which also helps to reduce pain, to make your blend extra spicy.

ESSENTIAL OIL: Back to Normal Bath Salts

These bath salts will make you feel better on their own, but when you add this powerful mix of essential oils, you will get help in ending the pain with this recipe's euphoric, nervine and sedative properties.

Yield: 5-6 applications

5 drops ylang-ylang oil

5 drops vetiver oil

5 drops helichrysum oil

3 cups salts

2 tablespoons carrier oil

1 tablespoon milk (optional for adults, recommended usage for children)

Use any type of salt you prefer: Pink Himalayan salt, sea salt, Epsom salts, Etc. Add essential oils and carrier oil to salt but add milk to bath water. Stir until essential oil and salt mixture is well blended. Put into jar with lid. Let sit 24 hours and stir again. Do not make the water too hot, as the oils will dissipate.

Do not add the salts when the water is running but add ½ cup of the bath salt mixture to bathwater as you get into the tub. Store remainder in a jar with a tight-fitting lid, in a cool, dark area for up to 3 months.

ALTERNATIVE REMEDY: **Hot/Cold Alternative Method**

Using heat and cold packs has been around for centuries to combat pain. The Heat relaxes the muscles and the ice numbs the pain receptors.

Heat Pack: fill a water bottle up with hot water, wrap a towel around it and place it on the painful muscle or joint. Leave it there until it begins to cool off, then replace the hot water.

Ice Pack: using a zip lock bag, fill with crushed ice. Wrap a thin towel around the bag and place it on the site of the pain.

Alternate these methods every 20-30 minutes.

PANIC ATTACKS

An overwhelming, hysterical feeling consumes a person, and they feel they cannot breathe or that they are going to die during a panic attack. Many physical symptoms accompany the panicky feelings. Calming the person and getting them in control of their breath is the number one goal during an attack. Thwarting an attack altogether is the ultimate objective overall. These recipes using essential oils, natural remedies, Ayurveda and herbs have been used for thousands of years to instill a sense of calm and well-being in a person prone to panic attacks. Medications and therapies also have recently advanced and work wonders in controlling panic attacks.

***AYURVEDA:* Stone of Peace**

Sodalite is considered the stone of peace and calming. Using this crystal in the following method is said to relax and calm someone. Crystal therapy has once again come to the forefront of modern healing. Thousands of years ago people used crystal therapy in their lives daily. Many people keep a piece of sodalite handy for panic attacks.

During crystal therapy you can use sodalite, moonstone, howlite or rose quartz. All of these stones are reported to help people who suffer from panic attacks. Using your stone, if you are alone, lay on the floor or on a bed. Place the stone on your heart, or on your third eye or forehead. Breathe while feeling the stone and the energy from the stone. Stay in position for 5-10 minutes.

If you are in public, take your stone and hold it. Squeeze it while slowly breathing in and out. You should experience feelings of serenity and tranquility. You can carry your crystals with you wherever you are to get the additional comfort when it is needed.

***HERBS:* Panic Salve**

This salve can be worn daily. It contains herbs that bring a sense of stillness, while at the same time sharpening your focus. These herbs have been used for millenniums for calming a person.

Yield: 2 Cups

2 cups lemon balm leaves, ground

2 cups lavender (or chamomile or passion flower) ground

2 cups carrier oil

1-2 ounces beeswax

Place the ground herbs into a pan and stir in the oil. Cook on extremely low heat for up to 1 ½ hours. Strain the mixture through a finely woven sieve, or cheesecloth. Add 1-2 ounces of beeswax, to get the consistency you desire. Pour into mason jar, label and date. Apply to chest, neck or arm area 2-3 times daily. You may cover area with linen or gauze and affix with tape to protect furniture and clothing. Store remainder in containers with tight fitting lids in a cool dark area for up to one year.

ESSENTIAL OIL: Panic Roll-On

Essential oils have long been known for their calming and sedative therapeutic properties. Making a roll-on to carry with you during or before a panic attack is widely recommended. They are easy, smell great, and they work.

Yield: 1 Ounce

4 drops linden blossom oil

4 drops ylang-ylang oil

2 drops lavender oil

3 drops vitamin E oil

1-ounce carrier oil

Combine the ingredients into a small bowl. Using a tiny funnel, pour the mixture into roller bottles. Label and date. Roll on pulse points such as wrist, temples or soles of feet as desired, 2-3 times daily. Do not roll onto open wounds, mouth, eyes, genitals, sensitive areas or mucus membranes. Store, upright, in a cool, dark area for up to 6 months.

ALTERNATIVE REMEDY: **Panic Salt Bath**

Himalayan salts contain properties to promote healing, calm and wellness. Many people start out their daily rituals with a salt bath to protect them throughout the day. This bath can be so healing to your mind and soul and may prevent a panic attack.

Yield: 1 Application

½ cup Himalayan salt

Run your bathwater as hot as you would like it. Add the salts and swirl them around so that the salts dissipate into the bath. Relax in the tub as long as the water is a comfortable temperature. If you decide to add any essential oils to the water, ensure that you add a tablespoon of milk to disperse the oils. Once you are done, dry your feet very well to avoid slipping.

PASSION

The first thing everyone thinks of with the word passion, is love and romance without boundaries. I personally think of the passion that inspires a person to fulfill their life's purpose. I have a passion for Ayurveda, essential oils, herbs, self-help books, my home, writing and my family. Each member of my family fuels and feeds their passions through various activities, research and action. These delightful recipes can help to fuel your passion for another person, a project, or a deep desire. These recipes have been used since before Cleopatra's reign on Earth. Now they are yours for the making!

AYURVEDA: Heart Chakra

The heart chakra is what is associated with all types of passion in Ayurveda. They use many tips and tricks to keep that passion burning. Try incorporating a few of these into your daily practices.

> Affirmations: *say words or phrases to yourself daily that are in line with your passion. For example, if you are working on and passionate about a quilt, say "I open my heart to finish-*

ing my quilt." Or "I open my heart to finishing this project." Repeat the phrase to yourself many times daily.

Color Therapy: *using the color green is synonymous with passion. Surround yourself with this color. Wear green jewelry or jade, paint your craft or writing room green. Wear green clothing, walk under green trees, sit on green grass.*

Crystal therapy: *Jade is the stone of passion. Hold a piece of jade while you meditate on what you want or desire.*

Diet: *eat soups or salads. It has been shown that eating salads with a lot of greens can help you to be focused and remain on task for that which you are passionate about.*

Doshas: *balance your doshas. If you lose passion for a person or a project, your doshas are out of balance. Use essential oils, herbs, yoga, and diet to balance your doshas.*

HERBS: Passion Balm

This balm contains herbs that are known far and wide for their passion inducing properties. Making this balm is fun and easier than it may sound. Wear the balm on your wrists or soles of your feet. Massage it in and let the herbs do their magic.

Yield: 1 cup

½ cup of a combination of one or more of rose petals, passion flowers, cinnamon stick, or jasmine petals

1 cup carrier oil

1 oz. beeswax chopped

Add the herbs to the oil in a small pan or double boiler on the stove. Cook on extremely low heat for 1 hour, stirring occasionally. Strain the oil and herbs through cheesecloth. Discard the herbs. Add the beeswax and stir until melted. Pour into containers, label and date. Once cooled, apply to areas desired. Reapply 2-3 times daily. Store in a cool, dark area for up to one year.

ESSENTIAL OIL: Passion in the Air

Permeating your home or office with these essential oils can have you once again feeling the fire for that project or person. Run this diffuser while focusing on what you desire.

Yield: Application

5 drops rose oil

5 drops jasmine oil

water

Each diffuser has different amounts of water and oils that can be used for that particular diffuser. Adjust the recipes according to your diffuser. Add the water, then add the oils and run your diffuser for the desired effect.

ALTERNATIVE REMEDY: Lover's Passion

To bring passion to people is an on-going, life-long process. It's not something you work on once and then let nature take its course. You have to work at keeping love alive in a relationship. Some tips below can help you to restore passion to a dull and lifeless love life.

Hold hands: *holding hands and hugging are ways to simply express your interest. Whether you have been together 5 days or fifty years. Showing you care is the number one way to keep passion alive.*

Date nights: *schedule a time to focus on your partner. Don't take for granted that they will cut a chunk of time out specifically for you, take the lead and do it yourself. Just let them know you miss spending one on one time with them, and then focus solely on them when you go out. Everyone likes to feel special.*

Change initiation: *if your partner always initiates intimacy between you two, then it is time for you to step up and make the first move. This will add an aura of excitement and change that is needed in every relationship.*

Try new things: *Eat at a new restaurant, wear new lingerie, try a new position when making love, change up the routine. New is exciting!*

PATIENCE

Being patient is NOT a quality I possess. But it is a quality I desire. When I know I need to be patient with a project, a person or time, I use one of these blends to release my inner calm and conquer those pulse racing thoughts I am prone to. Patience is a virtue, and sometimes it's a necessity. Impatience is a very vata trait. Balancing your doshas helps a great deal with patience.

AYURVEDA: Passion Pranayama

Breathing exercises are a huge part of Ayurveda. This particular exercise will force you into a state of relaxation and patience. Try it one time and you will become a believer.

> *Diaphragmatic – Find a comfortable position and lay in corpse pose, on your back. Arms down at sides, palms up. Eyes closed, and feet relaxed. Place a 5-10-pound comfortable, soft weight (such as a sand bag, or a large bag of rice) onto the diaphragm, right below the rib cage. Continue lying in corpse pose and breathe as normal as possible. The weight*

will strengthen the diaphragm and force the patient to take long, slow, deep breaths. This exercise can be performed for 5-15 minutes a day until diaphragm is strengthened. It can also be used in times of significant stress, anxiety or fear, as it has many calming properties.

***HERBS:* Echinacea/Rose Sachet**

This sachet is beautiful to smell, and the aromas released with a gentle squeeze bring patience and calming to the recipient. These herbs are as beautiful to look at as they are therapeutic.

Yield: 1 Application

1-2 Tablespoons echinacea flowers, dried

1-2 Tablespoons rose petals, dried

1-6-inch square linen or cheesecloth

1-piece ribbon (optional)

Dry the herbs until no moisture present to prevent mildewing. Crunch the herbs in a bowl with your fingers until crumbly. Do not crunch so much as to make a powder of them. Next, fold the material until it forms a square with the printed sides facing each other. Sew the edges of two of the sides together, until you have a pocket formed. Turn the material right sides out. Place the herbs inside the pocket, then continue sewing until it is closed. You may fashion a loop out of a scrap of material and attach to one corner of your sachet for hanging purposes. Set the sachet in a spot where you will be meditating or doing most of your thinking. I place mine on my desk by my computer. Each day give it a few squeezes with your fingers to release a new round of aromas. When not in use, you can store in a zip lock bag to retain the fragrances. I use mine for a month or two before I can no longer detect any smells.

ESSENTIAL OIL: Patience Bath Bombs

What better way to have patience essential oils delivered straight to your brain other than using bath bombs in an incredibly soothing bath. These oils are known to promote patience, calming and relaxation.

Yield: 10-14 bombs

1 cup baking soda

½ cup citric acid

½ cup corn starch

½ cup Epsom salts, fine grained

15 drops lavender or rose oil

15 drops ylang-ylang or patchouli oil

½ teaspoon carrier oil

¾ teaspoon water

spray bottle (water)

You will need a small bowl and a large bowl. In the small bowl, add your wet ingredients (and food coloring, if you desire), and combine with a fork or a whisk. In the large bowl add your dry ingredients, mixing well. Very gently and slowly, while whisking, add your wet ingredients to the dry bowl. If it begins to fizz, pour the wet ingredients at a slower pace, and whisk rapidly until the mixture quits fizzing.

When the ingredients are mixed well, you can add 2-4 sprays of water to the mixture, it will have the consistency of wet sand. When it is as malleable as you would like it, then quickly form into balls. It will dry out quickly, so you must work fast making the balls, or smashing it into the molds.

Leave, uncovered, sitting out 12-24 hours. I usually leave mine out overnight. In the morning, I place the balls into a large container with a tight-sealing lid. You can place one bomb in the shower, in the corner, so that the aromas and the oils will slowly release into the air. Or you can simply put one or two bombs in the completely filled bathtub when you get in. The oils will mix with the water, and the fizzing is soothing and exhilarating at the same time. Store your bath bombs in an air-tight container for up to 6 months. I store mine in a dark area so that the color won't fade.

***ALTERNATIVE REMEDY*: Patience Mantra Remedy**

One of the things about an impatient person is that they have no tolerance for meditation. But force yourself to meditate for 5 minutes, and you will find your thoughts becoming more under control and induce a sense of calm in yourself. Reciting a mantra to yourself is a great way to bring patience to yourself. Use this well-known mantra or make one for yourself such as reciting the words

"I am calm."

So Hum mantra - Sit in a comfortable spot and close your eyes. Pay close attention to your breathing and notice your inhales and exhales. After a few minutes quietly say the word "so" as you inhale through your nose. Follow by saying the word "hum" as you exhale. For every inhale, the word so. For every exhale, the word hum. If your thoughts wander, return them to your breath. Repeat this cycle for 5-20 minutes.

PEACE

Whether it be world peace, peace of mind, or harmony between family members, peace has been sought since Cain slew Able. The therapeutic properties in the ingredients release natural chemicals in your brain to promote peaceful thoughts and feelings. The rituals involved in this section promote peace and well-being to everyone.

AYURVEDA: Music Peace Therapy

Utilizing music to bring peace is well known by every culture and throughout all time periods. The saying "music soothes the savage beast" has been said for a thousand years for a reason. It works.

> *Choose soothing, meditative music such as Krishna Das, or some classical music. Sit quietly in an area free from distractions. Think pleasant thoughts while concentrating on the sounds of the music. Your mind will settle, and your shoulders and jaw will relax, and you will be overcome with stillness and quiet.*

HERBS: Peaceful Tea

This tea invokes a certain charm, calm and peace to the drinker. I love this tea at nighttime as it also has many sedative properties and ensures a peaceful night's sleep.

Yield: 1 Cup

Combine 2 teaspoons of any of the following herbs: chamomile, passion flower, lemon grass, St. John's wort, lemon balm or green tea.

Honey

Water

Boil one cup of water. Add the herbs, flowers, seeds or stems. Slowly pour the boiling water over the herbs. Cover the cup of herbs and steep for 6-10 minutes. Strain the tea and discard the herbs. Add honey, cream, or sweetener if desired. Drink when at comfortable temperature.

ESSENTIAL OIL: Peace Rub

These peaceful and calming properties in this blend of essential oils promotes peace and happiness. Rub this on as you go throughout your day to bring peace to everyone you come in contact with.

Yield: 1 Ounce

10 drops German chamomile oil

10 drops myrrh oil

3 drops neroli oil

1-ounce carrier oil

4 drops vitamin E oil

Using a bowl or a jar, combine the ingredients together using a whisk or a fork. Using your fingertips, spread the rub onto your pulse points, such as wrists, neck, or soles of feet, ensuring that you do not get into eyes, ears, mouth, open wounds, genitals, mucus membranes, or other sensitive areas. You may cover area with light gauze or old clothing to prevent staining furniture. Leave mixture on until you are ready to reapply. Store remainder in a dark colored jar, in a cool, dark area for up to one year.

***ALTERNATIVE REMEDY:* Tips for Peace**

Peaceful feelings inside and out can come from a multitude of areas. Following are some of the ways people of various cultures bring peace to their individual lives.

Salt lamps; using a salt lamp dispels the negative energy in an area. I use salt lamps in almost every room of my home, every day.

Gratitude: I use either a journal or mala beads to state my thankfulness for everything I have or want every day. Try writing down 5 things you are grateful for, or say some prayers starting every sentence with the words "thank you."

Declutter: Organize a space or clean out a cabinet or closet. Clutter can lead to negative feelings and a general sense of unease. Cleaning up a space can also help to clean out your mind.

Mantra: try saying mantras to yourself to give yourself peace and calm. Simply repeat the words to yourself "I have peace in my life" several times with your eyes closed. Try it right now. Works, right?

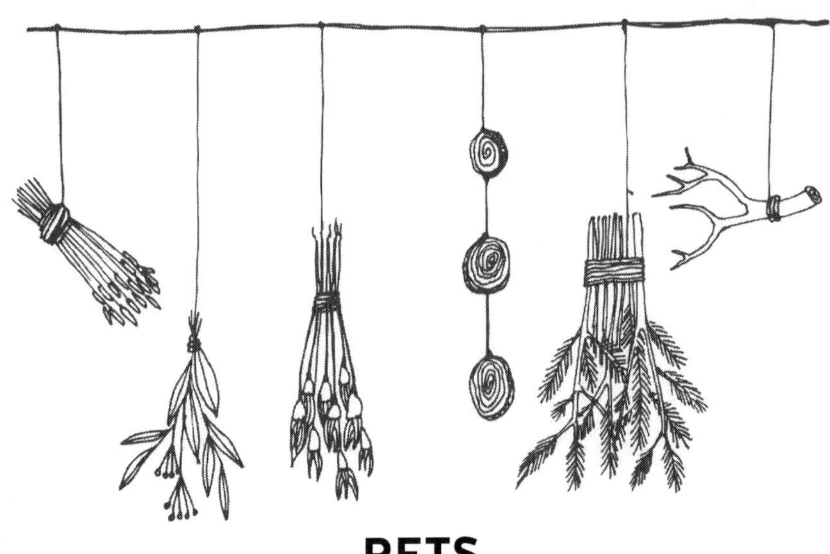

PETS

(over-stressed dogs)

The same way that moving to a new location, going to new surroundings, or any type of event can cause our stress levels to skyrocket, even if it's something good, the same can be said about our pets. Using one of these remedies can bring serenity and peace to your dog when going through a difficult ordeal or change in environment.

***AYURVEDA:* Pet Dosha Balancing**

Ayurveda beliefs also say that dogs and other animals have doshas. Balance your pet's doshas in the following ways:

> *Vata: a nice little massage of the back and shoulders should work wonders on calming down a pet overcome with vata hyper tendencies.*
>
> *Pitta: If your pet has the tendency to have aggressive or angry outbursts, try letting them swim. Swimming works out the aggression in pets the same way that it does people.*

Kapha: getting your couch potato pet to exercise can be trying at times. Take a run with your pet. Have fun while running and your pet will too.

HERBS: **Pet Chamomile Tincture**

This tincture is used to calm down your dog or cat. The recipe is for an animal 10-15 lbs. You can adjust according to your pet's weight.

Yield: 1 pint

2/3-pint chamomile flowers

1-pint vegetable glycerin

Place herbs in a pint jar until it's 2/3 full, and cover the herbs with vegetable glycerin, 1 – 1 ½ inches from the top of the jar. Cover tightly and place in a cool, dark location. Shake vigorously every day for 2 weeks, then let it set without shaking for one month. Strain, bottle, label and put the date you decanted it (strained herb). Use ½ - 1 dropper-full in tea, water or other liquid.

ESSENTIAL OIL: **Pet Peace Spray**

Using essential oils on pets is becoming more popular. Ensure that you research exactly which oils are good for which pets. Just because something is good for a dog, doesn't mean it is good for a cat. These oils are universal in calming our furry friends.

Yield: 1 Ounce

10 drops orange oil

5 drops lavender oil

1-ounce water

1 tablespoon apple cider vinegar

Spray bottle

Combine all the ingredients into a spray bottle. Label and date bottle. Use one of your hands to shield your pet's eyes, and the other to lightly spray your pet's coat. Apply daily or as needed. Store in a dark cool area for up to 6 months.

***ALTERNATIVE REMEDY:* Secret Pet Calmer**

These secret tips are known throughout the world for calming your pet. Find the ailment your pet has and discover the healing method most sought after.

Anxiety: give hugs

Stress: give hugs

Change: give hugs

Depression: give hugs

Pain: give hugs

Illness: give hugs

PLEASURE

Increasing our endorphins and promoting pleasure center activity is a multi-billion-dollar industry world-wide. But you don't need drugs, alcohol or any number of expensive products to bring your pleasure awareness front and center. Follow a few of these recipes and you can ensure bringing yourself and those around you a happier and more pleasurable experience.

AYURVEDA: Non-Attachment

In Ayurveda, life's happiness begins with an eight-fold path. First and foremost, on this path, is non-attachment. This means having too great of an attachment to the physical world. When we love our "things" so much that we place value on them above humanity, we are creating fear and worry in ourselves. In order to have pleasure, we must concentrate on what is truly valuable.

> *Family: show your family you love them every day. Tell them you love them. Give to them what they need.*
>
> *Helping Others: Give what you have to someone who needs it.*

If you have clothes you love, give them away. If you have spare food, cook a meal for someone. If you have time, share that time with an elderly or needful person. Give.

Clear clutter: When you become attached to things, you spend an unnecessary amount of time worrying about and protecting your things. Things are not important in the journey to having pleasure in your life. Begin by getting rid of a lot of your things. Give them to charities or thrift shops.

***HERBS:* Pleasure Infusion**

This infusion is meant to be taken slowly and throughout the day. These herbs bring peace, calm and pleasure so that you may experience what is truly valuable to you.

Yield: 1 Cup

1 teaspoon lavender flowers

1 teaspoon Rose petals

1 teaspoon peppermint leaves

1 cup water

honey (optional)

Bring one cup water to boil. Add the herbs and remove from heat. Cover and steep for 20-30 minutes. Strain and discard herbs. Sweeten if desired. Drink by the teaspoonful within 12 hours. Refrigerate any remainder for up to 3 days.

***ESSENTIAL OIL:* Pleasure Bath**

The pleasure you get from taking a bath and soaking in a hot tub is sometimes the greatest thing on Earth. Add to that experience by adding these oils reported to increase the pleasure centers of our brains.

5 drops clary sage oil

5 drops ylang-ylang oil

5 drops sandalwood oil

5 drops lavender oil

1 tablespoon milk

Add the oils to the water as it is running. After filling the tub with water, you may add milk to keep the oils from sticking to your skin. Milk helps the oils combine with the water. Ensure that the water is not too hot, as the oils will be rendered ineffective. Relax and enjoy your bath as long as you are comfortable.

***ALTERNATIVE REMEDY*: Pleasure methods**

People all over the world try daily to incorporate things into their lives that will bring pleasure. Some of those things work well, so are developed into rituals. I am including a few well recommended rituals below for you to use to bring pleasure into your life.

Self-awareness - to receive what you want, you must be aware of what it is you truly want. Become more self-aware by not saying "I want to be happy," but saying "I want" and list a particular thing, idea, or goal. Set your intention as specifically as you can. List the steps you will need to reach that goal.

Life's Purpose - To be happy and receive pleasure, it has been reported by most people that discovering their life's purpose led them to experience their greatest pleasure in life. Figure out what you were meant to do and go do it. Figure out what you were meant to be and go be it. Figure out your life's purpose and go live it. All of these goals will change over time. You can keep changing with your goals. Don't feel like because you want to start a balloon business that for the rest of your life, this should be your goal. As you age and change, so will your life's purpose. You can have many.

Moderation - Living excessively has caused more pain than happiness. Eating too much causes unhealthy weight gain. Spending too much money leads to debt. Try to moderate what you think is good in life. Living in moderation brings us pleasure in the long run, while living excessively brings us many problems.

POSITIVITY

Have you ever been around those types of people that after your interaction with them, you just feel good about yourself and good about life? Even if they are going through some bad times, they look at the bright side of life and are thankful for the things in their life that is positive. Building up your positivity can only do one thing for you, make everything better. These recipes are still being used all over the world to bring joy, happiness and positivity to people from all walks of life.

AYURVEDA: Oats Energizer

Oftentimes when negative energy surrounds us, we become tired, sad, lethargic, depressed and really don't feel like carrying on with our daily tasks. This recipe has the ingredients needed to boost our energy and dispel any bad feelings.

Yield: 1 Cup

½ cup oats

1 cup water (directions may use varying water to oat ratios. Follow directions on box)

½ teaspoon turmeric

Sprinkle of cinnamon

½ teaspoon honey (or any sweetener you desire)

Dried fruit (optional)

Almonds (optional)

Cook the oats according to package directions. Add the remaining ingredients and stir. Enjoy a healthy, energy inducing breakfast. Discard remainder.

***HERBS:* Positivity Herbal Bath**

This recipe is one I like to use because of the beautiful aromas, the peaceful feelings and the positivity imparted by this bathing experience. These herbs have long been known for dispelling negativity and bringing delightful thoughts and experiences to the user.

Yield: 1 Application

1 teaspoon Jasmine flowers

1 teaspoon peppermint leaves

1 square linen, muslin, cheesecloth or gauze

6 inches ribbon or string

Make a sachet for the tub by laying out a piece of material. Place the herbs in the middle of the cloth. Bring the ends of the fabric together and tie off with a string. Once the tub has filled with water, place the sachet into the water. You may remain in the tub as long as the water is comfortable. Discard the herbs after using.

ESSENTIAL OIL: **Positive Citrus Diffuser**

These aromas can make just about anyone happy. Use this recipe if you want to bring some positivity and joy into your home, not to mention the boost of energy these essential oils can provide. I like to use this recipe when I am having family holidays to ensure everyone leaves their troubles outside on the doorstep.

Yield: 1 Application

3 drops orange oil

3 drops grapefruit oil

3 drops neroli oil

3 drops lemon/lime oil

Water

Each diffuser has different amounts of water and oils that can be used for that particular diffuser. Adjust the recipes according to your diffuser. Add the water, then add the oils and run your diffuser for the desired effect.

ALTERNATIVE REMEDY: **Positive Thinking**

There have been so many books, documentaries, studies and research done to prove that how you actually think affects yourself not only emotionally, but physically as well. Learning to train your brain is simple and at the same time it seems almost impossible. Your negative thoughts will always, always come back. But the sooner you realize this, the quicker you learn how to control your thoughts.

This exercise should be completed in a quiet, peaceful area. Low music may be played. Try to find an area free of negativity and distractions.

- *Sit on a pillow, folded towel, or a rug. Cross your legs comfortably. Sit erect, but not stiffly.*
- *Closing your eyes, think of peaceful things that make you happy. Controlling the mind is difficult and you may find your thoughts returning again and again to negativity. Just tell those negative thoughts to go away and replace with happy thoughts. Just brush the bad thinking away. It's as easy as that.*
- *Breathe. Each time your negative thoughts return to you, direct your thoughts to your breathing patterns. Try to completely empty the lungs of air with deep, slow, inhales and exhales. Continuously return your thoughts to your breathing.*
- *For 5-30 minutes, sit in silence, or softly chanting a mantra or an affirmation, and give your mind the positivity it needs to get you through another hectic day. You will find each day becoming easier, and your thoughts beginning to reflect the positivity you focus on each time you meditate. Problem solving, spirituality, communication,*

love, social interaction and peace all become deeply affected by meditating.

PRAYER

Praying can be done in moments of crisis, as a ritual, in times of need or distress, or unceasingly with every thought. Praying to a higher power has been done since time began. Increasing your devotion and focus during prayer can be so beneficial to us emotionally, physically, mentally and spiritually. I have researched some of the most popular ways to increase focus and worshipfulness and combined them into the recipes below.

AYURVEDA: Sacred Space

In Ayurveda, everyone has a sacred space. Whether it is an altar, a room, a kneeling pad, a yoga mat or a field. Find a space with no distractions, no social media, no sounds other than nature or music. Decorate your space with those things that mean the most for your spirituality. Your bible or other spiritual reading material, candles, photos, mala beads, yoga mat, whatever you want in your space. Use this space for the wonderful time of prayer.

Praying: you can pray however you want to, to whomever you want to in your space. You can kneel on a mat, pray on your knees, sit on a bolster, with a rosary or mala beads, whichever way is the most comfortable for you.

Journaling: I use my space for my gratitude journal. This is the greatest form of prayer for me. Each day I sit on my bolster and write ten things I am grateful for. Each gratitude begins with the words "thank you."

Affirmations: Sit in your sacred space and say your affirmations. These are prayers to yourself and your brain. You can write them down, as many as you want. Set your intentions for your specific goals and say them to yourself "I will save $20 a week in my savings account," "I am strong and confident." Stating these intentions out loud will rewire and retrain your brain.

Meditate: Sitting on your bolster in your sacred space and meditating will bring many answers to you about your daily life struggles. People help themselves more by meditating than by any other activity. Meditation can be a very powerful form of prayer.

HERBS: **Spiritual Bowl**

Using aromas to increase our attention during spiritual times is utilized in all cultures. Make this potpourri for your sacred space and breathe deeply of these aromas while you pray.

Yield: 1 Application

1 small piece of frankincense resin

1/8 cup Mugwort

1/8 cup chamomile flowers

1/8 cup nettle leaves

1 cinnamon stick

Dried orange peel

Dried lemon rind

Combine all ingredients in a bowl. Break the larger pieces into halves or fourths. Each day give the potpourri ingredients a squeeze to release the new aromas. To make the potpourri last longer, you may cover when not in use. After a month, discard into compost heap and replace with new ingredients.

ESSENTIAL OIL: **Prayer Spray**

Essential oils have been used in every religion on Earth. There is something calming and focusing in these aromas. These essential oils are well known for helping us to get in touch with our spirituality. This spray, in particular, can help us dive deeper into our souls and to become one with our Higher Power.

Yield: 2 Ounces

5 drops Palo Santo oil

5 drops frankincense oil

5 drops angelica oil

5 drops bergamot oil

3 drops vitamin E oil

Water

Using a funnel, pour all of the ingredients into a spray bottle. Label and date bottle. Oils and water separate, so you will need to shake very well before each usage. Spray your sacred area lightly as desired. Ensure that you do not get spray into eyes, ears, mouth, open wounds, or other sensitive areas. Store spray bottle in a dark, cool area for up to 6 months.

ALTERNATIVE REMEDY: Gratitude Remedies

I believe the greatest activity I have ever undertaken in my life concerning prayer has been to begin each prayer with gratitude. I had heard this for years but didn't believe it until it was an exercise I had to complete during my yoga teacher training courses. Gratitude is everything.

Be grateful daily for the things you have, and more importantly, be grateful for those things which you have yet to receive. If you give thanks for the future you desire, show belief that you will achieve your dreams, and thank your provider for allowing you to have that which you do not yet have…it will be yours.

PROSPERITY

Being prosperous means to be financially secure by doing that which we love. It means to have enough of something that you can share that something with others. For centuries, people have looked for ways to increase their prosperity for themselves, their communities and their nations. These rituals, tips and recipes include blends from all over the world that have been used to increase one's prosperity in all things.

***AYURVEDA:* Prosperity**

In Ayurveda, having prosperity means to have significantly grown spiritually. We must concentrate daily on empowering our souls to do good. It does not matter your religion or beliefs; every belief has room for growth. These are some of the ways that Ayervedics use to grow in prosperity.

Meditation: meditate daily. Every day. Even if it is only for 5 minutes.

Prayer: pray to whomever you wish. But pray multiple times daily.

Give: give what you can to others in need. You will be more thankful for what you have.

Read: read spiritual material daily. It should be something you are interested in learning about.

Gratitude: Increase your spirituality and prosperity by being grateful for what you already have, and for what you have yet to receive.

HERBS: Prosperity Wash

Bathing yourself in these herbs has been reported to bring great prosperity to many people. Make a bowl of this heavenly aromatic blend and wash yourself with this scent to attract what you want.

Yield: 1 Cup

1 tablespoon lemongrass stems chopped

1 tablespoon honeysuckle flowers

1 tablespoon basil leaves

1 cup water

Add the chopped herbs, stems or seeds to one cup boiling water. Simmer slowly for up to 20 minutes. Remove from heat and allow to cool to room temperature. Strain and discard herbs. Dip linen or gauze in the liquid and apply as a wash to body, without getting into any sensitive areas. Allow to air dry. Store remainder in refrigerator for up to 24 hours in a jar or bowl with a tight-fitting lid.

***ESSENTIAL OIL:* Prosperity Diffuser**

These essential oils have been reported since time began for making a person prosperous. Try running this blend in your home, office, or anywhere you spend a lot of time.

Yield: 1 Application

5 drops spikenard oil

4 drops spruce oil

4 drops allspice oil

water

Each diffuser has different amounts of water and oils that can be used for that particular diffuser. Adjust the recipes according to your diffuser. Add the water, then add the oils and run your diffuser for the desired effect.

***ALTERNATIVE REMEDY:* Prosperous Home**

This recipe has been used throughout India for centuries. Try it and see what results you get.

Take seven pieces of turmeric and place them in the western most corner of your home. Replace the pieces annually on the new year. Wrap them in cheesecloth to protect flooring or furniture.

PROTECTION

Covering oneself for protection outside of physical means is a practice that has been handed down from one generation to the next. From those of us who "cover ourselves in the blood of Jesus" to those who invoke guardian angels to safely guide loved family members homes, protection for ourselves and our loved ones is a daily practice. Various cultures, religions and countries have used unconventional methods to bring protection from outside forces to themselves. Below is just a small sampling of different ways you can protect yourself and your family from evil.

AYURVEDA: Sage Protection

Ayurveda uses sage as a means of protection from harm, evil and enemies. This remedy is as old as time and I have done it many times myself.

> *Purchase a sage stick, which has been dried, wrapped and trimmed by a professional. You can buy these at herb shops and alternative healing stores. Get a shallow bowl or plate*

that can withstand heat. With fire, light the end of the sage stick. Once it is burning good, blow out the fire and it will begin to smoke. With your feather or your hand, push the smoke outward as you walk from room to room. Say your positive thoughts out loud, such as, "everyone here will be healthy", or "Only love, health and happiness reside here," and "My home and everyone in it will be protected against_______." Ensure once you have completed this ritual that you put out the burning sage and rest it on a metal or glass plate.

***HERBS:* Protective night**

This is the simmer pot I run on evenings I feel I need extra protection if I am alone. These herbs have been labeled with the properties of protection and security. Not to mention they make the whole house smell good.

Yield: 1 Application

2 cups water

1 tablespoon Betony leaves

1 tablespoon Agrimony leaves

1 cinnamon stick broken into pieces

¼ cup calendula flowers

Mix all ingredients into a small sauce pan with the water. Bring to a low boil and turn down heat. Let pan simmer until water starts to run low. Add more water as needed. A beautiful/protective fragrance fills the home. Ensure you turn off the burner before bedtime.

ESSENTIAL OIL: Protective Clothing

These essential oils have the protective properties needed to give you strength and assurance as you travel outside your home. This laundry detergent works well for low-sudsing washing machines and leaves your clothing smelling great and clean.

Yield: 2 gallons

¼ block Fels Naptha, grated

½ cup washing suds or powders

25-30 cups water

8 drops petitgrain oil

8 drops myrrh oil

Pour one cup water and the grated Fels Naptha into a small pan and heat on very low, stirring constantly, until Fels Naptha is melted. Do not boil. In a very large bowl add the melted Fels Naptha, the washing suds and 10 cups of water. Stir vigorously with a whisk until well blended. Pour, ½ each, into 2 one-gallon size jugs. Put the caps on the jugs and shake well. Let sit undisturbed for 12-24 hours. Add 10 cups of water to each jug. Shake well. Add the essential oils to the jugs. Shake well before each usage. Use ¼ cup for each load of laundry.

***ALTERNATIVE REMEDY:* Protective Sachet**

This sachet has been worn by kings seeking protection and by beggars fearful of the night. Throughout centuries this protective recipe has been reported to save many people from evil.

Yield: 1 Sachet

1 tablespoon caraway seeds

1 teaspoon cloves

1 teaspoon lavender flowers

1 teaspoon rose petals

Dry the herbs until no moisture present to prevent mildewing. Crunch the herbs in a bowl with your fingers until crumbly. Do not crunch so much as to make a powder of them. Next, fold the material until it forms a square with the printed sides facing each other. Sew the edges of two of the sides together, until you have a pocket formed. Turn the material right sides out. Place the herbs inside the pocket, then continue sewing until it is closed. You may fashion a loop out of a scrap of material and attach to one corner of your sachet for hanging purposes. Use a safety pin to attach the sachet to your clothing or wear in your pocket. Each day give it a few squeezes with your fingers to release a new round of aromas. When not in use, you can store in a zip lock bag to retain the fragrances. I use mine for a month or two before I can no longer detect any smells.

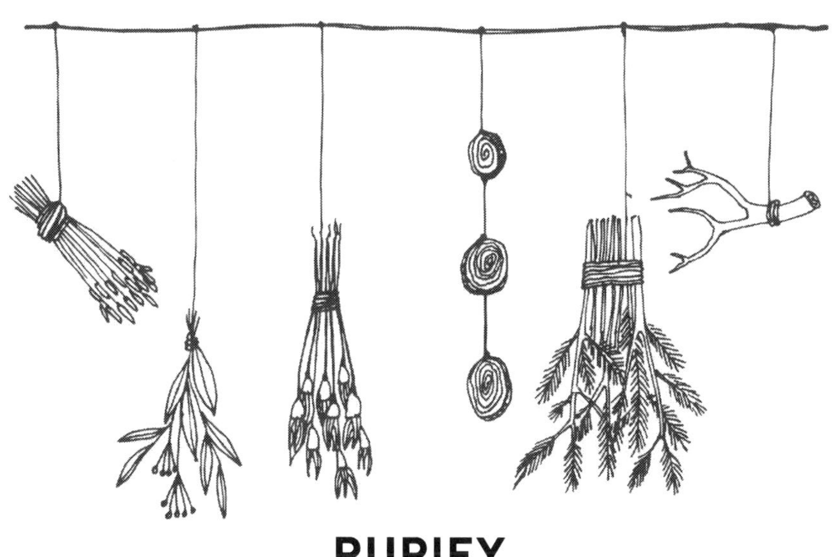

PURIFY

In researching and studying Ayurvedic medicine, I have learned that it is very important to purify the body before undertaking a healing session of any kind. Ridding oneself of evil and negativity is not just an Ayurvedic practice but is a ritual that can be found in every religion and culture in the world. These recipes have been gathered from far and wide to bring you the most ancient, and the most up-to-date purification rituals known to man. Enjoy!

AYURVEDA: Pancha Karma for Purity

This used to be quite a horrific process of detoxification involving blood-letting and vomiting. But throughout the years Ayurveda practioners have changed the steps for Panchakarma, although the old ways are still practiced in some areas. Panchakarma is time consuming, involved, emotional and extremely healing. Ensure through your physician that panchakarma techniques are safe for you, especially if you are on any medications or have any illnesses. Panchakarma is usually practiced for 3-5 days. Ensure that you are away from technology, in a quiet, peaceful area, with no distractions or stress. This is my own interpretation of present day panchakarma. The following steps will help you to detox and purify your body.

- *Wake up early with the sunrise. Go outside if weather permits, if not, have a dedicated quiet room. Sit and meditate, followed by a gentle, stretching yoga practice.*
- *Clean your teeth, have an oil pull, clean your ears. You may also perform tongue scraping and nasya at this time, if you wish. Cleansing and purifying the body involves the outside as well as the inside.*
- *Drink a cup of herbal tea. The most common detoxifying and purifying herbs to use in this process are dandelion, burdock, nettle, ginger and hibiscus. You can use other herbs suitable for your dosha if you prefer.*
- *Sesame oil body massage. Oil yourself from your scalp to your toes. Do not get in eyes, ears or mucus membranes. You can add essential oils to the sesame oil if you wish. Leave on for 15 minutes to 1 hour. Wash off in a warm bath.*
- *Kitcheree for lunch.*
- *Spend the afternoon alternately in nature or in meditation. Some light reading of self-help materials is permitted. Being alone with your thoughts for such a long time is mind-expanding, emotional and draining.*
- *At this point, you can take an enema (overseen by doctor or Ayurvedic practitioner), or you can have another*

head to toe oil treatment with sesame oil.

- *Eat kitcheree for supper, or you may have light, steamed vegetables with rice.*
- *Drink a relaxing, calming cup of detox herbal tea and add some relaxing herbs such as St. John's wort, lemon balm, valerian root or chamomile.*
- *Meditate, pray, read, journal, say your affirmations, use visualization techniques for your future (addiction free), do a few gentle yoga stretches, or sit under the moon light. Use your evening hours to relax, unwind, and prepare for the night.*
- *Eat 1-2 tablespoons ghee. This will work its way through the system all night, leaving you with a gentle elimination upon wakening.*
- *Coat the feet with sesame oil. Sleep with thick socks on to keep the oil from getting on your furniture, or to help you to not slip when you walk.*
- *Read a favorite and deeply meaningful inspirational chapter from a book, then sleep with a deep, satisfying, relaxing sleep.*

Repeat for 3-5 days.

HERBS: **Sage Smoke Purification**

Sage smoke is one of the oldest known forms of purification. You can use sage to purify your home, place of worship, your body or anywhere that you think evil or negativity is pervasive.

Yield: 1 Application

7 sage stems with leaves. Dried

1-foot thin string

Lighter

Plate

Feather, hand fan, or paper

Twist the sage stems together once they are dried. You can use a string to wrap and ensure the stems are tightly bound together. Light the end with fire, carefully holding over a plate so that the embers won't fall on the carpet or floor. Carefully fan the smoke away from your body while walking from room to room. Think positive and healthy thoughts and wishes as you pray while traveling into each room. Ensure that you don't lay the sage stick down anywhere except in a glass or metal dish.

ESSENTIAL OIL: **Oily Roller**

These essential oils are known far and wide for their ability to purify and protect. Use this roll-on before meditation, prayer or before opening yourself spiritually.

Yield: 1 Ounce

3 drops petitgrain oil

3 drops white birch oil

3 drops anise oil

3 drops hyssop oil

1-ounce carrier oil

3 drops vitamin E oil

Combine the ingredients into a small bowl. Using a tiny funnel, pour the mixture into roller bottles. Label and date. Roll on to pulse points such as wrist, neck and soles of feet as desired. Do not roll onto open wounds, mouth, eyes, genitals, sensitive areas or mucus membranes. Store, upright, in a cool, dark area for up to 6 months.

***ALTERNATIVE REMEDY:* Abhyanga for Purification**

People use many methods of purifying themselves before any spiritual ritual. Abhyanga is the term used during a self-massage purification/protection ritual.

1/8 Cup oil

- Warm the oil (sesame, grapeseed or olive) by placing it into a small glass container and sitting in a bowl of hot water for 5 minutes.
- Pour the warmed oil into a bowl with any added ingredients, such as essential oils, that you may desire.
- Gently massage entire body (avoiding eyes, mucus membranes, genitals, open wounds or other sensitive areas), starting with the scalp, down to the soles of your feet.

- While massaging yourself, repeat words of affirmation, calming and self-love. It is of paramount importance that you be good to yourself during a purification ritual.
- Ensure that you are standing on a towel, or sitting, to avoid slipping with the oil on your feet.
- When done, towel off the excess oil, or shower.
- Take note of how you feel. Enjoy the pleasant emotions that you are experiencing.

RAGE

Rage is the most fearful of all emotions. A person consumed with rage cannot control themselves in word or action. To be on the receiving end of someone's rage is terrifying to say the least. If you or a loved one are prone to fits of rage then anger management, medications and therapies are useful tools to help combat this all-encompassing emotion. These instructions from around the world can help you to learn to control your rage and bring you some calming and peaceful ways to deal with situations that are beyond your control.

AYURVEDA: Pitta Rage Control

In Ayurveda, the pitta dosha is responsible for outbursts of rage. This cooling breathing exercise (Sheetali) is perfect for using in conjunction with diet and exercise to balance your doshas and bring pitta under control.

> *Sit comfortably with erect spine. Open mouth and rest tongue on lower lip. Curl tongue to resemble a straw. Slowly breath*

in and out through your tongue for cooling breaths. Repeat cycles for 2 minutes.

***HERBS:* Rage Reducing Herbal Tea**

These herbs are renowned for their calming properties. Just sitting down and drinking a cup of hot tea can calm the soul and is a balm to the emotions, but you can add ice and drink it cold if you desire.

Yield: 1 Cup

1 teaspoon lemon balm leaves

1 teaspoon chamomile flowers

1 cup water

honey

Boil one cup of water. Add the herbs, flowers, seeds or stems. Slowly pour the boiling water over the herbs. Cover the cup of herbs and steep for 6-10 minutes. Strain the tea and discard the herbs. Add honey, cream, or sweetener if desired. Drink when at comfortable temperature.

***ESSENTIAL OIL*: Soothing Oil Bath**

This bath contains a blend of essential oils known for their calming and cooling effects. The therapeutic properties in this recipe will soothe rage and replace it with relaxation.

Yield: 1 Application

5 drops mandarin oil

4 drops bergamot oil

4 drops jasmine oil

4 drops vetiver oil

1 tablespoon milk

Add the oils to the water as it is running. After filling the tub with water, you may add milk to keep the oils from sticking to your skin. Milk helps the oils combine with the water. Ensure that the water is not too hot, as the oils will be rendered ineffective. Relax and enjoy your bath as long as you are comfortable.

***ALTERNATIVE REMEDY:* Rage Remedies**

These tips to control rage are new and old, from all cultures. Each one can have good effects on emotions, but when you combine two or more, the effects can be profound.

- *Find an area in your home devoted solely to your spiritual practices. You can fill with things you love such as candles, diffuser, music, mala beads, self-help books, pillows, whatever you want to make your morning routine all about you and your spirituality.*
- *Create ambiance. Light your candles, turn on your Zen music, burn incense, or run your diffuser. Create a devotional area that gets you in the mood to have a great day.*

- *First meditate for at least 5 minutes. Sit on a comfortable pillow and close your eyes. As you breathe in, think the word "peace." As you exhale, think the word "calm." After you practice meditating for a while, you can try different meditation techniques to see which ones you like the best.*

- *Read some sort of spiritual material, or self-help material. This step is so very important. Even if you can only read for 3 minutes. Learning how to advance in our spiritual journey from others is an on-going, life-time journey. Never quit.*

- *Pray. Say your prayers however feels comfortable to you. I use mala beads to ensure that I am saying over 100 prayers of gratitude each and every day. I thank God for each member of my family, my material possessions, for my positive thoughts, for the things I don't yet have, and for my spiritual journey. Gratitude is the key.*

- *Affirmations. Don't forget to say some pretty amazing things about yourself. Use positive language. Instead of saying "I am losing weight," say "I am thin and healthy." Say affirmations about the things you want to accomplish on your day. Today I said, "I will finish ten recipes today." And I will.*

- *Write a few things in your gratitude journal. You won't believe how happy and thankful this will make you. This step right here has turned around some of the most difficult relationships in my life. Instead of concentrating on the negative aspects of my relationships, I thought and was grateful for the positive aspects. Wow! Talk about stress relieving.*

- *Do some morning stretches. Yoga, jumping jacks, walking, karate, whatever gets you moving and your heart racing. Try to move for 5 minutes. It makes all the difference. I have a 7-minute routine that I complete each morning. Then when I can't do my regular yoga practice, I feel great knowing I have done at least the minimum of what I need.*

- *Completing even a few of these steps each day will have you on a path of devotion, love, worship, and peace like you have never experienced. You will get rid of negative emotions like rage, anger, depression, anxiety and lethargy. You will find that on days you are unable to perform your morning routine, you are longing for your space and prayers. But remember, you can pray and be thankful anytime, anywhere.*

RELAXATION

There is a time meant for energy, and a time to relax. Many of us, myself included, find it hard to attain peaceful relaxing moments. I always have a list going on in my head of things that need to be done before I can enjoy a relaxing moment. And the list is never-ending. I have experimented and used these hints, tips and recipes from various cultures to help myself to relax each day. They actually work. Some of them take practice, but I just add them to my list! The important thing is that every day we must take time for ourselves and relax for just a few minutes in our own surroundings. You don't need to go away on vacation or to a spa to relax. With these techniques you can master relaxation in your own home.

AYURVEDA: Relaxation Self-Massage

Abhyanga is a form of massage that you can do on yourself following the steps below. Sesame oil is very relaxing and warming.

Yield: 1 Application

2 Tablespoons sesame oil

- *Warm the oil by placing it into a small glass container and sitting in a bowl of hot water for 5 minutes.*
- *Pour the warmed oil into a bowl with any added ingredients (such as essential oils).*
- *Gently massage entire body (avoiding eyes, mucus membranes, genitals, open wounds or other sensitive areas), starting with the scalp, down to the soles of your feet.*
- *While massaging yourself, repeat words of affirmation, calming and self-love. It is of paramount importance that you be good to yourself.*
- *Ensure that you are standing on a towel, or sitting, to avoid slipping with the oil on your feet.*
- *When done, towel off the excess oil, or shower.*
- *Take note of how you feel. Enjoy the pleasant emotions that you are experiencing.*

***HERBS:* Relaxation Herbal Tea**

This is one of my favorite teas to have before an evening of friends and conversation. It helps me to calm down and releases all of my nervous energy.

Yield: 1 Cup

1 teaspoon passion flower

1 teaspoon chamomile flowers

1 cup water

Honey

Boil one cup of water. Add the herbs, flowers, seeds or stems. Slowly pour the boiling water over the herbs. Cover the cup of herbs and steep for 6-10 minutes. Strain the tea and discard the herbs. Add honey, cream, or sweetener if desired. Drink when at comfortable temperature.

***ESSENTIAL OIL:* Vacation Spray Aromas**

These essential oils make you feel so relaxed, you'll think you're on a beach in the Bahamas. They have calming, sedative and relaxing therapeutic properties to help you feel your best.

Yield: 2 Ounces

5 drops clary sage oil

5 drops jasmine oil

5 drops neroli oil

5 drops ylang-ylang oil

1 tablespoon witch hazel

2 ounces water

Using a funnel, pour all of the ingredients into a spray bottle. Label and date bottle. Oils and water separate, so you will need to shake very well before each usage. Spray the area lightly as desired. Ensure that you do not get spray into eyes, ears, mouth, open wounds, or other sensitive areas. Store spray bottle in a dark, cool area for up to 6 months.

ALTERNATIVE REMEDY: Crystal Relaxation Therapy

Crystals hold so much power, which can be transferred to us. Some stones put out high frequencies of energy, and other give the bearer a calming, soothing presence. Choose a few and try them out to see which one works best for you.

Choose one or more of the following crystals:

Fluorite, black tourmaline, blue lace agate

There are several ways to tap into the energetic frequencies given off by your crystals. Hold one while meditating or praying. Sleep with one under your pillow. Place one on your nightstand. Carry one in your pocket. You can simply hold and look at one while thinking relaxing thoughts.

REJECTION

We have all been rejected, more than once. Rejection hits us hard, no matter where it comes from; a job, a lover, a friend, a stranger, a critic, a keyboard warrior, or a relative. Some people take rejection very hard; others just say "well, I'll try again". I am of the former breed. I don't like rejection, but I do try to learn from it and understand the criticism, if it is constructive and not destructive. These recipes make it a little easier for me to bounce back in the positive, and not dwell in the negative. Try a few of these the next time rejection has you feeling like you want to give up.

***AYURVEDA:* Pitta/Kapha Balance**

In Ayurveda, they believe the kapha and the pitta are out of balance if one cannot get over a period of rejection. Try these foods to get yourself back into a balanced dosha frame of mind. Eat one or more of the following foods for a few days:

> *Ghee, soy, no hot spices, eggs, basmati rice, onions, eggplant, mango, mushrooms, peas, cauliflower, cabbage,*

broccoli, asparagus, apples, avocado, coconut and berries.

***HERBS:* Embracing Herbal Tea**

The herbs in this tea blend help us to accept others, no matter how we may feel rejected. Open your heart as you sip this tea and learn to forgive.

Yield: 1 Cup

1 teaspoon lemon balm

1 teaspoon St. John's wort

1 cup water

honey

Boil one cup of water. Add the herbs, flowers, seeds or stems. Slowly pour the boiling water over the herbs. Cover the cup of herbs and steep for 6-10 minutes. Strain the tea and discard the herbs. Add honey, cream, or sweetener if desired. Drink when at comfortable temperature.

***ESSSENTIAL OIL*: Air of Acceptance**

To dispel any lingering negative feelings from rejection, try diffusing this blend to give yourself some uplifting aromas.

Yield: 1 Application

4 drops pine oil

4 drops helichrysum oil

4 drops eucalyptus oil

3 drops cedarwood oil

water

Each diffuser has different amounts of water and oils that can be used for that particular diffuser. Adjust the recipes according to your diffuser. Add the water, then add the oils and run your diffuser for the desired effect.

***ALTERNATIVE REMEDY:* Crystal Embracing Therapy**

These stones have the power to help us get over the feelings of rejection and to accept and embrace those who we feel may have wronged us. It does us no good, when we feel rejected, to harbor feelings of resentment. We must learn from rejection and embrace those who gave it. Hold these stones close while you meditate or pray.

Lepidolite, selenite, rose quartz, amethyst, blue lace agate, or fluorite.

Place each of your crystals in your hand and close your eyes for a few seconds. Which crystal "feels" right to you in this moment, in your current state of emotions. Choose that crystal as your "rejection and forgiveness" crystal. You can carry that crystal with you, wear it as jewelry, or any number of ways you wish to keep your crystal close enough to you to absorb your negative emotions and to promote positive emotions. One of the best ways to incorporate the healing power of your crystal is to lie on a flat, comfortable surface. Place the crystal in the middle of your chest. Lay your hands loosely at your sides, and let your feet fall where they may. As you lie still for 5-15 minutes, think about that crystal. Imagine its healing effects coursing through your blood veins, your organs, your heart and finally through your brain. Once your emotions are calm and under control, sit up, take a few breaths and walk away.

REMORSE

Guilt, sorrow, shame, and regret are all negative emotions derived from remorse. I have remorse at times about things I say or that I do. I try to remedy the situation as best as I can. When the negativity takes over, I turn to these well-used, positive, calming and focusing recipes to take my mind off of the negative outcomes and find a brighter outlook from my actions.

AYURVEDA: ***Dahl***

In Ayurveda it is believed that all illness, physical and mental, begins in the gut. The same can be said of emotions. Negative emotions affect us in so many ways, and the first thing you notice after your negative thoughts, is negative feelings in your digestive area. This recipe is used for remorse and any negative thinking that may affect your digestion.

Yield: 4 servings

1 cup lentils (any type)

1 sweet potato diced

1 onion diced

1 hot pepper minced

3 cloves garlic minced

½ teaspoon cinnamon (optional)

¼ teaspoon cumin (optional)

¼ teaspoon curry powder (optional)

½ teaspoon turmeric

½ teaspoon salt

1 bay leaf (optional)

½ inch ginger, minced

2 tablespoons coconut oil

2-4 cups coconut milk (optional0

2-4 cups broth

1 cup spinach leaves (optional)

water

In a frying pan, lightly sauté the ginger, onions, garlic and pepper in the coconut oil. In a large pot, add the lentils, sweet potatoes, sautéed vegetables, and whichever spices you prefer. Add the coconut milk, broth, water, or desired liquid. Bring to a boil, stir, and reduce heat. Cook for 25-35 minutes or until lentils and sweet potatoes are tender. Add liquid as needed. When done, add spinach leaves, if desired, and stir until wilted. The end result will resemble a very thick stew. Serve with flat bread or any type of light bread or cracker. Store remainder in refrigerator, freezer, and just heat portions as needed.

HERBS: Rue for Remorse

There is an old saying that rue in the garden banishes any remorse in the household. Try growing a rue plant and bring positivity into your home. Never ingest rue. Especially harmful to fetuses.

ESSENTIAL OIL: Remorseful Spray

These oils are known to dispel any negative thinking and have you back to thinking positively and with an excitement for the future rather than regret over the past. Sometimes we play past events over and over in our mind, filling ourselves with negativity over things that most of the people involved in our perceived wrongdoing don't even remember.

Yield: 2 Ounces

5 drops linden blossom oil

5 drops sandalwood oil

3 drops angelica oil

3 drops melissa oil

1 teaspoon witch hazel

2 ounces water

Using a funnel, pour all of the ingredients into a spray bottle. Label and date bottle. Oils and water separate, so you will need to shake very well before each usage. Spray the area lightly as desired. Ensure that you do not get spray into eyes, ears, mouth, open wounds, or other sensitive areas. Store spray bottle in a dark, cool area for up to 6 months.

***ALTERNATIVE REMEDY*: Tips for Renewing the Spirit**

There is an abundance of advice, remedies and potions to rid oneself of the negative emotions of remorse and replace with spiritually renewing thoughts.

- *Develop new habits: Don't sit around feeling regret and remorse over the past. Think about the future instead. Try new things. They say for something to become a habit, you must do it for 30 consecutive days.*
- *Give: Do something good. The thing you do may not seem to be able to make up that for which you are remorseful, but to someone else it may mean even more.*
- *Counseling: Find a good Ayurvedic or alternative counselor who can help you to overcome that emotion that is eating away at you.*
- *Restore: Pray, meditate, yoga, say affirmations. Do a ritual or a practice that can restore your soul like any of the aforementioned. But there is so much you can do for yourself. Take a walk, in nature. Go fishing. Just let yourself do something that is totally for you and your soul.*

ROMANCE

We all look at romance differently. I think the most romantic thing in the world is when my husband would look at me with this particular smile. It got me every time. Others think gifts, travel, food, or foreplay are great romantic gestures. Chocolate, perfume, oysters, and other tangible objects have long been touted as the most romantic/aphrodisiacal substances in the world. These recipes have been used for thousands of years to bring romance into a home. Try some and see if you don't get some!

AYURVEDA: Dosha Balancing for Romance

In Ayurveda it is believed that if your doshas are out of balance, then you cannot give fully in the romance department. Here are some suggestions for balancing doshas of all types to obtain and stabilize a tridoshic constitution.

- *Diet: Eat fresh and locally. Cut down on pre-packaged foods.*

- *Yoga: balancing postures are great for all dosha types.*
- *Crystals: Amethyst, pearl and diamonds are the romance stones to balance those doshas.*
- *Color therapy: brown, red, orange, green, blue for doshas and romance.*

HERBS: Romantic Simmer Pot

These simmer pots are so sweet and adorable. You can use a small pan on your stove for this. These herbs promote romance and smell amazing. You can't help but turn to thoughts of love and romance with these aromas.

Yield: 1 Application

1 tablespoon rose petals

1 tablespoon jasmine

1-inch piece cinnamon stick

1 tablespoon lavender flowers

water

Place the herbs, stems and/or seeds into a small pan on the stove. Bring to a slight simmer after filling up the pan 2/3 with water. Ensure that you continue adding water throughout the day as it evaporates. After the day/evening is over, drain and put herbs in compost pile, and discard the liquid.

***ESSENTIAL OIL:* Romance is in the Air**

Permeate the air with these romantic aromas, full of aphrodisiacal properties. Use your diffuser to spread the love around your home or office.

Yield: 1 Application

3 drops angelica oil

3 drops jasmine oil

3 drops neroli oil

water

Each diffuser has different amounts of water and oils that can be used for that particular diffuser. Adjust the recipes according to your diffuser. Add the water, then add the oils and run your diffuser for the desired effect.

***ALTERNATIVE REMEDY*: Feng Shui for Romance**

Feng Shui is a method of displaying objects or placing them so that the energy that flows throughout your home portrays what you are feeling. These Feng Shui tips promote romance and love.

- *Ensure that you have a headboard for your bed that is strong and sturdy.*
- *Do not have a lot of extra pillows on the bed. You should have a pillow for yourself and one for your lover.*
- *The room should have flowers in it, whether real flowers*

or a painting, it's up to you.

- *Pink is the color of romance, so ensure that there are touches of pink throughout the room.*
- *No electronics of any type such as computers, iPads, televisions, etc.*
- *Candles and crystals can add a lot in the way of romance to a bedroom. Ensure you have both.*
- *Declutter. Nothing ruins romance like looking around and seeing a bunch of junk and piles of clothing. Your room should be free of all clutter.*

SADNESS

Some people seem to live in a state of perpetual sadness. It may be chemicals in the brain, it could be because they were raised in sadness, or maybe they just have a negative outlook on life. But sometimes relatively happy people are overcome with sadness due to circumstances in their lives. The human race has sought ways to dispel sadness and gloom for thousands of years. From smiling at someone, to making silly jokes, we try to brighten the days of others around us. These recipes and tips have been used world-wide to bring an end to that painful emotion.

AYURVEDA: ***Rasayana***

In Ayurveda, when one is feeling sad or down, a quick recipe of Rasayana is used to lift the spirits and provide instant energy. Many fruits are used to make a fruit salad, or Rasayana, but one of the favorites for sadness is a banana Rasayana.

Yield: 2 Servings

2 bananas sliced thin

1 cup coconut milk

1 tablespoon jaggery (Indian type of sugar)

½ teaspoon cardamom powder

1 teaspoon honey

Sprinkle of cinnamon or coconut flakes

Place the first 5 ingredients into a bowl, stir and chill for 1 hour. Taste to see if you need to add more jaggery or honey for sweetness preference. Sprinkle the cinnamon or coconut flakes on top before serving. You may toast the coconut if you prefer.

HERBS: Euphoric Rice

This rice dish is made often in families in various cultures to bring a sense of happiness or joy to a family member. The herbs and spices in this recipe are uplifting and have properties that promote happiness.

Yield: 4 servings

1 cup jasmine rice

2 cups water (amount may differ according to package recipe)

1-inch piece grated ginger

1 saffron needle

1-inch piece grated ginseng

1 teaspoon oregano

1 tablespoon ghee

Heat the ghee in a sauce pan. Add the grated ginseng and ginger. Once they are soft, add the rice and brown. Add the water and cook according to rice package directions. After done, add the oregano and saffron and stir. Remove from burner and cover with a tight lid and leave to steam itself for 5 minutes. Any leftovers may be tightly covered and stored in the refrigerator for 2 days.

***ESSENTIAL OIL:* Uplifting Rub**

This rub contains therapeutic properties that uplift the spirit and dispel sadness. You can use this daily on yourself to promote feelings of well-being. Even the act of doing something solely for yourself can end sadness and bring yourself a little bit of joy. It's not often that we do anything for only ourselves and no one else. Try it!

Yield: 1 Ounce

4 drops Palma Rosa oil

4 drops Palo Santo oil

3 drops clary sage oil

3 drops geranium oil

4 drops vitamin E oil

1-ounce carrier oil

Using a small glass bowl, mix all of the ingredients together using a small whisk. Using your fingertips apply the oils to the back, neck, temples, legs, soles of feet, or where desired. Ensure that you do not get any of the mixture into the eyes, ears, mouth, mucus membranes, genitals, open wounds, or sensitive areas. Store remainder in a dark colored jar, label and date, and place in a cool, dark area for up to 6 months.

ALTERNATIVE REMEDY: **Sadness Dispellers**

Sadness is so prevalent in sunshine-restricted areas of the world that the effects it has on people have been given the diagnostic label of "SAD." There are a few medicines that can help with this condition, but the easiest way to cure SAD is listed below.

- *Get as much sunshine as you can. If you can't get sunshine invest in the lights that will brighten and help you train your brain to believe you are getting sunshine.*
- *Vitamin D. We just can't get enough. Available readily and cheaply in tablet form, take vitamin D every day. Almost everyone has a vitamin D deficiency.*
- *Surround yourself with the colors yellow and orange. Paint your walls with these colors. Wear yellow/orange clothing. Buy some yellow flowers.*
- *Citrine. This gemstone is colored yellow/orange and helps dispel sadness. Meditate while holding this gemstone. Wear citrine jewelry. Place a piece on your desk.*

SELF-ESTEEM

There are various reasons why we may have low self-esteem; relationships, family, our perceived projection of ourselves, the ways in which we were raised, the list is on-going as to why we are inundated with these feelings. To build self-esteem is a path, a journey, and it starts with treating yourself better. Cultures around the world have experimented and devised methods of boosting people's self-esteem. Try one of these concoctions every day and see if you don't feel better about yourself.

AYURVEDA: Ojas

The essences that embody our very emotional health are prana, tejas and ojas. Ojas are responsible for promoting our vitality, self-confidence and happiness. There are many ways to increase your ojas and increase your happiness and self-esteem as well.

- *Herbs: ashwagandha, ginger, turmeric and basil are hot action herbs which increase ojas.*

- *Food: the ojas diet is spicy and hot, but also includes milder foods such as basmati rice, ghee, milk, honey, greens, nuts, dates and grains.*
- *Sleep: Ojas grow with well-balanced sleep. Go to bed early and rise before sunrise.*
- *Yoga: Hold yoga poses and take deep, long, slow breaths.*

***HERBS:* Self-Esteem Tea**

This tea can provide you with a feeling of well-being and strength. These herbs have properties to help you focus, stay on task, and to be more open and honest with yourself and others.

Yield: 1 Cup

1 teaspoon peppermint

½ teaspoon red clover flowers

1 clove

Water

Honey

Boil one cup of water. Add the herbs, flowers, seeds or stems. Slowly pour the boiling water over the herbs. Cover the cup of herbs and steep for 6-10 minutes. Strain the tea and discard the herbs. Add honey, cream, or sweetener if desired. Drink when at comfortable temperature.

ESSENTIAL OIL: Self-Esteem Spray

Essential oils can pass through the blood/brain barrier through the olfactory senses or through skin. These essential oils can help to boost our self-esteem through their therapeutic properties that make us feel better about ourselves.

Yield: 2 Ounces

4 drops bergamot oil

4 drops melissa oil

4 drops myrrh oil

4 drops rosewood oil

1 teaspoon witch hazel

2 ounces water

Using a funnel, pour all of the ingredients into a spray bottle. Label and date bottle. Oils and water separate, so you will need to shake very well before each usage. Spray your body lightly as desired. Ensure that you do not get spray into eyes, ears, mouth, open wounds, or other sensitive areas. Store spray bottle in a dark, cool area for up to 6 months.

ALTERNATIVE REMEDY: Tips for Increasing Self-Esteem

Really, no one can increase your self-esteem for you. This is something that depends solely on yourself. Making a formative plan and sticking to it, accomplishing it, and realizing you can do anything is number one in the ways to increase your self-esteem.

- *Set small goals. Write them on a chart. These small goals should lead to your ultimate large goal. You will feel so good about yourself at every baby step you take in reaching these goals.*
- *Complete each step on your goal chart one at a time.*
- *Write under each completed small goal how you feel about accomplishing that step.*
- *When you reach your ultimate end goal. Reward yourself. You deserve it. Then set a new goal.*

SERENITY

The blissful feeling of serenity can be obtained by many means. Accomplishing a major achievement, holding a baby, petting a dog and meditation are a few of the ways that I can attain serenity in my life. Some people like bubble baths, walks in the woods, or music. These recipes and musings below are from how people endeavor obtain serenity throughout the world. Much, love, bliss, peace and calm to you.

AYURVEDA: **Sattvic Life**

In Ayurveda, a Sattvic lifestyle is reached by doing our best…at everything, for everyone. In order to be there for others, we must reach this state to keep ourselves healthy and happy so that we can live a serene life and give to others what we are fully capable of.

- *Diet: eat fresh and wholesome ingredients. Do not eat packaged foods, and when possible, no fried foods. Vegetarianism can help us to lead a more serene and peaceful life. Eat seasonally and eat for your dosha.*

- *Exercise: Instead of working out at a frenetic pace, try a slower, more peaceful form of exercise such as hiking in nature or yoga.*
- *Spiritually: Stay connected with your spiritual side. Pay attention to your higher power daily. Pray (asking and thanking) and meditate (listening.) Read spiritual materials.*
- *Give: Serenity is most upon us when we are happy with ourselves. Nothing makes us happier than to help others and give. Give your time, a smile, a donation.*

HERBS: **Serenity Tea**

Just simply making a cup of herbal tea can bring a sense of serenity to me. Drink this tea as you sit and think about and be grateful for your day, your life, and your loves.

Yield: 1 Cup

1 teaspoon lemon balm

1 teaspoon spearmint

1 cup water

Honey

Boil one cup of water. Add the herbs, flowers, seeds or stems. Slowly pour the boiling water over the herbs. Cover the cup of herbs and steep for 6-10 minutes. Strain the tea and discard the herbs. Add honey, cream, or sweetener if desired. Drink when at comfortable temperature.

ESSENTIAL OIL: Serene Air

This blend of essential oils contains properties that can make you feel calm, relaxed and bring a smile to your face. The next time you are stressed out, try this recipe to bring some balance to your emotions and serenity to your whole being.

Yield: 1 Application

3 drops marjoram oil

3 drops vanilla oil

3 drops ylang-ylang oil

Water

Each diffuser has different amounts of water and oils that can be used for that particular diffuser. Adjust the recipes according to your diffuser. Add the water, then add the oils and run your diffuser for the desired effect.

ALTERNATIVE REMEDY: Serenity tips

These alternative tips are some of the things that people do in cultures all over the world to bring serenity and calm to themselves. I try to practice a few of these every day of my life. We live in such a fast-paced world, it really does something for your mental health to take at least ten minutes a day to do something for yourself.

- *Gratitude: It cannot be stressed enough how a gratitude*

journal can change your life. Simply write down five things that you are grateful for every day. When you are done writing, the serenity and calm that overtakes you cannot be bought.

- *Thoughts: Train your brain to stray away from negative thoughts. Simply brush that thought aside and replace it with a beautiful thought. Worry does nothing but harm you. Serenity heals you.*
- *Kindness: your acts toward others can set the tone for how you feel the entire day. Giving something of your-self to someone in need can produce a feeling of serenity quite unlike anything else.*
- *Read: reading self-help books or spiritual material of any kind can promote self-love, serenity, self-confidence and understanding. Try reading "Unicorn Untamed by Lin Reynolds." Full of humor, love and an over-all self-empowering book.*

SHAME

An oftentimes unbearable feeling combined with guilt or remorse. Shame can make us feel less than what we are and significantly lower our self-esteem. Shame is often caused by our own actions. Either by something we have done, or that we have let another do to us, either willingly or unwillingly. Placing the blame on ourselves for something beyond our control is another area in which we often feel shame. These recipes have been handed down for generations to help people to get over that useless feeling of shame. Bring some positivity back in to your life and get rid of all of those negative thoughts and emotions.

***AYURVEDA:* Cooling Diet**

According to Ayurvedic thinking, all illness of the body and mind is brought forth from the digestive tract. Shame is associated with hot feelings, so in the Ayurvedic tradition, shame should be cooled off through the gut.

Eat a cooling diet. Light airy foods such as cauliflower,

broccoli, salads, seasonal vegetables (either raw or lightly steamed), berries, and nuts. Avoid hot foods, spicy foods and heavy foods.

HERBS: **Shame Tea**

This tea helps you to think positively and to be in a more stress-free, peaceful state of mind.

Yield: 1 Cup

1 teaspoon St. John's wort

½ teaspoon chamomile flowers

½ teaspoon passionflower

1 cup water

Honey

Boil one cup of water. Add the herbs, flowers, seeds or stems. Slowly pour the boiling water over the herbs. Cover the cup of herbs and steep for 6-10 minutes. Strain the tea and discard the herbs. Add honey, cream, or sweetener if desired. Drink when at comfortable temperature.

ESSENTIAL OIL: **Empowering Air**

These essential oils have the ability to bring us self-confidence, self-love and forgiveness. Try running this diffuser when those negative thoughts and emotions take over.

Yield: 1 Application

3 drops petitgrain oil

3 drops palmarosa oil

3 drops Palo Santo oil

Water

Each diffuser has different amounts of water and oils that can be used for that particular diffuser. Adjust the recipes according to your diffuser. Add the water, then add the oils and run your diffuser for the desired effect.

***ALTERNATIVE REMEDY*: Herbal Aromatics**

Making this simmer pot and filling the air with these delightful scents works through our olfactory senses to bring self-empowerment and love to our home, thereby reducing feelings of shame and guilt.

Yield: 1 Application

1 tablespoon chamomile flowers

1 tablespoon spearmint

1 cinnamon stick

water

Place the herbs, stems and/or seeds into a small pan on the stove. Bring to a slight simmer after filling up the pan 2/3 with water. Ensure that you continue adding water throughout the day as it evaporates. After the day/evening is over, drain and put herbs in compost pile.

SPIRITUALITY

Spirituality is the foundation of all of the things. No matter where you are in life, increasing your faith and your spirituality should be at the top of your everyday list of things to do. It doesn't matter how you work on it, either through prayer, mala beads, reading positive books, going to church, serving others, just ensure that you do it. You will find that all the problems and issues in your life are manageable and you are able to more fully serve others if you have a strong spiritual foundation.

AYURVEDA: Mala Bead Praying

I am a firm believer in prayer. Praying to your higher spirit is communicating your gratitude, thoughts and wishes. Using mala beads is the way that I ensure I am praying about everything I need to pray about and communicating everything I have had plaguing me. Each set of mala beads has 108 regular beads and one special large bead. You can order them from Amazon or pick them up at a lot of stores that sell spiritual artifacts.

Sit in a nice comfortable area free from distractions. If you have music playing, turn it down low.

You can do this with eyes opened or closed, however you feel best suits your needs.

Hold your mala beads in front of you, grasp the small bead next to the largest bead (the God bead). Using your fingers, slowly grasp each bead, stating a prayer while holding each bead. Similar to how you would finger through a rosary.

Begin each prayer with the words "thank you." Even if you are asking for something in the future such as "Thank you that my book is a #1 bestseller." State it like it has already happened.

Believe what you pray for on each bead. Feel how you would feel as if you had already accomplished it.

When you have completed a prayer for each bead, say a special prayer on the God bead for God. This ensures you have said 109 prayers.

HERBS: **Spiritual Tea**

This tea blend has been used to open communications between our world and the next. To increase your spiritual acceptance and openness, drink a cup of this tea before your prayers or rituals.

Yield: 1 Cup

½ teaspoon fennel seeds

1 teaspoon hibiscus flowers

1 teaspoon lavender flowers

1 cup water

honey

Boil one cup of water. Add the herbs, flowers, seeds or stems. Slowly pour the boiling water over the herbs. Cover the cup of herbs and steep for 6-10 minutes. Strain the tea and discard the herbs. Add honey, cream, or sweetener if desired. Drink when at comfortable temperature.

ESSENTIAL OIL: **Spiritual Spray**

This recipe has the essential oils that have been used for thousands of years for a multitude of sacred rituals and religions. Use these in your sacred space to help you open up to spiritual enlightenment.

Yield: 1 Ounce

4 drops angelica oil

4 drops fir oil

4 drops frankincense oil

4 drops melissa oil

1 teaspoon witch hazel

1-ounce water

Using a funnel, pour all of the ingredients into a spray bottle. Label and date bottle. Oils and water separate, so you will need to shake very well before each usage. Spray the area lightly as desired. Ensure that you do not get spray into eyes, ears, mouth, open wounds, or other sensitive areas. Store spray bottle in a dark, cool area for up to 6 months.

***ALTERNATIVE REMEDY:* Sacred Sungazing**

One must be barefoot and connected directly to the Earth to sun gaze. Sit comfortably and wear comfortable clothing. The time is very important. Sun gazing must be within 30 minutes of sunrise or sunset. Gazing at the sun any other time of the day will damage the optic nerves and the retinas of the eyes. At sunrise or sunset, sit before the sun and gaze at it while either chanting, praying, meditating or other spiritual activities. Start out with 10-20 seconds the first day. Increase by 10-20 seconds daily until you can gaze at the sun for 30 minutes. It will take several months to reach this stage. The sun is said to be one of the most powerful healing agents known to man. Caution is strongly advised to only perform this ritual at sunrise and sunset. This practice will get you in touch with your Higher Power and bring you closer to that which you seek.

STRESS

Stress causes only bad things to happen. Stress can be the trigger to illness, to fight and argue irrationally, and to lose track of ourselves. We can use recipes from around the world to reduce the stress in our lives and to bring us a sense of peace and stillness. When you feel your blood pressure rising, your pulse racing and your thoughts turning towards negativity, you can know that the chemicals in your brain are also going crazy and doing all sorts of things to you, none of which you need. Stop this downward spiral and focus on the solution and not the problem. Bring positivity in to yourself and try to naturally end stress related symptoms with these blends and tips.

AYURVEDA: Brahmi Milk

According to the Vedic texts, all illness, physical and mental, begins in the digestive tract. Brahmi is very soothing and gentle to your stomach, as well as having therapeutic properties that calm and de-stress you as you drink it. Drink this milk about an hour before you go to bed.

Yield: 1 Cup

1 teaspoon brahmi powder

1 teaspoon gotu kola powder

1 cup milk

Dash of cinnamon or ginger

Honey

Using a small pan, heat the milk until warm. Add the brahmi and gotu kola powder and bring to a slow boil. Remove from heat. Cool slightly and add cinnamon, ginger and honey if desired. Drink slowly 1 hour prior to retiring for the night.

***HERBS:* Stress Ointment**

Using these herbs is a practice that has been going on since time began. You can make this ointment to apply, as needed, to your pulse points to give you the calming and stress-reducing properties throughout the day.

Yield: 2 Ounces

½ ounce meadow sweet, chopped

½ ounce lemon balm, chopped

½ ounce valerian root, chopped

1 cup carrier oil

1-ounce beeswax grated

Combine the oils and the herbs and cook on very, very low heat in oven (250) for 1-3 hours. Strain, discard herbs, add one ounce of beeswax, melt and stir. Pour mixture into a jar with a lid. Label and date. Apply to pulse points when cool. Store in a jar with a tight-fitting lid in a cool, dark area for up to one year.

***ESSENTIAL OIL:* Stress Massage Rub**

A massage can relieve many of the tension and muscle problems associated with stress. Combine that massage with the properties of these essential oils, and your stress will evaporate. You can even give yourself a self-massage, it's worth it to get rid of all that anxiety and worry.

Yield: 1 Ounce

5 drops melissa oil

5 drops St. John's wort oil

5 drops clary sage oil

4 drops vitamin E oil

1-ounce carrier oil

Mix all of the ingredients together in a small bowl. Using fingertips, apply mixture to areas you wish to massage, keep away from eyes, mucus membranes or sensitive areas. Reapply as needed. Store remainder in a small jar for up to a month.

***ALTERNATIVE REMEDY:* Morning Routine**

This routine is the main thing that helps me if I am suffering from prolonged anxiety and stress. This routine seriously leaves no room in your spirit, body or mind that will allow for stress. You will become a much more grounded and level-headed person, not to mention the growth spiritually after a few weeks of this routine.

- *Find an area in your home devoted solely to your spiritual practices. You can fill with things you love such as candles, diffuser, music, mala beads, self-help books, pillows, whatever you want to make your morning routine all about you and your spirituality.*
- *Create ambiance. Light your candles, turn on your Zen music, burn incense, or run your diffuser. Create a devotional area that gets you in the mood to have a great day.*
- *First meditate for at least 5 minutes. Sit on a comfortable pillow and close your eyes. As you breathe in, think the word "peace." As you exhale, think the word "calm." After you practice meditating for a while, you can try different meditation techniques to see which ones you like the best.*
- *Read some sort of spiritual material, or self-help material. This step is so very important. Even if you can only read for 3 minutes. Learning how to advance in our spiritual journey from others is an on-going, life-time journey. Never quit.*
- *Pray. Say your prayers however feels comfortable to you. I use mala beads to ensure that I am saying over 100 prayers of gratitude each and every day. I thank God for each member of my family, my material possessions, for*

my positive thoughts, for the things I don't yet have, and for my spiritual journey. Gratitude is the key.

- *Affirmations. Don't forget to say some pretty amazing things about yourself. Use positive language. Instead of saying "I am losing weight," say "I am thin and healthy." Say affirmations about the things you want to accomplish on your day. Today I said, "I will finish ten recipes today." And I will.*

- *Write a few things in your gratitude journal. You won't believe how happy and thankful this will make you. This step right here has turned around some of the most difficult relationships in my life. Instead of concentrating on the negative aspects of my relationships, I thought and was grateful for the positive aspects. Wow! Talk about stress relieving.*

- *Do some morning stretches. Yoga, jumping jacks, walking, karate, whatever gets you moving and your heart racing. Try to move for 5 minutes. It makes all the difference. I have a 7-minute routine that I complete each morning. Then when I can't do my regular yoga practice, I feel great knowing I have done at least the minimum of what I need.*

- *Completing even a few of these steps each day will have you on a path of devotion, love, worship, and peace like you have never experienced. You will get rid of negative emotions like rage, anger, depression, anxiety and lethargy. You will find that on days you are unable to perform your morning routine, you are longing for your space and prayers. But remember, you can pray and be thankful anytime, anywhere.*

VITALITY

Vitality is that energetic, youthful, healthy feeling that is the difference between us having a bad day and a wonderfully productive day. Acquiring vitality begins with the mind, positive thoughts, and just doing it! We can use some of the hints and tips from the rest of the world to learn to increase our vitality and to begin to live the life we have always wanted. It's all up to you.

AYURVEDA: Vitality Pancha Karma Cleanse

This used to be quite a horrific process of detoxification involving blood-letting and vomiting. But throughout the years Ayurveda practioners have changed the steps for Panchakarma, although the old ways are still practiced in some areas. Panchakarma is time consuming, involved, emotional and extremely healing. Ensure through your physician that panchakarma techniques are safe for you, especially if you are on any medications or have any illnesses. Panchakarma is usually practiced for 3-5 days. Ensure that you are away from technology, in a quiet, peaceful area, with no distractions or stress. This is my own interpretation of present day panchakarma. The following steps will help you to reinvigorate and fill your body, mind and soul with vitality.

- *Wake up early with the sunrise. Go outside if weather permits, if not, have a dedicated quiet room. Sit and meditate, followed by a gentle, stretching yoga practice.*
- *Clean your teeth, have an oil pull, clean your ears. You may also perform tongue scraping and nasya at this time, if you wish. Cleansing and purifying the body involves the outside as well as the inside.*
- *Drink a cup of herbal tea. The most common detoxifying herbs to use in this process are ginger, burdock root, dandelion, turmeric, and lemongrass. You can use other herbs suitable for your dosha if you want.*
- *Sesame oil body massage. Oil yourself from your scalp to your toes. Do not get in eyes, ears or mucus membranes. You can add essential oils to the sesame oil if you wish. Leave on for 15 minutes to 1 hour. Wash off in a warm bath.*
- *Kitcheree for lunch.*
- *Spend the afternoon alternately in nature or in meditation. Some light reading of self-help materials is permitted. Being alone with your thoughts for such a long time is mind-expanding, emotional and draining.*
- *At this point, you can take an enema (overseen by doctor or Ayurvedic practitioner), or you can have another head to toe oil treatment with sesame oil.*

- *Eat kitcheree for supper, or you may have light, steamed vegetables with rice.*
- *Drink a relaxing, calming cup of detox herbal tea and add some relaxing herbs such as St. John's wort, lemon balm, valerian root or chamomile.*
- *Meditate, pray, read, journal, say your affirmations, use visualization techniques for your future, do a few gentle yoga stretches, or sit under the moon light. Use your evening hours to relax, unwind, and prepare for the night.*
- *Eat 1-2 tablespoons ghee. This will work its way through the system all night, leaving you with a gentle elimination upon wakening.*
- *Coat the feet with sesame oil. Sleep with thick socks on to keep the oil from getting on your furniture, or to help you to not slip when you walk.*
- *Read a favorite and deeply meaningful inspirational chapter from a book, then sleep with a deep, satisfying, relaxing sleep.*

Repeat for 3-5 days.

***HERBS:* Re-Vigor**

These herbs can bring some vitality and energy to your life, and also have the properties to reduce depression and melancholy. This is a great tea for a pick-me-up.

Yield: 1 Cup

1-inch ginger chopped or ½ teaspoon ground ginger

1 teaspoon peppermint leaves

Honey

1 Cup water

Boil one cup of water. Add the herbs, flowers, seeds or stems. Slowly pour the boiling water over the herbs. Cover the cup of herbs and steep for 6-10 minutes. Strain the tea and discard the herbs. Add honey, cream, or sweetener if desired. Drink when at comfortable temperature.

ESSENTIAL OIL: **Vitality Spray**

Use this spray to increase your vitality and bring energy, purpose and well-being to your body and soul. These essential oils have been around for a long time, and the reason is because they work. The therapeutic properties help to fill you with a sense of purpose and the wherewithal to get it done.

Yield: 2 Ounces

4 drops bergamot

5 drops spearmint

4 drops pink grapefruit

1 teaspoon witch hazel

2 ounces water

Using a funnel, pour all of the ingredients into a spray bottle. Label and date bottle. Oils and water separate, so you will need to shake very well before each usage. Spray the area lightly as desired. Ensure that you do not get spray into eyes, ears, mouth, open wounds, or other sensitive areas. Store spray bottle in a dark, cool area for up to 6 months.

***ALTERNATIVE REMEDY:* Vitality Diet**

These foods are well known throughout time, cultures and the world over for their vital life-giving properties. Try incorporating one or more of these foods into your diet daily.

Spicy foods, Oysters, tomatoes, fish, coffee, nuts and saffron.

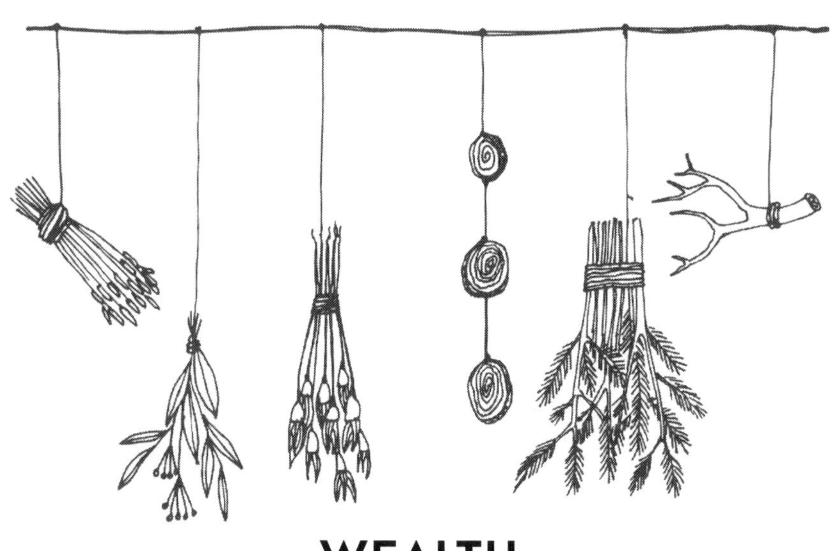

WEALTH

People all over the world, since time began, have looked for ways to accrue wealth. I have researched the various means that people have used throughout time and have compiled them here so that you too can gather some of the wealth for yourself and your loved ones. Of course, hard work, saving your money, and following your dreams are ways to have wealth in your life, but it sure won't hurt to use some of these recipes to give yourself that needed boost!

AYURVEDA: Karma

Religions and people all over the world live by the laws of karma. Give and you will receive. Take and it will be taken. I have seen this work out many times in my own life. Try living by the Karmic laws for a month and see if you notice a difference in your life.

> *Give to get. Give of your time, your money, your friendship or whatever you have. It is said that whatever you give, good or bad, you will get back 10-fold. Try it. Find a friend in need or*

give your time to a charity. Go to a hospital, a nursing home or a local charity and find out what they need and help out. Giving of itself is one of the most joyous things a person can do. Try giving and see if things don't get better for you. Amass your wealth by giving it all away. This is one of the big secrets of life and now it's yours to do with what you will. But the same can be said of evil. If you do bad things, then ten times that number of bad things will happen to you. Simply do good.

***HERBS:* Wealth Rub**

Try wearing this scent with money attracting herbs incorporated into the recipe. These herbs have been used since the dawn of time to bring prosperity to the wearer. You can wear this rub on your wrists, neck, or use it as a moisturizer. Hopefully you will attract a raise in pay, a check in the mail, or some form of money that you want.

Yield: 1 Cup

½ ounce rosemary, chopped

½ ounce peppermint, chopped

½ ounce thyme, chopped

1 cup carrier oil

1-ounce beeswax grated

Combine the oils and the herbs and cook on very, very low heat in oven (250) for 1-3 hours. Strain, discard herbs, add one ounce of beeswax, melt and stir. Pour mixture into a jar with a lid. Label and date. Apply to pulse points when cool. Store in a jar with a tight-fitting lid in a cool, dark area for up to one year.

ESSENTIAL OIL: Money in the Air

These essential oils have been reported to bring money to the user of the oils. It won't hurt to run these in a diffuser for a time and see if your wealth increases.

Yield: 1 Application

3 drops ginger oil

3 drops patchouli oil

3 drops jasmine oil

Water

Each diffuser has different amounts of water and oils that can be used for that particular diffuser. Adjust the recipes according to your diffuser. Add the water, then add the oils and run your diffuser for the desired effect.

ALTERNATIVE REMEDY: Crystals for Wealth

Crystals have been used forever to attract wealth and prosperity. Take your crystals and let them sit out in the moonlight overnight to get cleansed and re-charged. Once you do that, sleep with them, wear them, put one in your pocket, on your nightstand or on your desk at the office. Each month try to remember to recharge your crystals. The following crystals are the most popular for obtaining wealth into your life.

Peridot

Tiger's eye

Clear Quartz

Pyrite

Citrine

jade

WORRY

I was a born worrier. I could never sleep due to worrying about problems and issues that never happened and were likely to not ever happen. I learned to swat away negative thoughts and have gotten pretty good at it. I have used several of the recipes here to help me to focus on the positive and eradicate the negativity in my brain.

AYURVEDA: Meditate Your Worry Away

I learned that when I meditate, to look at my thoughts as an observer. When negative thoughts intrude, I just push them aside and focus on my breathing. This has helped me so much to train my brain to not actively participate in negative thinking. It takes practice, and meditation is the perfect environment for practicing thought control.

- *Meditation should be completed in a quiet, peaceful area. Low music may be played. Try to find an area free of negativity and distractions.*

- *Sit on a pillow, folded towel, or a rug. Cross your legs comfortably. Sit erect, but not stiffly.*

- *Closing your eyes, think of peaceful things that make you happy. Controlling the mind is difficult and you may find your thoughts returning again and again to negativity. Just tell those negative thoughts to go away and replace with happy thoughts. Observe your thoughts, don't react to them. Just watch them as if you are watching a movie, then send each thought on its way. Answers will come.*

- *Breathe. Each time your thoughts return to you, direct your thoughts to your breathing patterns. Try to completely empty the lungs of air with deep, slow, inhales and exhales. Continuously return your thoughts to your breathing.*

- *For 5-30 minutes, sit in silence, or softly chanting a mantra, and give your mind the positivity it needs to get you through another hectic day. You will find each day becoming easier, and your thoughts beginning to reflect the positivity you focus on each time you meditate. Problem solving, spirituality, grounding, communication, love, social interaction and peace all become deeply affected by meditating. It is said that praying is "asking" God for what you need. Meditating is "listening" to what God is telling you.*

***HERBS:* Worry Reliever**

These herbs have the most peaceful, calming, anti-anxiety effect. Sip a cup of this before bedtime and have a wonderful night's sleep without any negativity cloaked in worry.

Yield: 1 Cup

1 teaspoon lemon balm leaves

1 teaspoon lavender flowers

Honey

1 cup water

Boil one cup of water. Add the herbs, flowers, seeds or stems. Slowly pour the boiling water over the herbs. Cover the cup of herbs and steep for 6-10 minutes. Strain the tea and discard the herbs. Add honey, cream, or sweetener if desired. Drink when at comfortable temperature.

ESSENTIAL OIL: **Worry-Free Air**

These essential oils promote peace and productivity and eliminate any worrisome and negative thinking.

Yield: 1 Application

3 drops tangerine oil

3 drops eucalyptus oil

3 drops spruce oil

Water

Each diffuser has different amounts of water and oils that can be used for that particular diffuser. Adjust the recipes according to your diffuser. Add the water, then add the oils and run your diffuser for the desired effect.

ALTERNATIVE REMEDY: Worry Free Rituals

There are so many rituals and practices the world over that have been used for centuries to rid the home of negativity and give you peace of mind. Try one or more of these and see if you can set your mind at ease.

- *Salt: sprinkle salt in four outer corners of your home and sprinkle a little over all thresholds.*
- *Mantra: say a protection mantra as you walk from room to room. Say anything you want that makes you feel safe and protected. A favorite is "Angels protect this home and all who reside in it. No negativity shall reign here."*
- *Crystals: Charge your crystals overnight under a full moon. They will protect you and discharge any negative ions in the home.*
- *Colors: surround yourself with white, blue and yellow. These are colors of the spirit, the sun and purity.*
- *Tea: drink herbal teas to calm the nerves and promote well-being.*
- *Essential oils: Run your diffuser with some essential oils to help banish worry and regret.*

WORSHIP

Worshiping is the highest praise coming from deep in our hearts straight to the divine. To enhance your spiritual moments and give more freely of your soul to the creator, try some of these recipes. People the world over have tried numerous ways in which to increase their focus and insight while worshiping. I have researched some of these ways and chosen the ones that did seem to help me to be more in tune with those giving, grateful, holistic thoughts and ideas.

AYURVEDA: Sacred Space

Everyone needs their own sacred space. I have many friends who simply use a tray with crystals, spiritual books, crosses, mala beads, candles, or whatever brings them peace on it. I also have friends who have entire rooms made into a small sacred area complete with bolster, yoga mat, alter, incense and chair. However, you decide what your sacred space should be, just make sure it is yours and make it to reflect your current spiritual needs. It can be large, small, hidden, open, however you want it. But it should be private.

Your sacred space should reflect who you are and what you want to draw from on your sacred journey. If you are Christian, maybe you want a nice mat to kneel on, an alter with a cross, incense, rosary beads and a bible on it. If you are wanting to develop a closer relationship with your higher power, you might want a yoga space, mala beads, buddha statue and candles. Whatever you want in your sacred space, you can have it. It is for you alone. Spend time there each day, wheth-

er praying, saying mantras, burning sage, diffusing essential oils, journaling your gratitudes, doing yoga, meditating, or simply sitting in peace and gazing at your crystals. This is a space for you to feel open to receiving gifts for your spirit. You will grow here more than anywhere else on Earth. Make it perfect for you.

HERBS: Frankincense Worship

Frankincense is a resin type substance that has been used for worship forever. You can purchase it in its resin form. The aroma is heavenly. Frankincense is the most widely used herb in the bible. You can also buy electric incense burners and frankincense burners. Use this when beginning a time of worship.

Yield: 1 Application

1-ounce frankincense

In your incense burner or electric burner, place a small piece of frankincense resin. Light with fire or plug in. Never leave unattended.

ESSENTIAL OIL: Worshipful Air

Aromas can get us in the mood for so much. In order to use essential oils in your place of worship, or your sacred space, use these oils which have been used since worship first began among humans.

Yield: 1 Application

3 drops frankincense oil

3 drops angelica oil

3 drops myrrh oil

Water

Each diffuser has different amounts of water and oils that can be used for that particular diffuser. Adjust the recipes according to your diffuser. Add the water, then add the oils and run your diffuser for the desired effect.

***ALTERNATIVE REMEDY:* Worship Meanderings**

I often sit at the computer, or with my journal, or with just a pad and pen and record my spiritual thoughts. Sometimes they may not make sense, but sometimes they seem profound to me. Try just writing as you pray, you may be surprised what you end up with, what you ask for, and what you really want. Use some of the ideas below to begin your spiritual writings.

- *List five things you are grateful for.*
- *Write what you want most in life.*
- *Write what you want most for your family and friends.*
- *Write what steps you want your higher power to help you with to attain that goal.*
- *Thank your higher power for helping you to attain your goal before you ever reach it.*

- *Feel the feelings of gratitude you will feel when you reach your goal.*
- *Write your prayers for your day and how you want things to go.*
- *Write your blessings you wish for others.*
- *Read spiritual material.*
- *Write spiritual material.*

ACKNOWLEDGMENTS

I would like to thank my daughters, Lin and Colleen, without whom I would never have had the courage to write that first book. You girls are everything to me. Well, except for the grandkids. So, ALL of y'all are everything to me.

I would like to give my greatest appreciation to Murphy Rae for the beautiful cover art. Murphy is a book cover genius. I love you Murphy and thank you. I would like to thank my agent, Jane Dystel and Miriam Goderich for supporting me in my foray into self-pubbing. Dystel, Goderich and Bourret are the literary agent giants of the world! Thank you to Alyssa Garcia of "Uplifting Author Services" for her brilliant formatting of a book that I had no idea how to format. So, if you like the spacing, design, font and everything else a formatter does…she's your girl! And lastly a huge thank you to Amazon for making Kindle Direct Publishing a great outlet for authors.

I would like to give my respect to all the record keepers, story tellers, cultural healers, shaman and indigenous people the world over for keeping the old healing traditions alive and passing them down throughout the generations and sharing them with the world. I did so much research on various cultures and their healing traditions, rituals and methods. It was so eye opening and spiritually thought provoking for my journey. I appreciate deep in my soul all of the educators in the world who so freely share their healing tips and recipes with the world.

Thank you to my family for continuing to support my many absences, ideas, trial runs, healing techniques, passions and seclusions. Y'all are the best. There are none better.

Index

A

B

C

D

E

F

G

H

I

LIST OF METHODS

Balm
Bandage
Bath
Bath Salts
By Mouth
Compress
Decoction
Diet
Diffuser
Drinks
Foot Bath
Gargle
Infusion
Inhale
Lotion
Massage Oil
Meditation
Neat
Oil
Oil Pull
Ointment
Paste
Poultice
Powder
Rub
Sachet
Salve
Spray

Spritz

Steam

Syrup

Tea

Tincture

Tips

Treatments

Wash

Wrap

Yoga

RESOURCES

@. (2015). 10 Best Healing Herbs. Retrieved August/September 2016, from http://www.prevention.com/mind-body/natural-remedies/best-healing-herbs-top-10

Alborzian, C. (2013). The One plan: A week-by-week guide to restoring your natural health and happiness. New York: HarperOne.

Alternative, Holistic, Natural & Spiritual Healing Methods. (n.d.). Retrieved April/May 2016, from http://www.allthingshealing.com/

Augur, W. D. (n.d.). Healing Herbs Natural Remedies. Retrieved October/November 2016, from http://herbsandnaturalremedies.com/

Ayurvedic Tips for Healthy Nutrition taken from Dr. Deepak ... (n.d.). Retrieved May 1, 2016, from http://ayurvediccookingclasses.com/ayurvedic-tips-for-healthy-nutrition-taken-from-dr-deepak-chopra/

Bricklin, M. (1982). Rodale's encyclopedia of natural home remedies: Hundreds of simple healing techniques for everyday illness and emergencies. Emmaus, PA: Rodale Press.

Consumer health. (n.d.). Retrieved January/February 2016, from http://www.mayoclinic.org/healthy-lifestyle/consumer-health/in-depth/alternative-medicine/art-20045267

Diseases and Conditions. (n.d.). Retrieved August 04, 2014, from http://www.mayoclinic.org/diseases-conditions

H. (2016). Do You Take a Holistic Approach to Life? Retrieved December 01, 2016, from http://healing.about.com/od/faq/p/holistichealing.htm

Dodt, C. K. (1996). The essential oils book: Creating personal blends for mind & body. Pownal, VT: Storey Communications.

Ferrell, V., Ferrell, V., Vance Ferrell, Harold M. Cherne, M.D., FERRELL, Vance; ARCHBOLD, Edgar E, M D; CHERNE, Harold M, M D, Ferrell, Vance; Archbold, Edgar E.; Cherne, Harold M., & Vance H. Ferrell and Harold M. Cherne, M.D.

(1970). Natural Remedies Encyclopedia. Retrieved August 08, 2016, from https://www.abebooks.com/book-search/title/natural-remedies-encyclopedia/author/vance-ferrell/

Ferrell, V. (1998). Natural remedies encyclopedia: Topically arranged home remedies for over 500 diseases. Beersheba Springs, TN: Pilgrims Books.

Fite, V. G., McDaniel, M. G., & Reynolds, V. L. (2016). Essential oils for healing: Over 400 all-natural recipes for everyday ailments (1st ed., Vol. 1, Ser. 1). New York: St. Martin's Griffin.

Fite, V. G. (2020). Llewellyn's book of natural remedies: Over 400 ayurvedic, herbal, essential oil, and home remedies for every-day ailments. Woodbury, MN: Llewellyn Publications.

Fite, V. G. (2018). Essential Oils for Emotional Wellbeing: More Than 400 Aromatherapy Recipes for Mind, Emotions and Spirit. Llewellyn Publications.

Frawley, D. (1999). Yoga and Ayurveda: Self-healing and self-realization. Twin Lakes, WI: Lotus Light Pub.

Keville, K., & Green, M. (2009). Aromatherapy: A complete guide to the healing art. Berkeley, CA: Crossing Press.

Kowalchik, C., Hylton, W. H., & Carr, A. (1987). Rodale's illustrated encyclopedia of herbs. Emmaus, PA: Rodale Press.

Lad, V. (1998). The complete book of Ayurvedic home remedies. New York: Harmony Books.

List of plants used in herbalism. (n.d.). Retrieved November 11, 2016, from https://en.wikipedia.org/wiki/List_of_plants_used_in_herbalism

McDaniel, M. G. (2019) Words in Amber. Kindle Direct Publishing.

Organic Herbs & Spices. (n.d.). Retrieved October 30, 2014, from https://www.mountainroseherbs.com/

Shealy, C. N. (1998). Illustrated encyclopedia of healing remedies.

Shaftesbury, Dorset: Element.

Sondhi, A. (2006). The modern Ayurvedic cookbook: Healthful, healing recipes for life. Vancouver: Arsenal Pulp Press.

Spear, H. E. (2011). The everything guide to chakra healing: Use your body's subtle energies to promote health, healing, and happiness. Avon, MA: Adams Media.

WebMD – Better information. Better health. (n.d.). Retrieved December 11, 2015, from http://www.webmd.com/

WebMD – Better information. Better health. (n.d.). Retrieved March 30, 2015, from http://www.webmd.com/herbs

What Is Ayurveda? Treatments, Massage, Diet, and More. (n.d.). Retrieved January 07, 2016, from http://www.webmd.com/balance/guide/ayurvedic-treatments

Worwood, S. E., & Worwood, V. A. (2003). Essential aromatherapy: A pocket guide to essential oils and aromatherapy. Novato, CA: New World Library.

Made in the USA
Columbia, SC
21 October 2021